SHAPING BELOVED
COMMUNITY

SHAPING BELOVED COMMUNITY

Multicultural Theological Education

Edited by
David V. Esterline and Ogbu U. Kalu

Westminster John Knox Press
LOUISVILLE • LONDON

Scripture quotations from the New Revised Standard Version of the Bible are copyright © 1989 by the Division of Christian Education of the National Council of the Churches of Christ in the U.S.A. and are used by permission.

Book design by Drew Stevens
Cover design by Eric Handel, LMNOP

First edition
Published by Westminster John Knox Press
Louisville, Kentucky

This book is printed on acid-free paper that meets the American National Standards Institute Z39.48 standard. ♾

PRINTED IN THE UNITED STATES OF AMERICA

06 07 08 09 10 11 12 13 14 15 — 10 9 8 7 6 5 4 3 2 1

Library of Congress Cataloging-in-Publication Data

Shaping beloved community : multicultural theological education / edited by David V. Esterline and Ogbu U. Kalu.—1st ed.
    p.   cm.
  Includes bibliographical references (p.   ) and index.
  ISBN-13: 978-0-664-22937-5 (alk. paper)
  ISBN-10: 0-664-22937-9 (alk. paper)
  1. Theology—Study and teaching.   2. Multicultural education.   3. Multiculturalism—Religious aspects—Christianity.   4. Christianity and culture.   I. Esterline, David.
II. Kalu, Ogbu.
  BV4020.S53   2006
  230.71'1—dc22   2006041360

Contents

Introduction

Every time academics write, they must ask again the crucial questions, why do we write, and for whom? This book has emerged from an institution's soul-searching about its place, engagement, and concerns in multicultural theological education. It is not a lonely journey; as the racial and cultural diversity in society and in congregations increases and the opportunity of working with immigrant churches in ministerial formation unfolds year by year, many seminaries are working at keeping pace. The Association of Theological Schools (ATS) reports that racial/ethnic enrollment grew from 2.7 percent of total enrollment in member schools in 1969 to 19.9 percent in 1999, and then to approximately 28 percent by the fall of 2004. The gender profile is also changing: in 2004, 36 percent of all seminary students were women, and 48 percent of the African American students were women. The percentage of racial/ethnic faculty has also increased, but not as rapidly as students: from 4 percent of all full-time faculty in ATS schools in 1980 to 14.5 percent in 2004.[1]

Many seminaries are committed to establishing and maintaining diverse learning/worshiping communities of faculty and students. Equal commitment is needed in the area of teaching and learning, that is, to the development of a pedagogy appropriate for diverse classrooms and communities. This collection of essays by members of the faculty at McCormick Theological Seminary addresses this issue: commitments and practices in multicultural theological education that move beyond diversity to the shaping of community and new ways of learning for both students and faculty.

McCormick's commitment to diversity and to learning across cultures has been evolving since the 1970s, as described by Deborah Mullen in chapter 6, "From Sideline to Center." By 1991 there was no single racial majority among the masters level students, and that balance has been maintained until the present. In 1991, 45 percent of the students were Euro American, 17 percent were African American, 17 percent Asian American, 13 percent Hispanic, and 8 percent nonresident visa holders; 43 percent of the students were women. By 2004 the numbers had changed, but still without a racial majority: 39 percent Euro American, 38 percent African American, 12 percent visa, 6 percent Hispanic, and 4 percent Asian American; 55 percent were women. Among the faculty in 2004, African and African American, Asian American, and Latino made up 35 percent, and 39 percent were women. As many of us find ourselves saying to each other, we still have some way to go—and that way is not only about numbers; it is also about ways of learning and teaching.

One of the most significant centers of learning at McCormick is the Language Resource and Writing Center (LRWC). Established in the early 1990s as a language lab, the LRWC has developed into a center of hospitality, openness, care, and cross-cultural understanding. Within the framework of language work relating to the skills necessary for critical reading and listening and coherent writing and speaking, the LRWC helps students understand cultural differences and the values informing those differences. With the LRWC, McCormick has been able to maintain a policy of admitting international students who are not proficient in English and has provided support for students in their growth and reflection beyond course work. The opportunity to learn with and from students may well be more important than our own need, as faculty, to teach. Nurturing a multicultural community has at least as much to do with listening and learning as it has with teaching.

MULTICULTURAL EDUCATION

We are well aware that the term "multicultural" is used in so many different ways and in support of such widely differing commitments that it must be defined before it can be used meaningfully.[2] "Multicultural education" in North America over the last thirty years has had a wide variety of meanings, and even now there is hardly an emerging consensus about definitions, practice, or objectives. Still, there are broadly shared commitments and a basic understanding that multicultural education must be incorporated into every aspect of education and involve every learner, teacher, and administrator. At its most fundamental, multicultural education can be defined as the commitment to making full, complete education equally available to all students. All dimensions of the education enterprise are involved, including knowledge construction, curriculum, pedagogy, school culture, and all decision-making processes. Multicultural education can be understood as an attempt to reform educational institutions so that students from all groups—such as those identified by race, ethnicity, social class, and gender—will be treated with equity and will have equal opportunity for educational success.[3] These shared definitions also form the foundation for multicultural *theological* education.

Two of the most widespread misconceptions about multicultural education (including multicultural theological education) are that it is intended primarily for students from "minority" groups and that it has to do mainly with curriculum reform. Students from the "majority" culture in the United States are often in desperate need of an education that includes exposure to the world majority as well as nurturing of awareness and respect for the diversity in North America. Without the opportunity for multicultural learning, "majority" students are not receiving a just or complete education and are likely being miseducated about their place and role in the world.[4] The reforms called for by multicultural education go far beyond changes in the curriculum (which are themselves not insignificant) to include the understandings, commitments, and behaviors of teachers and administrators; teaching and learning styles; and the objectives, policies, norms, and culture of educational institutions. Multicultural education is relevant to everyone involved in the education process and calls for change in every dimension, with the goal of fostering educational equity.

DIFFERENT WAYS OF UNDERSTANDING HUMAN DIFFERENCE

Multicultural education theory and practice extend across a very broad spectrum, from programs that do little more than encourage assimilation into the "mainstream" to those deeply committed to radical social and political reform. To make sense of this range of understanding and practice, a number of typologies have been developed in the last fifteen years framing the various approaches to multicultural education and the underlying conceptions of culture, race, and difference.[5] These conceptualizations provide a significant framework for any discussion of multiculturalism and are as helpful in thinking through multicultural theological education as they are for the wider world of K–12 and post-secondary multicultural education.

In the following list we describe the five main ways of understanding human difference, in order to uncover the assumptions underlying the various definitions of "multicultural" and the related approaches to education. Each way, or type, has specific implications for teaching and learning, and each has both positive and negative aspects. We suspect that most educators incorporate parts of different types into their work, even though they may find one particular type to be the most fitting for their approach as a whole. (Of course, as is usually the case with typologies, we recognize that reality is not nearly this tidy or well organized.)

1. Everyone is essentially the same. At a fundamental level, no matter their race, ethnicity, or culture, all people are understood to be essentially the same. This view holds that the difference between individuals is more significant than identity based on any group association. The focus in education is on the individual as unique; the reality of race, ethnicity, culture, and other frameworks (such as gender and age) is not denied, but focusing on them is considered undesirable and even harmful to the education process. This is the conceptual framework of much of the education system in the United States and the ways that system has undertaken historically to assimilate "minorities" into the "mainstream" of the dominant white culture. In this view the majority or dominant group assumes that its understanding of education is correct for everyone, as differences of race and culture (and histories of oppression and domination) are not thought to be significant for teaching and learning. (Gary Rand describes this as the Epcot approach in the *Power* section of chapter 13.) This view has the advantage of pointing out the reality that all people do have many characteristics in common and that individuals, even within racial, cultural, and other groups, are unique. The difficulty is that it does not take into account cultural worldviews, the very real differences that result from social/political/economic history, or the relationships of oppression and domination between groups. It also assumes that there is little difference between group memberships, a viewpoint held in common with the following type.

2. All differences are equally important. All group differences are considered cultural differences, so "multicultural" comes to mean inclusion of all differences: gender, ability/disability, sexual orientation, race, nationality, and so forth. Many use the term "multicultural" in this way, as an umbrella to cover all differences and to give all types of difference equal importance. The positive aspect of this view is that it demands that all differences be recognized and celebrated. No one is marginalized; everyone's group-related identity is accepted. On the negative side, this view is ahistorical and so does not deal with sociopolitical context or the history of oppression. In teaching and learning, this view stresses the need to accept and celebrate all group-related identities and promotes learning about the "other," about those who are different from the mainstream. The acceptance and teaching advocated by this view, however, is usually done without regard to issues of power relations, privilege, and race.

3. *Nation of origin or ethnicity is most important.* Difference is understood primarily as having to do with one's ethnicity and the related values, customs, beliefs, behaviors, and so on. Where one was born (or where one's parents were born) and the related worldview are central. Culture is equated to ethnicity in this view; other aspects of difference are recognized, but they are not as significant as the overarching cultural experience, which is directly related to nation of origin or ethnicity. The advantage of this approach is the way it builds on the traditional understanding of culture and the interrelatedness of society and the meaning of learned behaviors and values. The disadvantage is that difference between individuals within groups is overlooked; as individuals are seen primarily as members of their "culture," stereotyping is likely. Immersion experiences and exposure to cultures different from one's own are preferred ways of teaching and learning.

4. *Race is central.* The primary locus of difference in the United States is race. Advantage or disadvantage, inclusion or exclusion, are based on perceived skin color, other physical characteristics, and (sometimes) language—that is, on race. The understanding of racism as a system of advantage based on race fits within this view. Other group memberships, such as gender or religion, exist within the context of race; the experience of belonging to a racial group is more significant than all other group memberships. One of the most significant aspects of this framework for understanding difference is the recognition of the variation between members of a particular racial group in the ways that they identify with race, both their own and others—so the tendency toward stereotyping is greatly reduced. This view takes advantage of recent work on racial identity, which has to do with the psychological consequences of living in a society in which everyone is either privileged or disadvantaged because of his or her racial classification. For those who are not part of the majority or dominant race (that is, those who are not white), racial identity development models provide insight into the ways that individuals resolve, or do not resolve, the identity conflicts they face as

"nonwhites" in a predominantly white society. For whites, it provides a framework for a process by which they might come to understand their whiteness as part of developing a nonracist identity. Advantages of this approach: attention is given to all individuals and racial groups, not only the marginalized or dominant; it reduces stereotyping of individuals; it requires that attention be given to power relationships, both past and present. The primary disadvantage might be seen in the very difficult personal work that is required for understanding and taking responsibility with regard to race and racism. Teaching and learning make use of racial identity development theories and give particular attention to the history of racism and the present social and political realities of race.

5. *Oppressed and oppressor are the most important categories.* At the center of this view is the reality of oppression experienced in many parts of the world. Difference is understood in the contrast between the culture of the oppressed and that of the oppressor, even as these two cultures develop in relation to each other. As the result of colonialism, slavery, and violence, oppressed peoples have become alienated from their own cultures and histories, and their oppressors have developed cultures of domination and violence. Paulo Freire's work fits in this view, as does postcolonialism. The advantage of this framework is its provision for a broad, global understanding of power relations throughout the world; on the other hand, by concentrating on oppression and the common experience of the oppressed, this view may overlook differences related to gender and race. Teaching and learning focus on the history of power relations and on understanding and overturning the cultures of the oppressed and the oppressor.

The lack of agreement among educators, including theological educators, about the meaning of "multicultural" is related to different understandings of difference, understandings that are themselves rooted in fundamentally different ways of viewing the world with regard to culture, race, power, and the significance of history. The five frames presented above are offered as a way to understand the worldviews that support these varying definitions and approaches. They can be found, in various forms and combinations, throughout the chapters that make up this volume.

OUTLINE OF THE VOLUME

The book benefits from a multidisciplinary approach that is sensitive to theoretical issues as well as the specific challenges within the various disciplines of theology. In the first section on theoretical and institutional frameworks, David Esterline outlines in chapter 1 the main aspects of theological education that are needed to develop leadership for a church with true multicultural understanding and commitments. The chapter begins with a vision of such a church and a definition of "multicultural" in terms of race, ethnicity, culture, and proactive work against racism. The focus of the chapter is on the way multicultural theological education can prepare women and men for ministry by creating a climate of acceptance and inclusion within seminary communities, by developing a pedagogy that affirms the experience and cultural location of the learner, and through a diverse and inclusive curriculum.

In the second chapter, José Irizarry explores common approaches to multiculturalism within the field of theological education and suggests that in order to move from the mere recognition of cultural "difference," theological institutions should engender "intercultural" perspectives in both their scholarship and their pedagogies. The author contends that an intercultural perspective yields educational practices that allow people from different cultures to influence the knowledge and faith formation of each other and to forge a shared community of theological discourse. Utilizing the concepts of movement and space, the author suggests new directions in the trajectory of theological education and new learning environments as necessary ingredients for an intercultural theological education.

In chapter 3, Anna Case-Winters inquires into the nature and purpose of theological education. Among other things, theological education prepares people for the living of the faith in the contemporary context. One important feature of the contemporary context is the phenomenon of difference (in race, class, gender, culture, religion, etc.) and the ways in which difference becomes the occasion for exclusion, oppression, conflict, and violence. Theological education should search for a means of addressing this challenge in the living of the faith. The chapter poses the question, "How may we do difference, differently?" It seeks wisdom from the lived experience of McCormick Theological Seminary, which is intentionally diverse in its character, as well as from ecumenical and interreligious dialogues of difference.

The force of Latino(a) presence in reshaping the North American religious landscape compels a reflection on the implications for theological education. In chapter 4, Luis Rivera proposes that seminary faculty need to tap into the theoretical resources and practices that U.S. "minority" theologians employ in their theological reflection and pedagogies, especially the increasing interest among Latino/a theologians in developing a theology and theological method that is inter- or cross-cultural. Rivera presents the concept of *intercultural dialogue* as a potential component for a theological educational model that works with an awareness of the plurality of cultures in its midst and around the world and is committed to form women and men for the practice of intercultural ministry in these societies.

Because theological librarians are given the power to name, classify, organize, mediate, and transform inherited traditions, seminaries *must* acknowledge librarians as part of the conversation regarding the institutional identities, purposes, and programs they are in the process of constructing. Ken Sawyer argues in chapter 5 that the *promise* of contemporary multiculturalism seeks a wider world and a broader mandate for religion, and is thus a good description of much of what active theological librarians currently do. The very *premise* of theological libraries seeks a wider world and a deeper reading of the complexity of religious communities, and is thus an ally to many forms of multiculturalism.

In chapter 6, Deborah Mullen delineates how the seminary has intentionally struggled to practice an ideological articulation. She uses both the statistics on enrollment and the development of special centers (African American, Latin American, and Korean/Asian American) to illustrate the changing face of theological education in McCormick Theological Seminary.

The second section of the book explores the challenges of multicultural education in biblical and theological studies. In chapter 7, Cynthia Campbell underscores the biblical roots for the conception and practice of multicultural theological education as a way of Christian living, reflection, ministerial formation, and pedagogy. This approach is grounded in an understanding of God as creator of all, in the belief that the gospel of Jesus Christ is for all people, and in the conviction that cultural diversity is part of God's providential ordering of life on earth. The essay includes discussion of the ways this view is expressed in various courses in McCormick's curriculum.

One dimension of teaching the Bible from a multicultural theological perspective in the contemporary period is the problem of power relations embedded in globalization, namely, that benefits from cultural diversity are compromised by some cultures dominating others, and that this has implications for the teaching of method, hermeneutics, and pedagogy in biblical interpretation. In chapter 8, Robert Brawley argues against one method trumping another and suggests *complementarity* among alternative methods. This method contends that hermeneutical moves depend on what is sought and the rationale supporting it. This chapter adopts Freire's dialogical peer reflection to engender new perceptions of reality that emphasize local and personal (over against universal) ways of construing reality. A high value is placed on autobiography within community, which by encountering alternative stories, induces disequilibrium and results in alternative visions, which are reinscribed in autobiography in an antiheroic mood.

The aim in chapter 9 is not so much to address the theoretical or conceptual aspects of multicultural theological education, but to describe an actual class that was uniquely successful in setting up a genuinely multicultural educational experience. Ted Hiebert argues that the key to this experience was a course in which the distinctive goal was writing a book for which each class member contributed a chapter. Writing a book together created a unique kind of learning community in which diverse voices became a more prominent part of the classroom culture, in which critical engagement and dialogue became more substantive, and in which diversity actually raised the bar of academic study and discourse.

In chapter 10, Jae Won Lee explores how to face the increasing challenge and need for reading and teaching the Bible from multicultural perspectives by focusing on two issues from a Korean American feminist biblical perspective. First is the issue of how to understand and conceptualize the nature and meaning of "difference" for multicultural readings of the Bible. Dealing with some key points in contemporary theoretical discourses on "difference," she highlights the necessity to construe the meaning of difference primarily in terms of the marginalized identities (race, gender, class, culture) in unequal social relations. Second is the issue of how to relate oneself to the differences of others in constructive ways. The chapter presents an alternative reading of Romans 14:1–15:13 as an example of the politics of difference that rejects an assimilationist approach to difference, but promotes radical mutuality based on the practice of solidarity with the weak.

Part 3 addresses issues of ministerial formation and the ways that multiculturalism is at the center of constructing viable strategies in many forms of ministry and practical theology. In chapter 11, Homer Ashby explores the strategies for practicing liberating cross-culturality in pastoral care. The author presents three approaches that have been proposed for teaching pastoral care and counseling in the cross-cultural classroom. The strengths and weaknesses of each model are identified. Using the best features of the three models the author describes how he structures his class in pastoral care and counseling for the cross-cultural classroom. The image of a "dance" is offered as a way of thinking about how persons from different cultures might engage one another in the pastoral care and counseling process.

Moving from the classroom to the field, Robert Cathey describes and analyzes how the 2004 Barcelona Parliament of the World's Religions served as the context for practicing theological education in interfaith and intrafaith dimensions. An interfaith teaching team from McCormick (Sarah Tanzer and Robert Cathey) designed and led a travel seminar to this beautiful, multicultural region in Catalan, Spain. Just before they set out to encounter religious diversity in Barcelona, "the great enchantress," terrorists struck Madrid on March 11, 2004. Nevertheless the seminar went forward with a theologically diverse group of students from the Hyde Park cluster in Chicago. Chapter 12 provides one model for how educators can engage their students intensively in learning about traditions other than their own, while exploring how their community acts in relation to religious "others." It calls for greater engagement between seminary faculties and populist interfaith movements to foster critical thinking about distinctive differences between religions (rather than slogans like "peace, love, and harmony"). Critical theological reflection should accompany interfaith partnerships for constructive change in our age disrupted by violence and counterviolence in the name of "the one true religion" and the national security state.

McCormick Theological Seminary is not only a teaching institution but a worshiping community. The central focus of chapter 13 by the seminary musician, Gary Rand, is the idea that a service of worship can be structured in such a way that it offers people many different ways to participate meaningfully. This openness creates a context of welcome and hospitality and is a significant building block of multicultural community. The chapter suggests three characteristics of open worship. First, open worship encourages congregational participation. Open worship reduces the spotlight on clergy and worship leaders and raises the light on the people. Second, open worship uses a variety of means of expression, since we do not understand the world or express our understanding in exactly the same way. Open worship incorporates many forms, styles, strategies and actions to help everyone find a familiar voice. Lastly, open worship embraces the complexities, the depths, and the mysteries of faith that call us to worship together. Easy formulas and thinned-down descriptions give way to surprise and wonder, richness and depth as we worship God, the mysterious, graceful, creator of this wonderful, diverse world.

In chapter 14, Joanne Lindstrom examines how experiential education serves as a contextual learning process and the role it plays in the development of ministerial authority and identity. It looks at the role of each of the partners in learning—student, the site, supervisor, community, and seminary. Using anecdotal information and reports from students, Lindstrom illustrates how cross-cultural experiential education can offer a broad range of valuable insights and growth opportunities as it encourages the formation of authority and identity for students.

The next two chapters bring to the fore the challenges of a global perspective on multicultural theological education. In chapter 15, David Daniels argues that the contemporary face of Christianity compels the need to develop a globalized narrative of Christianity that would provide materials for constructing new Christian identities, and thereby build new forms of solidarity and common witness. In this chapter, Daniels proposes a multicontinental approach for teaching the history of Christianity, the compatability of various models of church history, and the challenge of periodization and pedagogy in teaching church history from a global perspective. He touches on a fundamental problem, namely, that Western institutions give scholarships to international students to study in the West but fail to be attentive to their stories, the literature produced in those contexts, and the task of designing a pedagogy that could assist a wholesome ministerial formation.

In the concluding chapter, Ogbu Kalu uses the context of theological education in Africa to illustrate the implications of the issues of race and oppressive power relationship that were raised in the chapters by Esterline, Rivera, Brawley, Lee, and Daniels for multicultural theological education. Missionary education in Africa was characterized by a conservative ideology that ignored the indigenous worldviews, avoided social justice challenges, and hindered a critical reflection in the people's experience of God. Kalu reconstructs the various models in African theological education that contested the missionary vestiges and experimented with sustainable models in a globalizing environment. This chapter examines six of such models: (i) the voice and exit by the nineteenth-century movement dubbed Ethiopianism; (ii) the liberal multicultural ideology by indigenizers in the twentieth century and (iii) by the ecumenists in the 1970s; (iv) the pluralistic multiculturalism proposed in the Theological Education by Extension (TEE) project; (v) the implications of the rise of Christian universities in the twenty-first century; and (vi) the critical multiculturalism in the "ministerial formation-by-engagement" practiced within the emerging charismatic spirituality. The reshaping of

African theological education may privilege Afrocentric ideology but still faces the problems of quality control, adequate funding, and adequate infrastructure. At the background of all the chapters is the persistent question: how these reflections could impact theological education globally. The problems in multicultural theological education in North America are global and resonate with the experiences of non-Western peoples.

NOTES

1. Association of Theological Schools, *Folio on Diversity in Theological Education* (Pittsburgh: ATS, 2003), and "The Fact Book on Theological Education and Annual Data Tables 2004–2005," http://www.ats.edu/data/factbook.htm.

2. Several of the contributors to this volume develop and build on related definitions.

3. The multicultural education literature is vast and growing. For beginning points, see James A. Banks and Cherry A. McGee Banks, eds., *Handbook of Research on Multicultural Education* (San Francisco: Jossey-Bass, 2001); Patricia G. Ramsey and Leslie R. Williams, *Multicultural Education: A Source Book*, 2nd ed. (New York: RoutledgeFalmer, 2003); Carlos F. Diaz, *Multicultural Education for the 21st Century* (New York: Longman, 2001); and Maurianne Adams, Lee Anne Bell, and Pat Griffin, eds., *Teaching for Diversity and Social Justice: A Sourcebook* (New York: Routledge, 1997).

4. This is a point made regularly in the multicultural education literature. See, for example, Sonia Nieto, *The Light in Their Eyes: Creating Multicultural Learning Communities* (New York: Teachers College Press, 1999).

5. Christine E. Sleeter and Carl A. Grant, *Making Choices for Multicultural Education: Five Approaches to Race, Class, and Gender*, 2nd ed. (New York: Merrill, 1993); Joe L. Kincheloe and Shirley R. Steinberg, *Changing Multiculturalism* (Buckingham, UK: Open University Press, 1997); and Robert T. Carter, "Reimagining Race in Education: A New Paradigm from Psychology," *Teachers College Record* 102, no. 5 (2000): 864–97. We build especially on Carter's work in the five ways of understanding human difference.

PART ONE

Theoretical and Institutional Frameworks

CHAPTER 1

Multicultural Theological Education and Leadership for a Church without Walls

David V. Esterline

MCcCormick Theological Seminary is a community of learning and teaching, challenged by the Holy Spirit and grounded in God's transforming love for the world in Jesus Christ. The seminary's mission is to nurture the gifts of women and men for faithful Christian ministry and leadership in the church, in congregations and denominational agencies, and in the wider society. Preparation for church leadership is what seminaries do. In the terms used by the Association of Theological Schools, seminaries are "communities of faith and learning," they serve "religious constituencies," they are attentive to the "cultural realities and structures in which the church lives and carries out its mission," and they conduct research that should inform and enrich the life of the church.[1] An understanding of the church (including the surrounding "cultural realities and structures") and a vision of what the church might be should together form the foundation of theological education. What is the church for which leaders are being prepared? With a vision clearly defined, it will be possible to assess, redesign, and develop theological education that will provide leadership for the church.

A VISION OF THE CHURCH WITHOUT WALLS

Mestizo theologian Virgilio Elizondo presents a vision of an inclusive church that begins with a reminder of the original invitation to belong to the Christian family. "It offered equally to everyone, no matter their race or nationality, a new common bloodstream: the blood of Jesus. It flowed through everyone who joined, producing one close-knit unity:

the body of the Lord! . . . This new story would not destroy the histories of peoples, but would bring them into a new common space and time."[2] Elizondo's reminder is a worthy introduction to the vision in Ephesians 2 that leads us to imagine a church without walls of division or hostility. Christ came and proclaimed peace to those of us who were far off and to those of us who were near, so that we are no longer strangers and aliens, but citizens with the saints and members of the one household of God. Christ is our peace; he has broken down the dividing wall, creating in himself one new humanity. Though there is lively discussion among commentators about the specific allusion intended by the author in describing the wall that was broken down (*to mesotoichon tou phragmou* [Eph. 2:14], a redundant phrase meaning literally "the middle wall of the barrier"), the implication for the church and the larger meaning of the passage is as clear as can be. It was a "dividing wall of partition . . . constituted by all the expressions of social enmity, familiar to any Jew or Gentile in the Hellenistic world, the difference in place of residence, manner of worship, food and dress, politics and ethics, and above all the blank wall of mutual incomprehension, fear and contempt between the two groups . . . (an) apartheid between Jews and Gentiles."[3] The breaking down of the wall of division in this text stands for the overcoming of all divisions in the church, whether caused by culture, race, or class; it is the nature of the church to be undivided. The church is the place where women, men, and children are all to feel at home, as members of the one household of God.

But the promise of welcome and inclusion of earliest Christianity has not been realized. In fact, Christianity has often been exclusive or a force for segregation. If the walls of separation are to come down, there is work to be done in theological education and leadership formation for a new church. In Virgil Elizondo's vision, the new church has "a truly multicultural face and heart." In "Benevolent Tolerance or Humble Reverence?" he writes that we must move beyond "benevolent tolerance stemming from guilt feelings about the past, we need to undergo a deep cultural conversion from our previously unquestioned Western paradigm of truth itself. . . . We must all die a bit to our collective self-righteousness so that we may be more willing to listen and learn from others. . . . We have much to offer one another, if only we have the humility to accept it."[4]

The same should be asked of seminaries. Are those of us in the majority culture ready to recognize our ethnocentrism, to set aside our ownership of the normative culture, normative ways of knowing and ways of worship, and turn to listening, learning from and valuing those whose gifts are different from ours? If we expect all members of the household of God to be welcomed in our congregations, we need to give careful attention to the ways we listen, learn, and teach in our seminaries.

DEFINITIONS

Before turning to specific issues in theological education and preparation for ministry, I'll offer a few comments on the meaning of "multicultural" and the commitments I understand by the term. I use "multicultural" to indicate the inclusion of many different understandings of culture, especially those related to race and ethnicity, which are central to the discussion, and also, though to a lesser extent, those related to gender, age, sexual orientation, class, social location, language, and physical and learning abilities and disabilities. I also use the term to acknowledge the fundamental and provocative work of many who are working in the wider field of multicultural education, both in K–12 and in postsecondary education.

However, the term is not without its problems. Some educators find it problematic because it is often used in a manner that does not get at the basic issues of racism, power, and privilege. The commonly used inclusive definition (as set out in the paragraph above) can be seen as part of this problem. Multicultural education programs usually concentrate on developing awareness, fostering sensitivity, and increasing knowledge of many cultures and of culture understood in many different ways, but they often do not address racism and white privilege. Shawn Utsey and others stand in opposition to this broad approach to multicultural education because "it dilutes demands for racial equality by advancing an all-inclusive, pluralistic (or multicultural) perspective. . . . Multiculturalism maintains the status quo because it generally tends to ignore oppression, White privilege, and White racism."[5] Omowale Akintunde continues to use the term "multiculturalism," but he calls for a move toward a postmodern understanding. Rather than modernism's Euro American construction of the world, Akintunde sets out the goal of postmodernism as the "construction of a paradigm that does not recognize race as 'reality' and seeks to implement a sociocultural epistemology that is inclusive of all perspectives . . . and (to) reposition power in a more equitable way."[6]

Issues of race and ethnicity must be close to the center of any definition of "multicultural." Virstan Choy offers a shorthand exposition: by ethnicity we really mean issues of blood and belonging, and by race we mean issues of privilege, power, and prejudice.[7] Ethnicity is equated with culture in much of the literature,[8] and the term "ethnoculture" is often used to refer to a people group. Culture can be defined simply as the values, behaviors, customs, and consciousness learned from one's environment. More fully, people within a culture "have common and shared values, customs, habits, and rituals; systems of labeling, explanations, and evaluations; social rules of behavior; perceptions regarding human nature, natural phenomena, interpersonal relationships, time, and activity; symbols, art, and artifacts; and historical developments." Culture creates the sense of attachment and belonging; it is at the center of the concept of ethnic identity. Ethnicity can be understood as a birthright; each of us is born into an ethnic group, a cultural context of shared values, practices, and history. As Siân Jones observes: an ethnic group is "any group of people who set themselves apart and/or are set apart by others with whom they interact or co-exist on the basis of their perceptions of cultural differentiation and/or common descent."[9] Ethnicity is about blood and belonging.

Race, on the other hand, has to do with privilege that is often unearned, power that is inequitably distributed, and prejudice. Racism is clearly related to privilege and power, but not so clearly to prejudice. Beverly Tatum argues convincingly that prejudice and racism are not the same and that the two terms should not be used interchangeably. Racism cannot be understood simply as the result of racial prejudice. Rather, racism is "a system of advantage based on race."[10] In the United States, this system "clearly operates to the advantage of Whites and the disadvantage of people of color." The term "white privilege" is used to refer to the unearned advantages that are enjoyed by whites in this system. As Beverly Tatum explains, "it is more comfortable simply to think of racism as a particular form of prejudice. Notions of power or privilege do not have to be addressed when our understanding of racism is constructed this way."[11]

Understanding racism as a system of advantage based on race, in which some receive advantages they have not earned or deserve, contradicts basic conceptions of justice and flies in the face of the American idea of meritocracy. In the United States, understanding racism as a system of advantage based on race takes into account the experiences of *everyone* in the society and so is rightly understood as close to the center of the country's cultural reality. I understand the term "multicultural," even in its broad, inclusive definition, as a commitment to changing this reality.

In the remaining part of the chapter, I outline the main aspects of theological education that are needed to develop leadership for a church with multicultural sensibilities and commitments. These aspects are found in three broad areas: (1) the climate and culture of the seminary,

(2) the closely related issue of the ways that learning and teaching are understood, and (3) content—what is taught in seminary.

THE CLIMATE AND CULTURE OF THE SEMINARY

Learning develops in a social context and emerges from the interactions and relationships that take place among learners and teachers. Institutional climate and culture, along with the commitments and attitudes of faculty and administrators, either foster or hinder learning. This is especially important in seminaries, where we are concerned not only with the immediate nurturing of learning but also with the ways our graduates will nurture climates of acceptance and inclusion in their places of ministry.

Learning is always interactive with the environment of the learner. Ways of thinking, learning, and knowing are best understood as a socio-cultural process, as rooted in, and influenced by, social interaction. Russian psychologist Lev Vygotsky[12] is helpful here, with his theoretical framework that social interaction plays a fundamental role in cognitive development and that full cognitive development requires full social interaction. Learning cannot be separated from the social and cultural context in which it takes place, nor can education be separated from the ways that culture and society effect learning. This has remarkable significance for the ways that educational institutions organize themselves, as they reflect what is worth knowing and what it means to be educated.

Vygotsky's understanding is at some distance from the traditional view that learning is largely unaffected by context. According to the traditional view, if a child does not learn a skill, the failure should likely be attributed to the child's low intelligence or to some disorder or to a possible cultural difference. From Vygotsky's perspective, the situation is much more hopeful; everyone can learn if provided the opportunity for constructive social interaction. Failure to learn should not be defined immediately as individual failure, but possibly as related to systemic failure. There are important implications here for theological education— for faculty and administrators to accept and validate the cultures and languages of students, and by doing so create a climate of acceptance and constructive conditions for learning.

The collaborative relationship between learners and teachers is critical to learning, but it operates most effectively in the construction of knowledge only where there is affirmation of the learners' identities. As educator Sonia Nieto puts it, "When the context in which students learn is a caring and supportive one as well as respectful of their identities, students by and large learn. On the other hand, when they are asked to give up their identities for an elusive goal that they may never reach because of the negative context in which they must learn, students may be quite correct in rejecting the trade."[13]

The basic principles of multicultural education include fostering diversity in every aspect of the institutional environment, with special attention to the "hidden curriculum"—the ways the institution, in our case the seminary, conducts its affairs and organizes its common life. The commitment to diversity in multicultural education is particularly important for students from majority backgrounds; this is especially true in theological education, as learners from the dominant culture are called to listen to the ways that God is understood and God's work is undertaken in other locations. Multicultural education promotes the value of diversity (of all God's people) through fostering the understanding of the contributions and perspectives of all.

Multicultural education is about transformation—as, fundamentally, all good teaching is. Theological education is about the transformation that comes through conversion and God's work in our lives and ministry; it is also about our educational commitment to being transformed by listening and learning and engagement with students for their transformation. Transformation is needed at a number of levels—individual, community, and institution—with each required for the full fostering of student (and teacher) learning. Understanding the political and social aspects of the relation between learning and the environment is critical, not only for shaping the context of learning in theological education, but also for leaders in our congregations, denominations, and agencies. An understanding of the power relationships of dominant and nondominant cultures, and of who is privileged in these relationships, is critical in theological education and in Christian ministry. Multicultural education means working collaboratively, in ways that are equitable and mutually supportive of other members of the community. In seminary education this is often much easier to talk about than it is to do, yet it is one of the most significant of seminary commitments: to organize and conduct our life together in a manner that reflects God's reign and might serve as a model for students and their ministries.

LEARNING AND TEACHING

Closely related to the climate and learning context of the seminary are the ways that teaching and learning themselves are understood. One of the most significant components is the understanding that learning is constructed; education is not primarily about the transmission of ideas from teacher to learner, but about mutual discovery. This is an idea that is widely accepted, but much less widely practiced. Learning is not about the "banking" approach to education that Paulo Freire[14] disavowed, in which socially sanctioned, politically or religiously correct knowledge is deposited into the learner who may withdraw it (as from a bank vault) when examination time comes. Learning is not primarily about telling and being told. Rather, knowledge is constructed at the point of discovery, the point of experience (possibly gained before seminary) meeting new knowledge. In seminaries, even more than in other kinds of schools, learning should not primarily be about student ability to re-present the dominant attitudes or denominationally approved values and behaviors. Too often the replication of the accepted, sanctioned "knowledge" provides the measure by which teachers determine the extent to which learning has taken place.

This understanding is not at all new, but still we have a hard time putting it into practice. The idea that learning is not about telling and being told comes from John Dewey, who wrote in 1916,

> Why is it, in spite of the fact that teaching by pouring in, learning by a passive absorption, are universally condemned, that they are still so entrenched in practice? That education is not an affair of "telling" and being told but an active and constructive process, is a principle almost as generally violated in practice as conceded in theory. Is not this deplorable situation due to the fact that the doctrine is itself merely told? It is preached; it is lectured; it is written about.[15]

The usual explanation (which I believe to be correct) for this contradiction is the lack of trust in students and teachers to construct knowledge that is meaningful and significant. The mistrust happens at all levels and certainly on both sides of the liberal-conservative continuum, however that is construed, and is often as visible among students as among those responsible for the curriculum. In seminary education, especially, we are called to trust in the readiness and ability of students to listen, first of all to the voice of God's Spirit, and to learn. Of course, teaching texts and traditions and using tools are very important aspects of education, but learning is more complex than the provision of information or transmitting knowledge. More constructive is the development of "habits of mind" as described by Deborah Meier in *The Power of*

Their Ideas: Lessons for America from a Small School in Harlem.[16] Habits of mind such as, How do we know what we think we know? Whose perspective is it that we are using? How are things connected? Why is it important? Such questions keep us out of the banking approach, help us to consider options and learn to listen.

One of the most significant conceptual frameworks for working in diverse classrooms is provided by racial identity development theory.[17] Considerable attention has been given recently to issues of racial/ethnic/cultural identity and models of development by researchers and practitioners in the field of multicultural counseling, some of whom say that this approach is the most promising in the field.[18] Racial identity is defined by Janet Helms as "a sense of group or collective identity based on one's *perception* that he or she shares a common racial heritage with a particular racial group," and deals with the "psychological consequences to individuals of being socialized in a society in which a person is either privileged (i.e., White identity) or disadvantaged (e.g., Black or other People of Color identity) because of her or his racial classification."[19] Her work is especially important for its formulation of white racial identity theory and a framework for a process by which whites might come to understand their whiteness as part of developing a nonracist identity. The implications of racial identity development theory for seminary classrooms and communities are enormous, especially if it is understood first of all as a call for faculty members to work toward a solid sense of personal racial identity and awareness of privilege and power. Faculty will then be better able to guide and learn alongside students as they use the framework it provides for understanding the attitudes and reactions they find in themselves and others in their contexts of ministry.

Within the wide field of multicultural pedagogy, four additional notes are particularly important for seminaries:

1. As learning builds on experience, and as students arrive at seminary with a wealth of experiences and prior learning, it is for faculty and others in the community to support and build on that experience, affirm its cultural context, and provide a nurturing, fertile place for growth.

2. Cultural differences must be taken into account, but culture does not determine a student's ability or capacity to learn. As culture is not fixed, learning and cognition should not be understood as rigidly controlled by a specific culture; a culture's values are not known and expressed the same way by each member of the group. Broader ways of approaching the connection between culture and learning are needed—

such as the collective, interdependent / individualistic, independent continuum,[20] and understanding issues of authority and respect for elders. The competition / cooperation continuum is a significant example: competition is at the center of much of American higher education, yet many students, especially students of color, women, and international students, value cooperation and may have difficulty in classes that stress individual achievement. Still, it must be remembered that individuals always vary within groups and that culture, race, ethnicity, and language are "dimensions rather than definitions of each individual."[21]

3. There are significant links between language and learning. Research in the last two decades has consistently shown that students who are allowed to identify with and encouraged to use their first language have improved levels of learning and academic achievement, and that there are significant cognitive strengths among bilingual students.[22]

4. Eric Law, in *The Word at the Crossings: Living the Good News in a Multicontextual Community*, outlines a "pedagogy for the powerful." He begins with an invitation to honor Sabbath, to take time to step outside of our prescribed roles (which usually relate to positions of power) and encounter others. The internal culture of the powerful is almost always that of the surrounding culture, because the powerful have been the ones to shape it and often do not recognize that the norms, values, and beliefs they take for granted are not universal. Then Law asks us to create processes where the powerful and others can encounter and listen to each other, beginning (as he always recommends) with Bible study. Shift attention to God, ask about God's intentions, God's vision and Good News. He reminds us that "it is not we who transform the world, but God. . . . We do our parts the best we can, . . . but in the end it is the gospel of Jesus Christ that gives the courage for the powerful to let go of control, to open up their boundaries and honor Sabbath. . . . It is the gospel of Jesus Christ that calls us to find a new way to be in community that does not follow the destructive patterns of the world."[23]

SEMINARY CURRICULUM

At the center of multicultural theological education is an explicit curriculum that provides access to all perspectives. The inclusion of voices from diverse racial, cultural, language, and gender groups not only nurtures a climate of diversity and affirmation and invigorates the curriculum, but it also provides the voices *required* for the complete education of *all* students, not least those of the dominant culture. As Sonia Nieto

says of public school education, "multicultural education especially benefits majority group students, who may develop an unrealistic and
overblown view of their place in the world because of the unbalanced
and incomplete education they have received in the school curriculum
. . . (and) have been miseducated to the extent that they have been
exposed to only majority discourses."[24] How much more this might be
said of theological education, as Lamin Sanneh reminds us in his wonderfully titled recent book, *Whose Religion Is Christianity? The Gospel
beyond the West.*[25]

Peter Phan, Vietnamese American theologian, helps define the North
American theological context. He describes the immigrant experience—
living between two cultures without belonging fully to either but on the
margins of both—as a crucial source for the development of an "intercultural theology." (McCormick theologian Luis Rivera, with his work on
"diaspora hermeneutics," is the one who started my own thinking along
these lines.) Politically and socially, immigrants are not at the centers of
power of either of their two locations. In Peter Phan's words, "because
they dwell in the interstices between the two cultures, they are in a position to see more clearly and to appreciate more objectively, both as insiders and outsiders."[26] Theology in this reality is "intercultural" because it is
"shaped in the encounter between *two* cultures." But in North America
the situation is much more complex, because there are several cultures
encountering each other at the same time—not only the dominant culture and a single nondominant culture. Within each culture there are
many significant varieties, and all are constantly changing. So Peter Phan
speaks of and calls for a theology that is "inter-multicultural." This meeting place of theologies that emerge from the lived experiences of many
cultures, not just one or two, is exactly what we hope for at McCormick.
The commitment to fostering the engagement of many voices is at the
heart of the seminary's mission.

I find Peter Phan's notes on understanding culture especially helpful.
We need to move beyond the modern notion of culture as an internally
consistent, integrating whole into which individuals are socialized. Culture is evolving, inconsistent, conflicted—in contrast to the modern
view's "innocent cultural conventions." With a postmodern understanding of culture, intermulticultural theology cannot begin from a single,
general view of culture, that of the dominant culture, and then apply it
to other, local, ethnic cultures. Rather, as Phan says, we must begin with
"unmasking the asymmetrical relation between the dominant and
minority cultures and the forces of power at work in such a relation."[27]

Phan speaks, as many do, of a hermeneutics of suspicion, and then moves on to a hermeneutics of retrieval, including the stories of struggle and the stories of faith in the God who vindicated Jesus and how these stories have inspired and sustained stories of hope. We in theological education need to listen.

Multicultural theological education seeks to prepare women and men for ministry in a climate of acceptance and inclusion, through a pedagogy that affirms the experience and cultural location of the learner, and values the contributions of people of differing race, ethnicity, culture, language, gender, sexual orientation, and physical ability and disability. It fosters listening by removing barriers, nurtures learning, and encourages a readiness to being changed. Tearing down walls that divide, as clearly explained by the author of Ephesians, is God's work in Jesus Christ. We have an opportunity in theological education to participate in that work.

NOTES

1. *ATS Bulletin* 46, part 1 (2004): 48, 50, 53, 56.

2. Timothy Matovina, ed., *Beyond Borders: Writings of Virgilio Elizondo and Friends* (Maryknoll, NY: Orbis Books, 2000), 87.

3. John Muddiman, *The Epistle to the Ephesians*, Black's New Testament Commentaries (London: Continuum, 2001), 128.

4. "Benevolent Tolerance or Humble Reverence? A Vision for Multicultural Religions Education," in *Multicultural Religious Education,* ed. Barbara Wilkerson (Birmingham, AL: Religious Education Press, 1997), 387–88.

5. Shawn O. Utsey, Carol A. Gernat, and Mark A. Bolden, "Teaching Racial Identity Development and Racism Awareness: Training in Professional Psychology Programs," in *Handbook of Racial and Ethnic Minority Psychology,* ed. Guillermo Bernal et al. (Thousand Oaks, CA: Sage Publishing, 2003), 148–49.

6. Omowale Akintunde, "White Racism, White Supremacy, White Privilege, and the Social Construction of Race: Moving from Modernist to Postmodernist Multiculturalism," *Multicultural Education* 7, no. 2 (1999): 4.

7. Presentation at McCormick faculty consultation on Asian American ministry, April 2004. Dr. Choy is interim director of the Center of Asian American Ministries and visiting professor of ministry at McCormick.

8. Stacey J. Lee, "'Are You Chinese or What?' Ethnic Identity among Asian Americans," in *Racial and Ethnic Identity in School Practices: Aspects of Human Development,* ed. Rosa Hernandez Sheets and Etta R. Hollins (Mahwah, NJ: Lawrence Erlbaum Associates, 1999), 108.

9. Gargi Roysircar Sodowsky, Edward Wai Ming Lai, and Barbara S. Plake, "Moderating Effects of Sociocultural Variables on Acculturation Attitudes of Hispanics and Asian Americans," *Journal of Counseling and Development* 16 (1991): 194; Gargi Roysircar Sodowsky, Kwong-Liem Karl Kwan, and Raji Pannu, "Ethnic Identity of Asians in the United States," in *Handbook of Multicultural Counseling*, ed. Joseph G. Ponterottò et al. (Thousand Oaks, CA: Sage Publications, 1995): 123–54; Lee, "Are You Chinese or What?" 108; Siân Jones, *The Archaeology of Ethnicity: Constructing Identities in the Past and Present* (London: Routledge, 1997), xiii.

10. Beverly Daniel Tatum, *"Why Are All the Black Kids Sitting Together in the Cafeteria?" and Other Conversations about Race* (New York: Basic Books, 2003), 7; David T. Wellman, *Portraits of White Racism*, 2nd ed. (Cambridge: Cambridge University Press, 1993), 27–62.

11. Tatum, 7, 9. She points to the vast data supporting race as the primary predictor of social and economic well-being in the United States. See Neil J. Smelser, William Julius Wilson, and Faith Mitchell, eds., *America Becoming: Racial Trends and Their Consequences* (Washington, DC: National Academy Press, 2001), and Lee A. Daniels, ed., *The State of Black America 2004* (New York: National Urban League, 2004).

12. Vygotsky scholarship has boomed in the last few years. For his work in English, see *The Collected Works of L. S. Vygotsky*, ed. Robert W. Rieber and Aaron S. Carton (New York: Plenum Press, 1987–99), and *The Essential Vygotsky*, ed. Robert W. Rieber and David K. Robinson (New York: Kluwer Academic/Plenum Publishers, 2004).

13. Sonia Nieto, *The Light in Their Eyes: Creating Multicultural Learning Communities*, Multicultural Education Series (New York: Teachers College Press, 1999), 13. See also her *What Keeps Teachers Going* (New York: Teachers College Press, 2003).

14. Paulo Freire, *Pedagogy of the Oppressed* (New York: Continuum, 1984), and *The Politics of Education: Culture, Power, and Liberation* (New York: Bergin & Garvey, 1985).

15. John Dewey, *Democracy and Education: An Introduction to the Philosophy of Education* (New York: Free Press, 1944), 38.

16. Deborah Meier, *The Power of Their Ideas: Lessons for America from a Small School in Harlem* (Boston: Beacon Press, 2002).

17. Charmaine L. Wijeyesinghe and Bailey W. Jackson III, eds., *New Perspectives on Racial Identity Development: A Theoretical and Practical Anthology* (New York: New York University Press, 2001); Vasti Torres, Mary F. Howard-Hamilton, and Diane L. Cooper, *Identity Development of Diverse Populations: Implications for Teaching and Administration in Higher Education*, ASHE-ERIC Higher Education Report, vol. 29, no. 6 (San Francisco: Jossey-Bass, 2003); Beverly Daniel Tatum, "Talking about Race, Learning about Racism: The Application of Racial Identity Development Theory in the Classroom," in *Race and Higher Education:*

Rethinking Pedagogy in Diverse College Classrooms, ed. Annie Howell and Frank Tuitt (Cambridge: Harvard Education Review, 2003), 139–63.

18. Derald Wing Sue and David Sue, *Counseling the Culturally Diverse: Theory and Practice*, 4ᵗʰ ed. (New York: John Wiley, 2003), 207.

19. Janet E. Helms, ed., *Black and White Racial Identity: Theory, Research and Practice* (Westport, CT: Praeger, 1990), 9, and "Toward a Methodology for Measuring and Assessing Racial as Distinguished from Ethnic Identity," in *Multicultural Assessment in Counseling and Clinical Psychology*, ed. Gargi Roysircar Sodowsky and James C. Impara (Lincoln, NE: Buros Institute of Mental Measurements, 1996), 153–54. Janet Helms is "considered by many to be the mother of White racial identity theory" (Utsey, Gernat, and Bolden, 152).

20. See Uichol Kim et al., eds., *Individualism and Collectivism: Theory, Method, and Applications*, Cross-Cultural Research and Methodology Series (Thousand Oaks, CA: Sage Publications, 1994), and Geert Hofstede, *Culture's Consequences: Comparing Values, Behaviors, Institutions, and Organizations across Nations*, 2nd ed. (Thousand Oaks, CA: Sage Publications, 2001).

21. Eleanor W. Lynch, "Instructional Strategies," in Ann Intili Morey and Margie K. Kitano, eds., *Multicultural Course Transformation in Higher Education: A Broader Truth* (Boston: Allyn & Bacon, 1997), 62.

22. Carrol E. Moran and Kenji Hakuta, "Bilingual Education: Broadening Research Perspectives," in *Handbook of Research on Multicultural Education*, ed. James A. Banks and Cherry A. McGee Banks (San Francisco: Jossey-Bass, 2001), 445–62.

23. Eric H. F. Law, *The WORD at the Crossings: Living the Good News in a Multicontextual Community* (St. Louis: Chalice Press, 2004).

24. Nieto, *The Light in Their Eyes*, xviii.

25. Lamin Sanneh, *Whose Religion Is Christianity? The Gospel beyond the West* (Grand Rapids: Eerdmans, 2003).

26. Peter C. Phan, *Christianity with an Asian Face: Asian American Theology in the Making* (Maryknoll, NY: Orbis Books, 2003), 9.

27. Ibid., 13.

CHAPTER 2

Toward an Intercultural Approach to Theological Education for Ministry

José R. Irizarry

> To be with [God] is also to be with all who are, by their choice or the choice of others, non-citizens, non-belongers; it is to be part of a social order that depends on nothing but God's presence and self-gift, God's decision to be with the non-belongers.
>
> *Rowan Williams*[1]

In academic and popular circles, debates on multiculturalism range from the most conservative perspectives to the most radically critical, with liberals and moderates swaying in between. One wonders whether a common language of shared definitions is possible or even desirable. A theorizing of multiculturalism demands, in principle, a multiplicity of voices and even a multiplicity of definitions, each spreading out of a particular notion of culture and the cultural perspective of the theorist. Hence one of the central paradoxes of multiculturalism is revealed: any exposure of the topic is necessarily ethnocentric. There is no treatment of multiculturalism that "speaks out of" and for "all" cultural groups. However, this essential plasticity of the multicultural language cannot excuse the theorist or student writing about it from making explicit her choice of terms and the perspective by which she engages the discussion of cultural pluralism. After all, as linguist Noam Chomsky suggests, the meaning given to language guides its use.[2]

The specific questions when discussing the experience of cultural diversity determine the definition. Thus, some scholars have used alternative terms such as cross-culturalism, and interculturalism. Others add broader signification by coining terms such as transculturality, intraculturality, cultural difference, and identity politics. Since no singular concept is needed for meaningful engagement, it is important to make explicit the selection of our constructs and the reality we want to study by using very particularized language.

In this essay, I deliberately use the term *intercultural* as a preferable construct to speak about the multicultural experience. This term does not substitute or correct other terms, but refers to *a particular moment within the experience of the multicultural community where "culturally defined" groups engage each other in intentional ways in order to develop strategies to live together and to work together as distinctive members of the same community.* This stage of the experience presupposes that members of different cultural groups have recognized each other, learned something about each other, and agreed to show tolerance toward each other in some basic way.

To some extent, the years of multicultural experiments in education have laid down the basis for such elemental form of engagement. The boom of multicultural interests in education during the 1980s yielded an academic curriculum that supported the inclusion of various cultural perspectives in the overall learning process.[3] Commonly, the approach to this type of curriculum is *additive*, in that some courses are taught in *this or that* culture, while the core knowledge of the curriculum (formerly known as the canon) remains the same and undisputed. Multiculturalism then, from the educational perspective currently employed in institutions of higher education, is the recognition and validation of the presence of various cultural groups in the educational context. Simply stated, educational multiculturalism in higher education is the academic rendition of the inescapable social condition of cultural pluralism. This acknowledgment is in line with a more mundane attitude that declares we *are* multicultural and, therefore, we must "run with the program" and deal with it. In institutions of theological education, multicultural education took the form of courses on the theology of marginalized groups, the inclusion in more traditional courses of textbooks written from various cultural perspectives, and in some cases the establishment of programmatic centers created to help develop such a component of the academic offering and to offer institutional support to underrepresented students.

We should not be surprised to discover that the educational approach to multiculturalism took this form originally. The concept of multiculturalism itself, from the point of view of its linguistic determinants, is descriptive rather than prescriptive. Society is multicultural as a parking garage is multileveled, and a cake multilayered. Mere observation and description of the social configuration of our times will render a multicultural narrative. However, the concept of *inter*culturality (as well as *cross*-culturality) implies an active engagement among cultures. What is then given to the theorist or the student is a term that is linguistically conditioned to address the issue of agency and cultural dynamics. It is up to each student or theorist to use the term to describe how that cultural engagement happens and what are its objectives.

While the term "cross-cultural" is also a dynamic term, its constant usage in the literature of Christian missions has already charged its semantic content. A cross-cultural experience is commonly understood (although it is not essential to understand it this way) as the transit of one culture into the space of another culture and assumes that those "crossing" the line that divides one culture from another will give and receive from the exchange and come back to their initial cultural location. A cross-cultural experience has two (or more) distinguishable cultural configurations and presupposes an asymmetrical relation in principle, since the space in which the cross-cultural experience happens positions cultures as either observers or observed. I propose that an intercultural approach suggests a shift toward *a multicultural engagement that facilitates the possibility of various cultures sharing the same social configuration and therefore the possibility of negotiating values, practices, and even identities in order to live a more sustainable shared life.*

The intercultural experience is not additive, since the mere addition of cultures to a dominant understanding of reality does not challenge the centers of power in a multicultural experience. The intercultural experience is *transformative* in that power is first disclosed, analyzed, shared, and constantly renegotiated among the diverse cultural groups in the community. For this reason, interculturalism can be understood as the critical approach to multiculturalism. In an intercultural experience no one is guaranteed that their cultural identities will remain the same throughout the engagement. The purpose of living together is not mutual understanding and tolerance. As important as these objectives are for the process, they should not be the end of the multicultural experience. The purpose of intercultural education is the exploration of the possibilities for exchanging cultural meanings among groups in order to broaden our perspectives and change our own particular ways of thinking and living. In doing so, all groups immersed in the educational experience will be transcending the ethnocentric impulses of both cognition and praxis.

One of the most significant features of postcolonial thought is its acknowledgment that cultural assimilation and diffusion still happen, even when the old colonial regimes have disintegrated. However, since the dynamics of how neocolonialism operates are more evident and predictable, it is plausible in our globalizing context that "dominant" and "dominated" cultures can mutually acculturate and assimilate. These acculturations and assimilations produce new cultural identities, described by some as "hybrid" identities. In comparison to protocolonial experiences, postcolonialism does not assume that only the dominated culture will change, but the dominant one will also be transformed. What has been uncovered by the proponents of postcolonial theory is that the social groupings we call "cultures" are not unalterable configurations of essentialized identity but shared locations of meaning that are open to change through interaction either by agency or imposition.[4] The intercultural prospect opens the door to dialogical interaction regarding the power assumed in both agency and imposition, as well as a constructive appeal to uphold the value of the community in the midst of that critical dialogue.

The question is whether theological education can provide a suitable context where an intercultural experience can be promoted. If theological schools are about the mission of forming leaders for ecclesial communities seeking to foster *comm*(on)*union* in a diversified world, the question remains whether the current values, curriculum, and academic commitments of theological schools are adequate means to that formative end. As a social institution with a significant mission within a multicultural society, the church requires ministerial leadership that is able to communicate across the borders of both local groups and global cultures. In a theological sense, this leader should be equipped to navigate swiftly between the authorities of tradition (culturally defined) and revelation (open to the work of the Spirit in various cultural contexts). In some way, preparing ministerial leadership that can keep this dialogue in creative tension may be a more pertinent project in the American society of the twenty-first century than trying to sustain the tension of the old and exhausted dialogue between theory and practice. I argue that a new, intercultural approach to theological education can facilitate this sort of leadership and move the church toward fulfilling its vocation in the midst of a pluralistic society.

In order to respond to this question in a heuristic mode, I will use two terms, "movement" and "space," in order to build a conceptual framework for a discussion on intercultural theological education. Since I have established that the term intercultural is a dynamic concept, I should also imply some common elements of an active construct. First, any dynamic process is detectable by the movement produced within that process. An action presupposes the termination of inactivity and the initiation of some type of movement. Second, any activity is undertaken under the limits of a context or space; it has duration and a location. Taking into consideration these two features of a dynamic concept applied to interculturality, I suggest that an intercultural theological education should attend to the issues of movement and space.

THE MOVEMENT OF THEOLOGICAL EDUCATION

When David Kelsey traced the map of the cultural boundaries of theological education, the departure and destination points were already declared in the title of his book, *Between Athens and Berlin*.[5] Kelsey suggests that theological education has oscillated between two distinctive poles; a classical educational model that focuses in the formation of Christian character, in this case for ministry, and another model that focuses on the critical reflective skills required of any professional endeavor. According to Kelsey, "Athens" is "a movement from the *source* to personal appropriation of *the source*," in other words, from a revealed wisdom to the appropriation of that wisdom through the process of education.[6] The "Berlin model of theological education is a movement from data to theory to application of theory to practice."[7] The Berlin model, rather than being an alternative and conscious development of a new form of understanding theology in relation to culture, is basically the form that theological education took as it assimilated to the *Wissenschaft* mind-set of the modern German university.

From an intercultural perspective, one can easily point to the ethnocentric tendency of both these apparent "movements" in theological education. Rather than an oscillating movement between two distinctive and "irreconcilable" points, both models represent a collapsing toward the center of Western culture. While "Athens" and "Berlin" have distinctive perspectives and methods for doing theological education—which is to be expected, taking into consideration the historical setting in which they were forged—much of what is considered the "source" of wisdom and the logic of theological thinking remains unchallenged.

It would be unfair to declare the westernization of theological education accounts to be a historical flaw. After all, these models were developed in Western societies, and they obeyed, consciously or unconsciously, the exigencies of their contexts. The problem is not that theological education attended solely to the culture of the West, but that as the world beyond Europe became part of theological education efforts, such models were declared normative and universal. It was taken for granted that a normative model of theological education, with its epistemological and ontological assumptions, could address a cosmopolitan context and define the formative processes for the church catholic. With this assumption, many theological schools started to receive students from different cultural backgrounds under the assumption that knowledge produced under these models transcends cultural particularities. In other words, the "classic" and "scientific" models of theological education shape a system for teaching and learning that is cross-culturally invariant, even when it now includes the experience of various cultures.

A treatment of the implications of cultural pluralism in theological education is extensive enough as to constitute a major study in itself. Issues of theological authority, ecclesial traditions, socioreligious contexts for faith formation, and the structural arrangements of institutions in which theological knowledge is produced need to be comprehensively examined. To limit the scope of this article, I will focus on three aspects of the intercultural approach that render a critical view of theological education. These aspects are (1) the epistemological "source" from which we grasp theological understanding, (2) the existing "order" of theological reflection, and (3) the immediate "beneficiaries" of theological education.

While Kelsey suggests that theological education has a singular source, it is difficult to identify what this source is without immediately identifying it with Western culture.[8] To speak about a "source" in theological education is to suggest that there is a unified system of beliefs and ideas about God that can be apprehended, from revealed experience, via our intellects. In some way theological education has claimed a distinctive *object* of study, but it has maintained the accepted principle of higher education that grants cognitive skills a primordial role in defining the adequacy of knowledge. While other dimensions of knowledge have been validated, including the ethical, the aesthetic, and the experiential, these maintain a lower status in the hierarchy of knowledge in contrast to the cognitive dimension. Activities that heighten these "lesser" dimensions of knowledge in theological schools—such as worship, field education, community life, and public service—are seen as auxiliary to the core academic program, which is centered in curricular offerings.

A group of theorists has currently challenged the type of education that focuses on the cognitive-instrumental aspects of knowledge to the displacement of other pivotal components of understanding and meaning-making. Jürgen Habermas, for example, has deplored the sort of knowledge that is incapable of interacting effectively with the moral and the expressive dimensions of the rational person.[9] The critique offered by Habermas and others is not new. By the seventeenth century, Baruch Spinoza had already developed a full philosophical system on behalf of a holistic epistemology where affections and desire could play a significant role in the human production of knowledge. Spinoza's concept of "conatus" was elaborated in order to engage the whole person in the process of learning. However, the term and its implications fell in disuse under the overpowering influence of rationalistic thought in subsequent centuries.[10]

The point where interculturalism intersects with this proposal for a holistic understanding of theological knowledge is the recognition that this epistemology represents actual manners by which non-Western cultures engage already the construction of knowledge. Knowledge of God and religious experience find various sources in various cultures, and in teaching about theological matters, reason has not been given the primary role across the board. Take as an example the presentation of popular religion as a "locus" for interpreting theological meaning for many Hispanic/Latina believers and scholars. An analysis of theological knowledge through popular religiosity shows how the affective domain of individuals plays a central role in constituting religious knowledge.[11] In turn, Latin American liberation theology has been able to construct a rational system of theological declarations while claiming the importance of human volition as a primary source of theological knowledge.[12] With liberation theologies the experiential and the explicit disclosure of ideological stances become important in the declarative expressions of theological truths.

While in many theological education classrooms the liberationist take has been accepted as an appropriate methodology to be used by the culturally "other" (whether a "third-world" theologian or a feminist), the methodology is rarely incorporated in the interpretation of the so-called "classical" or "traditional" theology. When the intercultural dimensions of education are not taken into consideration, much of these important sources of theological insight is suppressed, under the current validation of cognition as the primary source of theological knowledge. When students of color or women in the theological classroom resist the subjugation of these insights and the impositions of cognition upon meaning, much of the knowledge they produce is deemed inadequate. Therefore, learning performance and motivation, as well as the evaluation of that form of scholarship by the instructor, can be affected.

The other aspect of *movement* that is clearly manifested in theological education is the order or logic of reflection. Kelsey and Farley describe this order as a movement from theory to practice. While theological educators invest mental energies defending the integrated character of theory and practice and resisting (philosophically) this binarism, the fact that it has to be constantly declared accounts for the permanence of this dualism. Something we have learned from Aristotle and his novel descriptions of the tripartite self (body, mind, and soul), for example, is how easily philosophical distinction becomes separation. The organization of theological disciplines reflects that distinction between the theoretical domains of education (classical fields) and the practical ones (ministry areas). We can also see how pervasive this separation is when we hear comments by students such as, "How do I translate what I learn in seminary to the congregational setting?" or the common remark of more seasoned leaders, "You will do things that you never learned in seminary."

In *A Fundamental Practical Theology*, Don Browning suggests that bridging the gap between theory and practice by a sustained engagement of theological reflection and the practices of ministry is the primary task of any institution fostering practical wisdom (*phronesis*).[13] While his book contains various articles, including some written from the perspective of communities of "color," thus providing models on how to navigate the tensions between theory and practice, this integration confronts a lack of models within the dominant culture. It is difficult to sustain an integration of theory and practice in a culture that socially benefits from the separation of labor and the social reproduction models that naturally emerge from this dualism. Theory and practice will remain fragmented as long as institutions of higher learning continue to support the Aristotelian law of the "excluded middle" in academic discourse.[14] While I agree that surpassing the theory/practice dualism is a primary challenge of theological education, both for pragmatic and ethical reasons, I contend that an intercultural approach to theological education can move seminaries and divinity schools from rhetorical apologetics about dualisms to an actual integration of theory and practice.

Taking advantage of the presence of a larger range of cultural subjects in the classrooms, we must attend to the various ways that cultural agents around the world have avoided falling into the theory/practice dualism. For example, the theology emerging from Asia acknowledges its debt to other traditional religions and philosophical schools within their national cultures.[15] Through this literature the contributions of both Buddhism and Confucianism in erasing the boundaries between theory and practice are well known. In these influential traditions of Asian theologies, the organic unity and integrity of the moral self is reflected not only in literary discourse but in art and symbols. It should not be surprising then to discover that when "enlightened" Europe needed to go out of the scientific enclave in order to get "practical wisdom," they looked into places like China to import the knowledge on productive techniques necessary for social functioning.[16] While the limits of this article do not allow for an in-depth exploration of other cultural variants (the American First Nations and the Islamic Tahwid principle come to mind), the distinction between theory and practice is a culturally specific problem, and only in comparative and integrative dialogue with other cultural groups can the dualism be addressed from a less essentialist and deterministic perspective.

One question that remains suspended on the debate on theological education is, Who is the beneficiary of the instructional and formative process that takes place within the theological institution? A perusal of mission statements across institutions does not shed clear light on the answer. Theological institutions claim to do something (train, equip, educate, prepare) for a certain type of individual (a leader, a servant, a professional, a clergy person) who will be serving a particular social institution (the church) in order to facilitate a certain development (change, transformation, responsiveness, sustained engagement) within the world. We can claim that either the individual learner, the church, or the world is the one that benefits from theological education. Perhaps the three of them benefit equally. But those who benefit can benefit only if what is given was needed in the first place. The individual needs of the learners are shaped, to great extent, by their cultural context. The church they serve retains (for good and ill) a strong cultural identity. And the world they are seeking to affect is a multicultural reality.

Theological education cannot claim that it is rendering benefits unless the needs-assessment process, in light of cultural exigencies, is part of the overall organization of its content, methods, and procedures. The school cannot have a monocultural understanding of its mission and the strategies for its organization and, at the same time, deliver an instruction that is beneficial for all cultural subjects who are represented.

Theological education, more than any other form of academic instruction, requires the incorporation of an intercultural approach to teaching and learning. The students who engage theological education are sent to religious communities that preserve a strong sense of cultural identity and ethnic consciousness. In many instances these churches become either absorbed into the dominant culture with its westernizing determinants or alienated from the major culture by a strictly cultural ghettoization. In light of this reality, the ministerial effectiveness that theological education will facilitate will be assessed by how well students are prepared to minister in context. But as theological institutions respond to these extremes of the cultural captivity of the church (assimilation and alienation), an intercultural experience can help learners avoid the perils of understanding the church in strictly cultural terms, by seeing culture as something that evolves, that changes positively through interactions, and that is inclusive of a diversity of influences. Moving towards heterogeneity in ecclesial identity will allow churches to embrace more than one model of being the church in relation to culture.

While the church is a natural beneficiary of theological education, one cannot advance an intercultural agenda if the church is not also a contributor to theological education. Having incorporated a variety of cultural groups into its history and tradition, the church possesses global voices that can offer the cultural knowledge theological education needs in order to break with its ethnocentrism. Theological scholarship around the world is important to this conversation, but much of that scholarship has been shaped by Western models of academia. Much of what scholars of the global church can contribute to the discussion of theological difference is borrowed from the experience of common people within the cultures they work to describe. The history of scholarship, in the West and elsewhere, has prompted theories of cultural diffusion that propose that rationality is produced by a few with intellectual capacities and then given to less creative and less civilized subjects. Theological education falls constantly into this understanding when it stresses the difference between the "educated" clergy and the lay person in the pew. To address the issue of culture adequately, theological schools will need to develop projects and strategies to observe, listen, and interpret a variety of "culturally labeled" congregations (racial ethnic) as well as ethnic immigrant cultures within society.[17] It will also need to apply the same cultural interpretation to congregations that identify with the dominant culture, so that these congregations can become an equal partner in the intercultural dialogue. The intercultural dialogue in theological education should be nurtured extensively by what cognitive anthropologists call folk knowledge—the subjugated knowledge of those who experience faith through "*lo cotidiano*,"[18] that which Michel Focault referred to as "*le savoir des gens*."[19]

CREATING SPACE FOR THE INTERCULTURAL EXPERIENCE
IN THEOLOGICAL EDUCATION

Two of my favorite novels, Gabriel Garcia Marquez's "Cien años de soledad" and Meir Shalev's "The Blue Mountain," have as a common theme a group of sojourners who struggle to create a new community in an unexplored place. The communities, with their values, rituals, institutions, history, customs, and organization, are created by these sojourners from pieces of memory and habits from the places they come from. In other words, they build a new culture out of diversity. These novels fall into a type of literature described by literary critics as "magic realism." In the building of these new cultures, events happen that seem marvelous to people (readers) outside the communities but that make perfect sense to those inside. In some way the novelists have created in the fictional town of Macondo and the illusory village in the Jezreel valley, what Brazilian dramatist Augusto Boal calls aesthetic spaces.[20] These aesthetic spaces are locations where the utopian possibilities that find restriction within the current social and cultural conditions can be rehearsed and practiced.

An aesthetic space serves as a restricted space where people bring memory and imagination to make things possible here and now. In a way the scriptural texts of the Judeo-Christian tradition contain a great number of aesthetic spaces. From the creation of a new religion and culture out of the pieces of memory of diverse migrant populations who shared the same "mythical" land (of milk and honey), to the many religious traditions carrying stories of possibilities, the Bible provides great models of aesthetic spaces. In the New Testament the most visible aesthetic space is named by Jesus "God's kingdom." Because the Bible is populated by these spaces, it gives us the best examples of intercultural experiences, where cultures sharing a religious and social space can shape each other into a common story of salvation, redemption, and liberation.

Theological education has in Scripture—as well as in the tradition of the church and the actual experience of believers—the sources for facilitating aesthetic spaces where intercultural communication and relations can be rehearsed and practiced for the time being. The classroom, the worship space, the intentional community, and ministry contexts can become spaces for exploring what it means to bracket one's own cultural positions in order to enhance knowledge and be transformed into a new community. For the spectators of the aesthetic space, the intercultural exchanges may be seen as unreal, idealistic, or lacking authenticity (as not representing an actual community outside the theological institution). However, in light of the current debate on the limits of great emancipating projects in education, it will help us to explore intercultural communities as a form of micropolitics. This is a way of organizing our life together to the extent to which we live together inside the boundaries of singular diverse community. In other words, while the school can offer motivation to work toward racial and cultural reconciliation through progressive theology and scholarship, it can offer also concrete experiences of interculturality that can then help the learner to see how these may operate in the world in which she is called to serve. These experiences will hopefully develop the sensibility, agency, and skills for leading a church where "us" and the "other" belong together because they belong with God.

I will try to describe briefly how the intercultural space can be constituted and the conditions of its formation. When learners and teachers enter the intercultural space, they all come with a consciousness of their particular cultures and enter into a shared learning space as pilgrims, as people constituting a new community out of the stories, memories, and values of those cultures represented. In this case, there are no normative or hosting culture and no "guest" cultures, since such a distinction already burdens the space with asymmetrical relations of power. But although the space is aesthetic (creative), it should not be naive, and it should recognize the unavoidable presence of power in sociohistorical structures of racial privilege.[21] But arriving as pilgrims to the intercultural space, we already assume a deliberate critical posture and an open transformative agenda in relation to power. Those who intentionally work at intercultural community will come to understand the need to change the power dynamics in the aesthetic space as a precondition for learning and growth.

There are some critical perspectives that condition the space where intercultural theological education happens and that significantly alter the power dynamics of learning. First, the intercultural learning community problematizes the issue of difference. The question of what makes people who are equally motivated to learn by a sense of vocation and belief "different" is at the core of new relationships among teachers and learners. While there is no doubt that difference will be manifested in the learning space, it is important to recognize the subjectivity and flux of group identities. In the intercultural space, learners and teachers assume that difference is contextual, in that cultural differences may be more or less relevant depending on the context in which they come up. Learners do not surface their cultural identities in a consistent way everywhere. A learner who brings forward the input of some aspect of his cultural identity in a theology paper may not do so explicitly in the context of worship.

While race may be a distinctive characteristic of difference in a classroom, people from the same racial group can demonstrate difference when they stress the identity of their religious upbringing in the liberal-conservative spectrum. Cultural groups cannot be essentialized a priori. All groups who have come together to constitute a "culture" because they share some affinities maintain significant differences among themselves. For example, the cultural group that has been socially labeled "Hispanic" shares affinities in the areas of language, spirituality, and immigration histories, but preserves distinctive differences in politics and values. In other words, the manifestation of cultural difference is not something we predetermine by observing the learners—it is something that surfaces in the interaction. In the intercultural experience cultural difference is not something that we necessarily "bring" into the community of learners, but something that emerges in the relation. Therefore, cultural difference is relational, in that we come to the realization of our cultural distinctiveness when confronted with others who point that difference to us, or as we recognize being different in contrast to others. One important characteristic of the intercultural experience is that it should emphasize, as it points to differences, that cultural groups share common experiences and therefore they are similar in many respects. A discussion of difference has to be balanced with a discussion of similarity as a reminder of the ever present possibility of an intercultural community, one that enters into contact with others to generate a new communal culture.

The intercultural space for learning should not be understood as a place where learners, carrying their particular cultural identities, come together to present a challenge to socialization and pedagogy. It should be better understood as a space where identity formation happens. In the process of identity formation, education should provide the largest variety of cultural perspectives from which learners and teachers can responsibly form their own theological knowledge and religious values. The inclusion of theological perspectives from cultural contexts that are different from that of the dominant group is not presented only in order to explain that culture and its beliefs, but to render them as alternative views that can be acculturated into the belief system of all learners. In that sense, for example, to talk about a theology *of* the "Third World" delimits the potential of its contribution as a theology *from* the "Third World" for the formation of the whole church. It is necessary then not only to bring the content of these theologies to bear into the learning experience but also to have a deeper understanding of the methods of theological construction and the epistemologies that engender those theological discourses. The same principle applies to other disciplines of theological education.

The intercultural space for a theological education that respects, includes, and dialogues with the diverse realities of today's cultural pluralism encourages learners and teachers to reflect on personal meanings and constructions of cultural difference, to face and negotiate differences in the context of relations and shared commitments, to disclose the power dynamics that are implicit in a curriculum that supports epistemological hierarchies and dualistic reasoning, and to encourage faithful responsibility in constructing a Christian identity that is increasingly more catholic. Responding to the call for catholicity as a tangible expression of God's reign, we can move from cultural determinations if we, regardless of cultural identity, claim "our common pilgrim heritage and practice the most pilgrim of virtues, hospitality."[22] In the intercultural experience, our hearts, yearning for a more inclusive community, are restless until they rest in God.

NOTES

1. Rowan Williams, *Seven Words for the 21st Century* (Great Britain: Cromwell Press, 2002), 4.

2. Noam Chomsky, "Explaining Language Use," *Philosophical Topics* 20 (1992): 205–31.

3. See M. A. Gibson, "Approaches to Multicultural Education in the United States: Some Concepts and Assumptions," in *Anthropology and Education Quarterly* 5:94–119. See also J. A. Banks, "Multicultural Education: Development, Paradigms, and Goals," in J. A. Banks and J. Lynch, *Multicultural Education in Western Societies* (London: Holt, Rinehart & Winston, 1986).

4. See Gayatri Chakravorty Spivak, *Other Worlds: Essays in Cultural Politics* (New York: Methuen, 1987). See also Homi K. Bhaba, *The Location of Culture* (New York: Routledge, 1994).

5. David H. Kelsey, *Between Athens and Berlin: The Theological Education Debate* (Grand Rapids: Eerdmans, 1993).

6. Ibid., 19.

7. Ibid., 22.

8. Although Edward Farley does not use the language of "sources" to refer to the organizing principle of theological education, as Kelsey does, he utilizes the concept of "theologia," which also refers to a unifying subject matter and criteria to evaluate the adequacy of theological formation. See *Theologia: The Fragmentation and Unity of Theological Education* (Philadelphia: Fortress Press, 1983).

9. Jürgen Habermas, *Reason and Rationalization in Society* (Cambridge: Polity Press, 1984).

10. For a discussion of Spinoza's holistic view of knowledge and "conatus," see Thomas Groome, *Sharing Faith: A Comprehensive Approach to Religious Education and Pastoral Ministry* (New York: HarperCollins, 1991), 26–35.

11. See Orlando Espín, *The Faith of the People: Theological Reflections on Popular Catholicism* (Maryknoll, NY: Orbis Books, 1997).

12. See *Mysterium Liberationis: Fundamental Concepts of Liberation Theology*, ed. Ignacio Ellacuria and Jon Sobrino (Maryknoll, NY: Orbis Books, 1993). Refer especially to Clodovis Boff's article "Epistemology and Method of the Theology of Liberation," 57–85.

13. Don S. Browning, *A Fundamental Practical Theology: Descriptive and Strategic Proposals* (Minneapolis: Fortress Press, 1991).

14. In Immanuel Kant's late essay *The Conflict of the Faculties*, he traces a blueprint of the educational components of the modern university as he proposes that "it was not a bad idea to handle the entire content of learning . . . by mass production, so to speak—by a division of labor" (*Der Streit der Fakultäten*, trans. Mary J. Gregor [New York: Abaris Press, 1979]). This statement has defined the purpose of higher education of the modern Western university since then.

15. Choo Lak Yeow, ed., *Doing Theology with Cultures in Asia* (Singapore: ATESEA, 1988).

16. Gregory Blue, "Chinese Influences on the Enlightment in Europe," in Ruth Hayhoe and Julia Pan, eds., *Knowledge across Cultures* (Hong Kong: Comparative Education Research Center, University of Hong Kong, 2001), 277–87.

17. Mark Griffin and Theron Walker, *Living on the Borders: What the Church Can Learn from Ethnic Immigrant Cultures* (Grand Rapids: Brazos Press, 2004).

18. A discussion on *lo cotidiano* (daily living) as a source for theological reflection and ethical discernment has been extensively exposed by Ada Maria Isasi-Diaz, *En la Lucha: A Hispanic Women's Liberation Theology* (Minneapolis: Fortress Press, 1993).

19. Michel Foucault, *Power/Knowledge: Selected Interviews and Other Writings, 1972–1977* (New York: Pantheon, 1980), 82.

20. See Augusto Boal, *The Rainbow of Desire* (New York: Routledge, 1995), 16–39.

21. David Esterline treats the topic of white privilege in chapter 1.

22. Griffin and Walker, 182.

CHAPTER 3

Multicultural Theological Education: On Doing Difference Differently

Anna Case-Winters

WHAT IS THEOLOGICAL EDUCATION AND WHAT IS IT FOR?

It has been said that the whole aim of education is "the formation of *good habits*."[1] What are the "good habits" to be formed in a theological education? The work of theology itself is, as Edward Farley has argued, not so much a specialized discipline for religious professionals to study, as it is a *habitus*[2]—a habit or practice of Christian faith as we reflect upon what we believe and why and the implications for our lives. The work of theology is seeking the wisdom that attends faith. In theological education the Christian faith is opening itself to inquiry and critical reflection for the sake of the living of the faith.

Among other questions to be asked in designing programs of theological education is "What does the living of the faith require of us today?" Such a question lifts our eyes beyond the student, even the church in which the student will serve, to focus upon the wider world in which the church seeks to serve God faithfully. What kind of world is it? What are its needs and challenges? How may people of faith be some earthly good in the present context? How may religious leaders lead in good directions?

In inquiring into the question "What kind of world is it?" one characteristic of the contemporary context that cannot be ignored is the way in which differences (of race, class, gender, sexual orientation, culture, religion, etc.) become the occasions of exclusion and oppression, conflict and violence. One of the critical needs of our contemporary world context is to learn to do difference differently.

Unfortunately, people of faith have not been particularly helpful in leading the way in the face of this challenge. This was brought home to me recently at a forum on globalization. A representative of the World Bank was sharing an account of the resistance she met when trying to get religious leaders included in the World Bank Dialogue on Ethics and Values. Her colleagues objected on the grounds that religion is—in my own shorthand—defunct, divisive, and dangerous. It is, at best, irrelevant (defunct) to the contemporary situation—which it has failed to address in ways that are compelling. At worst, where it does make an impact, the impact is negative (divisive, dangerous). These charges are not without foundation in our history and current practice. Religious leaders have not always helped in finding a way to do difference differently. Rather, religious difference has added to the occasions for discord, conflict, and violence. Jonathan Swift's acid observation is to the point: we have "just enough religion to make us hate one another but not enough to make us love one another."[3]

Some would even say that certain aspects of some religions have exacerbated the problem of how differences are addressed. Some critics have in fact attributed the tendency to deny and disrespect difference to the religious impulses of monotheism. There is one God, therefore one truth, one way. When this is the predominant mind-set, differences cannot be embraced. One option is *opposition*: difference is a threat. There is what Freud called "the narcissism of small differences." There is no difference so slight that it cannot, under pressure, be turned into a marker of identity and an occasion for mutual estrangement.[4] Another option is *denial*: difference does not exist. We dwell upon similarities and commonalities and treat apparent differences as superficial and trivial. This is to disrespect difference. Neither of these approaches holds much promise for a global future. For a way forward we will need, as Rabbi Jonathan Sacks has proposed, "a theology of difference: why it exists, why it matters, why it is constitutive of our humanity, why it represents the will of God."[5]

Can theological education contribute to such a project? Potentially, institutions of *multicultural* theological education can become places for working out a "theology of difference." Components of research, reflection, and writing in this area would surely be part of such an undertaking. Seminaries committed to multicultural theological education can construct themselves as laboratories for the "dialogue of difference." In Sacks's analysis, the present reality is that difference generates anxiety, and anxiety generates fear, and fear leads to violence. The greatest antidote to violence might be a committed dialogue of difference.

But there is also the formational component to be considered. How do we nurture and nourish in one another that capacity to do difference differently? What courses, exposures, and experiences might cultivate the gifts and graces we need? The requisite gifts might include, but are not limited to openness to difference, willingness to articulate and explore differences, self-awareness, habits of critical (and self-critical) reflection, ability to form communities that recognize and embrace difference. The graces or virtues needed—and which religious imagination may be especially well equipped to cultivate—include such things as reverence, humility, self-restraint, and openness to the other. The ideal setting to cultivate such gifts and graces, it seems to me, is a multicultural setting. Such a practice of theological education has the double benefit of broadening and deepening the understanding of one's own faith tradition while in the process of nurturing these distinctive capacities.

LEARNINGS FROM EXPERIENCE AT MCCORMICK SEMINARY

At McCormick Theological Seminary we some time ago made a decision to do theological education in an intentionally multicultural environment. We are very aware that we are preparing students to be religious leaders in a church and a world that are decidedly different—not only multicultural but also post-Constantinian and some would say post-Christian—from the one most of the faculty were prepared to serve. We have made a decision to embrace the changes and seek to prepare our students to lead in the world that *will be*, rather than in the world that was, the world of our comfort zone. The open-ended exploration that this has entailed is carried in the language of one of our former promotional pieces: "preparing leaders for a church we cannot yet envision."

This effort has meant, among other things, that we have become in our common life an intentionally open and multicultural community. As set out more fully in the introduction to this volume, in the fall of 2004 McCormick's master's level community was 39 percent Euro American, 38 percent African American, 4 percent Asian American, 6 percent Latino/a, and 12 percent international students. We are, in some ways, a community of communities. As a result of our configuration, we feel the challenges of hearing the gospel in, and addressing the gospel to, the wider cultures in which we find ourselves. We also daily face the challenges and feel the tensions of our own different cultural perspectives on what the gospel is. We live with competing constructions of what is central to Christian tradition and a rich diversity of ideas, customs, and rituals that we associate with "gospel." This circumstance is at the same time a challenge and a benefit of what we have decided we are called to do.

I do not mean to imply that creating a multicultural community, in itself, accomplishes the purposes laid out above. But it does become an environment in which we cannot avoid working at these issues of difference. We continue to face in our internal life the challenges of difference and the occasions when difference becomes the occasion of oppression and exclusion. We continue to fight the tendencies of cultural imperialism.

One of the places this came to a head for us was around the issue of language. Should we make English proficiency a requirement for admission? On the one hand, about half of our faculty speak only English fluently. Thus to get the full benefit what we have to offer, English proficiency is necessary. On the other hand, language is a carrier of culture. Is it not a form of cultural annihilation if we create an "English only" environment? We eventually came to a conclusion that we should not make English a requirement for admission, but should admit without prejudice to language. At the same time we committed ourselves to provide the needed support systems—through translation, courses in Korean and Spanish, more bilingual faculty, and the creation of a Language, Resource and Writing Center.

Another challenge we continue to face is how to move from being multicultural in the sense of existing in mutually respectful but somewhat isolated cultures—specific subgroups. How do we deepen the encounters across cultures? How do classroom conversations move from the polite and distant toleration of all points of view to critical reflection and willingness to engage and challenge one another?

LEARNINGS FROM ECUMENICAL AND INTERRELIGIOUS DIALOGUES OF DIFFERENCE

"Exorcising Plato's Ghost": Resisting Universalizing Tendencies

In the ecumenical endeavors of recent years, the call to unity is sometimes met with a certain amount of caution and suspicion. The skeptical ask, "Whose unity—unity on whose terms?" There is a concern that the dominant group—whatever that may be in a given conversation—has an agenda of assimilating all others and making their own values and practices normative in a kind of "hostile takeover." The vision of unity is the melting pot in which differences melt away and we all become the same. It has become increasingly clear in current ecumenical endeavors that pressures toward unity as *uniformity* will be resented and resisted.

The places where advance is being made are the places where differences are recognized and allowed to stand, where all the conversation partners can participate with integrity—keeping the particularity of their convictions and commitments in tact.[6]

There is today a refusal of "metanarratives and universalizing, essentializing habits of thought." Jonathan Sacks argues that in a quest for "the dignity of difference" this is a good thing; it amounts to the "exorcising of Plato's ghost." He refers to Plato's proposal in *The Republic*[7] that this world of particularities and difference is a mere play of shadows in a cave. What is really real is not this world of particular material existence but the world of forms and ideas where the particular gives way to the universal. The powerful and problematic idea is that "truth—reality, the essence of things—is universal."[8] Sacks insists that universalism, as an orientation, may be as dangerous and potentially conflictual as tribalism, the view

> that there is only one truth about the essentials of the human condition, and it holds for all people at all times. If I am right, you are wrong. If what I believe is the truth, then your belief, which differs from mine, must be an error from which you must be converted, cured and saved. From this flowed some of the great crimes of history.[9]

One of our tasks may be an "exorcizing of Plato's ghost," deciding that universality and uniformity are not what ground our life together. Instead of this universalizing pressure, we might more profitably yield to the opposite pressure—to allow our world to be enlarged by particularity and difference as we welcome the contributions of persons whose beliefs and practices are different from our own.

Maintaining Mutuality: Language and Power

A major challenge in all "dialogues of difference" is how to maintain mutuality, keeping the conversation a conversation among equals. Power differentials regularly interfere. It is easy for the dominant group to fall into deciding unilaterally what is important to talk about, setting the terms and language of the dialogue, and deciding who will be invited to the table of dialogue. Those in power may do most of the talking, while the designated "others" are expected to listen and accommodate. The dynamics are further exacerbated by issues of language. The majority of our English-speaking students, for example, are accustomed to being in the dominant group—others learn their language, not vice versa. They invite others into dialogue—their own place at the table is assured.

Whatever the power differentials may be, it is a discipline for those in this conversation to make it a genuine dialogue characterized by mutual listening and mutual respect.

Related to the question of language is the difficulty of stretching to understand the other in his/her own terms. So much does not translate linguistically or culturally. We are tempted to put what the other says into our terms and to oversimplify. In interfaith dialogue, for example, we have learned that for Christians to say that all religions "boil down to" the injunction to love God and love your neighbor is not only reductionistic, but actually skews the reality in the direction of a particular Christian affirmation. Likewise, when Christians say that all are seeking salvation each in their own way, this is not entirely respectful of the genuine differences among religions, for not all aspire to "salvation" as such.[10] How may we listen more deeply to one another and resist reductionism and distortion toward our own perspectives? This requires at the very least maintaining mutuality. Some of the ingredients of that would be admitting our ignorance, being genuinely open to the other, bracketing preconceived notions, resisting premature conclusions, and engaging in ongoing respectful inquiry.

Celebrating Differentiated Consensus

One of the places where we see genuine advances in ecumenical endeavors today is in the new format of "differentiated consensus." The remarkable agreement achieved between the Lutheran World Federation and the Roman Catholic Church on the doctrine of justification is a case in point. Many were taken by surprise that a joint statement around this matter—the church-dividing issue of the Protestant Reformation—was even attempted, much less successful! An ingredient in the success of this undertaking may have been the "differentiated consensus" approach. Instead of endless debates to hammer out exact wording aimed at complete agreement and uniform expression (unity as uniformity), this format allows both agreement and difference to be honestly presented. In this approach, the conversation partners say together what they can say together and articulate the differences that remain and the reasons that they remain. This is a great advance, in my opinion, upon approaches that gloss over differences or even compromise them "for the sake of unity." In its own way, the clear articulation of the differences and what is at stake for the partners in those differences is as positive an outcome of the dialogue as the points of agreement. This relatively new format for statements from the ecumenical dialogues holds much promise for future conversations.

Letting the Other Be Other

Edward Farley, in his book Good and Evil: Interpreting a Human Condition, underscores the place and importance of the genuine "other" as one of the elemental features of the interhuman. As he notes, "much of the literature on the interhuman is preoccupied with the challenge laid down by solipsism, the idea that each human individual is so utterly enclosed in its sphere of consciousness that it has no true knowledge or experience of any other consciousness."[11] The discussions of solipsism, though, usually yield a methodological path to the interhuman, rather than solipsism as a final conclusion. The truth about the human condition that solipsism uncovers is vitally important, however. It reveals the situation of the "irreducible and uninterchangeable 'I'" at the heart of all human experience; it is the "strange mystery of the interhuman."[12] The other's experiences, as such, can never be experienced by me. This is a given, not an obstacle that can be overcome by more information or various strategies of broadening one's perspective. Thus the interhuman is always a sphere of "alterity" in which the relations are between beings who are and remain irreducibly "other" to each other.

This very situation is in a sense destabilizing and decentering, for it challenges any claims one may have to be the only "I," the only perspective. There is within us that which seems to resist such recognition and tempts us either to objectify the other or to see the other as an extension of the self and seek to "con-form" the other to oneself. Here is another sense in which we need to do difference differently. For what is true of interhuman interactions generally is surely true in relation to interhuman interactions that are cross-cultural—perhaps all the more so.

One needs to break out of the centered self (egocentricity) in order to really engage the other as other. Gabriel Marcel goes so far as to say that this requires of us a reflective break, a kind of redemption.[13] It entails an opening up to and vulnerability to the other. This is the precondition of such things as dialogue, empathy, and our being with and for the other. Insights from the field of theology and from cross-cultural encounters may assist us here.

The theological line of thought from Martin Buber to Immanuel Levinas is especially insightful. Buber's discussion in I and Thou insists upon the full integrity and mystery of the other. It conscientiously resists a lapse into objectifying, "I—it" relations. Levinas, in his discussion of "face," sees the other as "infinitely strange," a presence of something that does not yield to our projections of meaning but has its own independent claims upon us. Thus the other will not conform to the self or the self's perceptions of the other. What the "face" of the other calls forth from us is compassionate obligation.[14] The sphere of the face is the sphere of empathy and emotional participation.

The mutual emotional participation that occurs in interhuman relations does not overcome the situation of irreducible difference. Rather, relation *depends* upon that difference—otherwise, what we are describing is self-relation and not relation with the other.

A concrete instance of "letting the other be other" is in the practice of religious toleration.[15] In the United Nations document *Declaration of Principles on Tolerance*,[16] the sociopolitical necessity of toleration is underscored: "Since every part of the world is characterized by diversity, escalating intolerance and strife potentially menaces every region. It is not confined to any country but is a global threat" (Article 3). However, these social and political pressures alone are not sufficient to cultivate attitudes of toleration. The commitment to religious toleration must be grounded in the central religious commitments themselves.

One such grounding might be found in the affirmation of the freedom of conscience that is argued from various religious traditions. The Vatican II documents, for example, argue that everyone has a right to religious freedom. The argument may be lodged in the notion of "conscience"—that each person possesses a knowledge of his/her religious/moral obligations. Or it may be lodged in the notion that each of us is fallible and therefore no one should declare what will be binding upon others.

Joyce Shin has posed an interesting argument regarding the employment of the notion of "conscience" in Christian tradition. She examines Paul's writings, where discussion of "conscience" first arises in Christian usage. His context is the cross-cultural and often conflictual relations between Jewish and Gentile Christians.[17] She argues that, in his usage, the appeal is not to "autonomy of conscience," assuming the individual in isolation from others. Rather it is a "social usage of conscience" that always entails the concern for the well-being of the other."[18] Furthermore, this concern takes the form of "ethical accommodation" of the other. As the other's conscience is accommodated, a kind of religious toleration emerges. The other is allowed to be "other."

Broadening the Dialogue: Gospel and Cultures[19]

Within the Reformed family of churches, a global/multicultural dialogue of difference is ongoing through the World Alliance of Reformed Churches.[20] *Proceedings* from the Gospel and Cultures Consultation in Indonesia affirmed,

> The incarnation of Jesus Christ demands that we take culture seriously: for there is no "flesh" that is not nourished by a culture. No "word" can be heard that is not the language of a culture. . . . We recognize that the gospel illuminates culture. (C)ulture also illuminates our understanding of the gospel. Different cultures can perceive in the gospel that which other cultures had failed to perceive.[21]

This recognition was pursuant upon realization of the extent to which European and North American cultural traditions have historically been privileged interpreters of the gospel for the world church. This is true to such an extent that it has been hard to separate gospel from *this* culture, and mission work of another era joined the preaching of the gospel to Western cultural imperialism, and in many places a kind of cultural annihilation attended conversion. Current conversations challenge this privileging of Western cultural interpretations and see it as resulting in an impoverishment of interpretation and church life. The World Alliance has lately become clearer that God is present and active in all cultures and not captive to any culture. Present publications urge that we look for the "good news" of God in diverse cultural forms while maintaining a culture-critical edge alert to places where the gospel may challenge and critique particular cultural norms and practices. New interpretations of the gospel are emerging from multiple particular cultures employing their own distinctive images and experiences.[22] These enrich the understanding of the gospel, even as they urge us to a broader cultural literacy in the dialogue.

The landscape of global ecumenical endeavors is changing today. One reality is that it is the former "mission churches," the younger churches, churches of the Southern Hemisphere, that are today vital and growing, whereas we have seen something of a decline in mainline denominations in Europe and North America. The churches in other contexts do not always conform in every way to the habits and prescriptions of their parent churches. Their particular embodiment of the gospel and ways of being church are distinctive. This is as it should be. As D. T. Niles observed, when you transplant a growing thing to a new place, you must first break the pot in which you transported it; only then can it take root in the native soil to which you have brought it. New and differently enculturated theologies and practices have emerged. Ecumenical dialogues are radically reshaped in these contests as the old denominational distinctions inherited from the parent bodies in Europe and North America do not apply in the same way. Churches from these regions ask why we are bogged down in sixteenth-century controversies. When the Lutheran–Roman Catholic agreement on justification came forward, Russell Botman, a Reformed theologian from South Africa, urged that unless we can connect justification with justice, the agreement is of little significance. He argued, "It is a scandal to people who are dying daily of poverty, violence, and oppression when we postpone discussion on the relationship between justification and justice, treating the latter as merely a matter of ethical application."[23] It was an important insight and an instance of challenging the right of the European and North American churches to determine what is "important" to talk about in the dialogues of difference.

The changing landscape in this dialogue of difference has enlarged the circle of interpreters and shifted power relations significantly. This global/multicultural dialogue is yielding a broadening and deepening of understanding of Christian faith and tradition.

CONCLUSION

What we are learning in our multicultural setting at McCormick Seminary and from various dialogues of difference is proving fruitful. A multicultural theological education not only broadens and deepens understanding of Christian faith, but also nurtures in all those involved new habits of doing difference differently. Multicultural theological education allows us to cultivate gifts and graces that make possible the embrace of difference and commitments to build communities that know the dignity of difference. Such communities may be of some earthly use in public ministry in the wider world contexts where differences are still the occasion for exclusion and oppression, conflict and violence. Multicultural theological education has an important contribution to make here.

The great faiths have the potential—too little realized—of becoming a force for peace and for the justice and mercy upon which peace ultimately depends.[24] The Latin root of the word "religion" means "to bind."

Religion has the potential of binding us to one another and to God. The religious imagination discerns that we are "utterly connected" and that the connection embraces differences and does not depend upon their elimination. How may we become and build communities of faith that more fully realize this potential? We seek to create a better kind of world, one in which difference does not automatically provoke anxiety, fear, and violence; a world in which we understand the "God-given, world-enhancing dignity of difference."[25]

NOTES

1. Mortimer Adler said that "the aim of education should be the same for all . . . (i.e., everywhere and formation of good habits always, in every mode of society, every condition of life, etc.). . . . Education should aim at the formation of good habits" (as quoted in Brian Gerrish, "Tradition in the Modern World: The Reformed Habit of Mind," in *Toward the Future of Reformed Theology: Tasks, Topics, Traditions*, ed. David Willis and Michael Welker [Grand Rapids: Eerdmans, 1999], 3).

2. Edward Farley, *Theologia: The Fragmentation and Unity of Theological Education* (Philadelphia: Fortress Press, 1983).

3. Jonathan Sacks, *The Dignity of Difference: How to Avoid the Clash of Civilizations* (London: Continuum, 2002), 4.

4. Ibid., 21.

5. Ibid.

6. One very obvious instance of this approach in contemporary ecumenical efforts is the work of the Churches Uniting in Christ (CUIC). This new effort, launched in January 2000, inherits the legacy of earlier ecumenical efforts such as the Consultation on Church Union (COCU) and builds upon advances made there. However, it is a very different kind of undertaking. In the earlier efforts, COCU cherished a hope for "union" that would mean visible, institutional union. That hope was not realized. CUIC takes a more modest approach of declaring "marks" by which participating churches will express their relationship with one another. These include such things as mutual recognition of one another as authentic expressions of the one church of Jesus Christ, mutual recognition of baptism, provision for shared celebration of Eucharist, engagement in shared mission, and other such marks. The agreements neither presuppose nor require institutional union.

7. Plato, *The Republic*, trans. H. D. P. Lee (Hamondsworth: Penguin, 1955).

8. Sacks, *The Dignity of Difference*, 49.

9. Ibid., 50.

10. Mark Heim, in his book *Salvations: Truth and Difference in Religion* (Maryknoll, NY: Orbis Books, 2000), makes this point very directly. There is a

pluralism of religious "ends." Not all religions aspire to "salvation" as such. To impose this framework upon them is to distort and misrepresent.

11. Edward Farley, *Good and Evil: Interpreting a Human Condition* (Minneapolis: Fortress Press, 1990), 34–35.

12. Ibid.

13. Gabriel Marcel, *The Mystery of Being*, trans. Rene Hague (London: Harvill Press, 1950), vol. 1, chap. 9 (as referenced in Farley, *Good and Evil*, 38).

14. Farley, *Good and Evil*, 38. Farley's helpful explication of these insights is summarized here. Farley notes that the situation of alterity is not only an experience of the other as cognitively illusive, but an experience of the "reciprocity of autonomies." Human beings are, according to Levinas, "mutual interlocutors" (Immanuel Levinas, *Philosophical Papers*, trans. Alphonso Lingis [Dordrecht, Netherlands: Kluwer Academic Publications, 1987]). There is in this, as Ricoeur terms it, a "co-disclosure of fragility" (Paul Ricoeur, *Fallible Man*, trans. Charles Kelbley [Chicago: Henry Regnery Co., 1965]). We experience ourselves as vulnerable to the interpretations of the other. We are exposed to and subject to each other's world. "This is why this mutually discerned fragility refers not just to the other's physical contour, the other's body which can be injured, but to the other's personal being which can be objectified, disapproved, assessed, insulted, violated in a variety of ways, and murdered."

15. In this discussion I am instructed by the work of Joyce Shin in an unpublished article on "Accommodating the Other's Conscience: St. Paul's Approach to Religious Tolerance."

16. The member states of the United Nations Education, Scientific and Cultural Organization (UNESCO) drafted this declaration in Paris in 1995.

17. Shin looks particularly at the discussion of whether it is allowable to eat meat offered to idols (1 Cor. 8:7–13; 10:27–29). If it were simply a matter of autonomous conscience, then there would have been no problem; each could do as his or her conscience dictated. But since the conscience of the other is taken into account, there emerges a kind of social ethic in the use of conscience. It is an ethic of accommodation. "But if someone says to you, 'This has been offered in sacrifice,' then do not eat it, out of consideration for the one who informed you, and for the sake of conscience—I mean the other's conscience, not your own" (1 Cor. 10:28–29) (Joyce Shin, "Accommodating the Other's Conscience: St. Paul's Approach to Religious Tolerance" [unpublished paper]).

18. Shin, 3–4.

19. It is an elusive business to say what a culture is. In many languages, the word "culture" is derived from the Latin verb *colere*, which means to plow the earth, to inhabit a house, to revere, to worship, to honor, to respect, to pay homage. It is a rich and multilayered term. Is culture coextensive with a geographical area or with a language or language cluster? Is it a function of shared histories or common customs? What does it mean for several places to share a culture, or for one place to have many cultures or recognized subcultures? Beyond language and

custom, is there a core of particular worldview and way of being that belongs to a culture?

20. The World Alliance of Reformed Churches (WARC) is a family of more than 200 denominations and church communions who share the legacy of the sixteenth-century Protestant Reformation. It is the stream that came most under the influence of the theology of John Calvin. WARC represents 75 million Christians in 100 countries the world over. What the Alliance aims to do is to strengthen the unity and witness for Reformed churches, particularly to work for peace, economic and social justice, human rights, the integrity of the environment, inclusive community, and dialogue with other Christian communions and other religions. There are regional iterations of the larger organization, but every seven years the whole body gathers in a General Council to organize its work globally. It also sponsors other global events such as the Consultation on Gospel and Cultures held in Torajaland, Indonesia, in 1996.

21. WARC, *Consultation on Gospel and Cultures: Proceedings* (Torajaland, Indonesia, 1996), 177–78.

22. For example, the African concept of *Unbuntu* has enriched our understanding of how the gospel is manifest in community and in life together, not simply to individuals.

23. Russell Botman, "Should the Reformed Join In?" *Reformed World* 52, no. 1 (March 2002): 15.

24. Sacks, *The Dignity of Difference*, 4.

25. Ibid., 209.

CHAPTER 4

Resources for Intercultural Transformation of Theological Education from the Latino/a Margins

Luis R. Rivera-Rodriguez

In this essay I propose that seminary faculty need to tap into the theoretical resources and practices that U.S. minority theologians employ in their theological reflection and pedagogies. I call particular attention to the increasing interest among Latino/a theologians in developing a theology and theological method that is inter- or cross-cultural.[1] Specifically, I present the concept of *intercultural dialogue* as a potential component for a theological educational model that works with an awareness of the plurality of cultures in its midst and around the world and is committed to form women and men for the practice of intercultural ministry in these societies.

Several Latino/a theologians are interested in expanding their theological reflection and political collaboration across the cultural borders and political concerns of Latina/o communities. They see the need to reflect and work in dialogue and solidarity with members of other cultural communities. This cross-cultural encounter and exchange becomes a new locus and practice that allows the emergence of intercultural theologies from marginal communities in the United States. Implicit in these practices are components of intercultural relations, reflection, communication, and praxis that can serve to develop theoretical/practical models for cross- or intercultural theological education. The notion of intercultural dialogue and its corresponding habits, found in the work of the Cuban philosopher Raúl Fornet-Betancourt, can be an important theoretical component both to understand critically the interest and practice for intercultural theology among Latino/a theologians, and to develop a cognitive/reasoning component in an intercultural model of theological education.[2]

The first section, below, illustrates the emergent interest and practice of doing intercultural theology among some Latino/a theologians. Then I provide a brief summary of Fornet-Betancourt's philosophical project as a background for the discussion of his concept of intercultural dialogue. Finally, I present a reconstruction of Fornet-Betancourt's understanding of the habits for intercultural dialogue.

INITIATIVES OF LATINO/A THEOLOGIANS FOR INTERCULTURAL THEOLOGY IN THE UNITED STATES

By the end of the twentieth century and the beginning of the twenty-first, several Latino/a theologians noted the need to expand theological reflection and political collaboration across the cultural borders and political concerns of the Latino/a communities. The Catholic theologians Orlando Espín and María Pilar Aquino made this call, influenced in part by the work of Raúl Fornet-Betancourt. From different perspectives, the Protestant theologian Benjamin Valentin and the Presbyterian religious educator José R. Irizarry have made similar calls.

In her contribution to the anthology *From the Heart of Our People*,[3] María Pilar Aquino, recognizing the influence of Fornet-Betancourt, claims that "U.S. Latino/a theology is, from its very beginning, *an intercultural enterprise* that has no other route to theological knowledge but interculturality itself." Interculturality means, among other things, the diversity, exchanges, and interrelations of cultural subjects and traditions that constitute the mestizo members of Latina communities and also characterizes the larger sociocultural environment in the United States and the world. Theology is an intercultural enterprise because it "apprehends revelation and salvation from within the historical, religious, cultural, and bodily context of Latino/a communities" and from the exchanges and conflicts of different cultural communities and churches in the world.[4]

Orlando Espín has appropriated the work of Fornet-Betancourt in developing a constructive proposal for an intercultural theology of tradition.[5] Espín claims that today's world is one characterized by globalization and diversity. In order to respect and promote the value of authentic diversity against the homogenizing forces of globalization, there is a need for intercultural dialogue and an intercultural theology. He describes the practice of intercultural dialogue as one that takes place "through mutual witnessing, contrasting dialogue, and non-colonizing reflection." Intercultural dialogue happens when people from different cultural backgrounds/identities meet, coexist, and share with one another, from their respective cultural horizon/experience, what they understand and live as truth. In this exchange they practice a mutual witness, and everyone engages in a discernment process that involves the comparison of the proposals and the examination of one's own in light of the other's. Out of this contrasting dialogue each interlocutor gains a critical and larger understanding of all the proposals. This interdiscursive dialogue opens the possibility for new self-understandings as well as the possibility of appropriations, new synthesis, or new constructions of the truths they witness.

In his book *Mapping Public Theology*,[6] Benjamin Valentin proposes reshaping Latino/a theology in such a way that two emphases and commitments are combined in moving it towards a "translocal and transcultural" public theology. The defense of particular culture, identity, and cultural difference must be balanced with concerns for and reflection on the quest for social justice on the basis of "coalition building across racial, cultural, gender, class, and religious lines."[7] Latino/a theologies should be developed as public discourse and praxis that are "translocal and transcultural" in building "social solidarity and emancipatory coalitional politics" with other sociocultural subordinated groups and progressive constituencies.[8] Social justice and liberation are tasks that require coalitional activism built on both recognition of and respect for differences, and the recognition and promotion of commonalities and interconnection in "common problems, aspirations, hopes, and humanity."[9]

José Irizarry proposes an intercultural understanding of the faith community, the religious education process, and the praxis of the religious educator.[10] He claims that the educational situation in communities of faith involves the actions and interactions of learners and educators who bring and negotiate their cultural identities and perspectives as they engage in the forging of a shared communal religious identity. Irizarry defines intercultural as the "process by which culturally bounded selves share a common social space in order to forge a shared identity."[11] From this perspective, the context and process of education is intercultural in nature and purpose. Learners and educators, as diverse cultural selves and agents, create and participate in a context and pedagogy where culturally diverse identities are affirmed and negotiated in the process of constructing a shared religious identity that includes a shared intercultural identity. The religious educator should see himself or herself as a cultural self, one among the many others, whose vocation is in part to become "the ethnographer of his own culture, the place he was called out from" in order to facilitate a critical and affirmative intercultural pedagogy in the formation of the community of faith.[12]

This call for an intercultural or transcultural transformation of theology among sectors of Latino/a theology is illustrated in four anthologies edited or coedited by Latino/a theologians in the early part of the twenty-first century. My claim is that these books represent a new stage in exploring the practice of doing theology interculturally, even though an explicit reflection of this method is still undeveloped. I suggest that these books show four modalities of practicing intercultural dialogue.

An Intercultural Caucus

A Reader in Latina Feminist Theology can be interpreted as a Latina caucus with intercultural interests.[13] The authors are a diverse group of Latina theologians joined by their experience as Latinas, their commitments to Latino/a theology, and their intention to be in critical dialogue and solidarity with feminist and womanist theologians in the United States.

They share a consciousness of the cultural, ethnic, gender, class, and ideological diversity within and without the Latina communities. They recognize, respect, and engage these differences in critical dialogue. In particular, they position themselves as one of the main cultural-ethnic groups in the "national tapestry of women experiences" in the United States: Euro American, African American, and Latina women. Interestingly enough, they do not speak explicitly about other groups of women in this national tapestry: Asian American, Native American, and others.

They see themselves as bringing forth the voices and experiences of Latinas as a contribution to feminist theology in the United States. They claim that their voices have been absent from previous anthologies on feminist theologies where the Euro American and African American perspectives have dominated, working with a white/black focus and framework. Recognizing and denouncing this exclusion, they seek to "transform and enlarge that tapestry and create a bridge that connects to the work of our feminist and womanist sisters."[14]

The contributors are aware of and celebrate the diversity in cultural backgrounds, religious affiliations, social locations, and theological orientations among Latinas. On the other hand, they share in some macro social conditions that define some commonality in their experiences as Latina women and feminists. They share the experience of racism, sexism, devaluation, and exclusion in the United States. They have experienced a history of colonization and domination from empires that have contributed to their present status as "intruders" in their own land or as migrant workers. They also live in between many borders and boundaries: national, cultural, racial, economic, professional.

Some of the authors engage in discovering sources and resources for Latina feminist theology in their own communities and histories. They bring validation but also criticism to the cultural sources and religious practices in their Latina communities. Others are more intentional in developing a critical dialogue and exchange with Euro American feminism, Latin American feminism, and postmodernism. All the collaborators work with the intention of building an inclusive and just world in which this intercultural exchange, inside and outside of the Latina communities, is a matrix for human transformation and liberation.

An Intercultural Colloquium

According to its editors Fernando Segovia and Eleazar Fernandez, *A Dream Unfinished* is a convocation of African American, Asian American, and Hispanic Latino/a theologians to reflect on their ambiguous identification with and critical acceptance of the concept of *American Dream* "from their respective positions in the margins as members and voices of minority groups."[15] The agenda of this project is twofold.

First, it is a strategy to develop a dialogue among minority theologians in the United States. This collaboration is a remedy to the lack of connection in their theological reflection and academic work. "Inside the West, theologians from the various minority groups have kept, for the most part, to their own respective circles and discussions and, as a result, have failed not only to engage one another but also to develop any sense of common agenda or discourse."[16] Second, the project is a means to begin a network of solidarity that might help in joining forces to challenge the "forces of closure" present in society, the academy, and the theological guild.

The short-term goal is to bring these minority voices into a conversation, in and from the margins, in search of mutual recognition, learning, and solidarity vis-à-vis the ideology, policies, and practices of the *American Dream*. The long-term goal is to move beyond the margins "toward a very different conception and practice of theological studies and, most important, toward the eventual fulfillment of our unfinished dream in the country."[17] Though it is not part of the editors' vocabulary, one goal of this book can be interpreted as *intercultural* connection.

The organization of the book looks like three "panels" from different racial/ethnic communities that address the concept of the "American

Dream" from their perspectives. It gives the impression of a colloquium, that is, an academic meeting of specialists that take turns in addressing a topic. The exposition does not involve engagement among the participants. In this sense, the book allows for an *intercultural meeting*, but does not engage in depth in *intercultural dialogue*. Nevertheless, some of the articles show a greater engagement with and appropriation of the theological reflection and literature of other minority groups. This is a commendable first effort in convening this kind of intercultural agenda between these three main minority groups.

An Intercultural Forum

The *Handbook of U.S. Theologies of Liberation* is an exercise in intercultural theological dialogue among different U.S. liberationist theologians.[18] Most of the authors are members of minority and marginalized communities in the United States: African American, Asian American, Native American, Hispanic American, feminist, gay/lesbian. The authors are conscious of and committed to the understanding and practice of theology from particular social/cultural locations, within the general dynamics of dominant and marginalized groups and cultures, but with a commitment to liberation for all.

The essays recognize the multicultural context of U.S. theology and issue a call to develop theology at the crossroads of the coexistence and conflicts of a plural sociocultural and religious society. Moreover, the authors express a desire to practice liberation theology in the United States within the framework of a larger solidarity among marginal groups. "The hold of the dominant culture upon societal resources will not be effectively challenged until separate marginalized groups begin to accompany each other toward justice, understood here as the dismantling of oppressive structures."[19]

The handbook pursues, among other things, two important objectives. First, it challenges the traditional Eurocentric and male-dominant way of doing and teaching theology in U.S. universities and seminaries by enlarging the table talk, agenda, and canon of theology through these multiple voices from the underside.

Its second objective is to convene these theologians for what I call an "intercultural" dialogue and way of doing theology. The authors in the first part of the book develop their chapters on different theological foci by presenting their particular constructive perspectives in critical dialogue with the contributions of theologians within their ethno/cultural/gender communities and in dialogue with the perspectives of other minority and majority theologians. Theology is done from particular perspectives in a polyphonic forum.

This book represents a step forward in the practice of intercultural dialogue in Latino/a theology, insofar as a Latino has been the convener of a multicultural group of U.S. liberation theologians and has invited them to speak from their own locations in recognition and engagement with the voices and perspectives of other minority theologians, encouraging them to practice solidarity across cultural borders for the liberation of all.

An Intercultural Symposium

According to the editors, Anthony B. Pinn and Benjamin Valentin, *The Ties That Bind* has a twofold purpose.[20] First, it explores an alternative to the parallel and distant way in which African American and Hispanic/Latino/a intellectuals and theologies have developed. It explores "the possibility and desirability of a cross-cultural dialogue of people of color within the United States."[21] Second, the contributors to this volume are convinced that similar historical experiences as minority groups in the United States and similar sociopolitical aspirations for justice and liberation among these two communities call for greater efforts of mutual recognition and political collaboration that require cross-cultural conversation.

The organization of the book follows the pattern of a symposium, that is, a meeting for the discussion of selected topics where participants both make presentations and form an audience. The editors, as conveners of this dialogue, created a mutual agenda on selected topics, paired up participants, and assigned them to write on a topic from their perspectives, followed by a mutual response in which they were to explore similarities and differences in method and content. The objective of this dialogue was to "promote better understanding through a discussion of similarities and differences with respect to a few theological issues."[22] This volume, though limited to two cultural groups, exhibits more than the others a deeper engagement and practice of doing theology interculturally, and the authors engage more clearly in the habits of intercultural dialogue.

In summary, there is an initiative growing out of Latino/as and other minority theologians who are working towards an *intercultural* transformation of theology in the United States. Their practices need to be studied and assessed in order to identify components that might serve the goal of creating models of inter- or cross-cultural theological education. Some of the practices that characterize the theological thinking and communication of these theologians can be appreciated fully if we incorporate the notion of intercultural dialogue in the work of Fornet-Betancourt.

THE INTERCULTURAL TRANSFORMATION OF PHILOSOPHY

Since the early 1990s, Raul Fornet-Betancourt has been working on the intercultural transformation of philosophy in general and of Latin American philosophy in particular. According to Fornet-Betancourt, philosophies in Latin America, including the recent philosophies of liberation with their project of philosophical inculturation, are different expressions of monocultural and ethnocentric philosophies in need of an intercultural transformation.[23] This proposal has a twofold task. One is to critique and avoid in philosophy the colonial and oppressive practice of hegemonic European-based ethnocentric and monocultural reflection that ignores, assimilates, or subjugates other cultural voices and philosophies. The other task is to articulate a way of doing philosophy that takes place from the dialogue within and between cultures, and recognizes, respects, and consults with different cultural voices and philosophies, including the task of reconceiving one's own reflection in light of them.[24]

There are new circumstances in the present world that call for the intercultural transformation of philosophy. First, there is a deeper awareness and appreciation of the plurality of cultures and cultural philosophies around the world and in each society. In the case of Latin America, Fornet-Betancourt argues for the recognition of a multicultural and intercultural America with many people, cultures, and philosophical traditions even before the colonial times.[25] Second, there is a new consciousness of the value and rights of these cultural communities to sustain and develop critically their identities and traditions as a contribution to the rest of the world. This new consciousness is in part the result of the struggles for survival and recognition of cultural communities with minority status against different forms of colonizing violence and oppression against them exercised by dominant cultural communities. According to Fornet-Betancourt, the most important cases for Latin American philosophy are the traditionally ignored and suppressed, but now emerging and emancipating, voices from the indigenous and African American cultures.[26] They are claiming their place and contribution as equal philosophical voices with their distinctive sources, concepts, methods, and canons.

Third, there is a critical and moral perspective developing about the need in all cultures to resist the dangers of ethnocentrism and its politics of suppression and homogenization of "the other" and their cultures. This politics has been evident in projects of national unification and in oppressive policies and practices against minority groups and immigrants in the world and in Latin America. For Fornet-Betancourt, the most dangerous project today is the economic and monocultural project of neoliberal capitalist globalization.[27]

In light of and in favor of this multicultural world and its intercultural dynamics, and against the monocultural practices and ideologies that negate this world, Fornet-Betancourt argues for an intercultural transformation of philosophy. This new philosophy will have two fundamental qualities: it will be intercultural and interdisciplinary. It needs to be intercultural in order to contribute to the reorganization of a world in which diverse cultures of humanity in Africa, Asia, and Latin America claim and exercise the right to make their proposal for a really universal and ecumenical humanity. It needs to be interdisciplinary because of "the new constellation of knowledge that we have confronting us with the challenge of specific models of rationality" and their limits that requires the method of consultation.[28] A contribution of intercultural philosophy is to allow human history to maintain and develop the "character of a symphony orchestra in which the plurality of voices is the secret of the miracle of harmony."[29]

At the center of Fornet-Betancourt's project is the concept of intercultural dialogue. *Intercultural dialogue* is like a mutual and permanent con-vocation among free and equal subjects with different cultural identities, locations, philosophical traditions, and equal rights, who engage in a conversation to exchange and assess critically, by sharing and contrasting in their own terms, their insights and perspectives on issues in a mutually agreed agenda.[30] It is a dialogical forum in which the philosophical *logos* appears in a culturally conditioned polyphony of rationalities.[31] It is in this intercultural and interdiscursive encounter and process, at the crossroad of different philosophical cultural traditions in humanity, that these models of cultural rationalities are verified or falsified.[32]

As we have seen, the work and vision of Fornet-Betancourt is influencing some U.S. Latino/a theologians. Some of these theologians, like the philosopher, are calling for an intercultural transformation of theology. Others, not in dialogue with Fornet-Betancourt, are nevertheless engaging in collaborative reflective practices and publications that illustrate the notion and praxis of intercultural dialogue. The works of these Latino/a theologians can become resources to explore and experiment

with the notion of intercultural dialogue as a main component in a theological education that is cross- or intercultural.

INTERCULTURAL DIALOGUE AND ITS HABITS

As we mentioned before, the concept of intercultural dialogue is central
to Fornet-Betancourt's project for the intercultural transformation of
philosophy. His principal analogy for intercultural dialogue is a political
forum where free and equal cultural agents and subjects, with different
identities, voices, interests, and social locations, meet and work together
a common agenda and praxis for a just, participatory, decolonized, pluralistic, and liberated world. The practice of intercultural dialogue
requires the development of at least seven thinking and communication
habits.[33]

First is the habit of sharing and contrasting.[34] Positively, this means to
be open to the presence, difference, and contribution of the other, whose
proposal and perspective might bring wisdom to the way I understand
the issue at hand; to know the other in the interaction; and to interpret
more critically my own perspective in and from this exchange.[35] This
requires listening to the other from their own perspective and to contrast
their perspectives with ours to learn more about ourselves. Negatively,
this means to combat the habit of "subsuming and reducing," that is,
looking at the other and his/her discourse as an object to be interpreted
only by and within my own monocultural frameworks that are taken as
normative and explanatory of reality. This would be a practice of assimilation that understands the other through reduction and dismisses the
originality, alterity, and dignity of the other.

A second habit for intercultural dialogue is to learn to think "respectively" in the midst of voices that convene in the "polyphonic choir of the
intercultural dialogue."[36] This "respective thinking" has two dimensions.
One is to learn to name and make explicit our propositions in light of the
cultural logos, ethos, and practices that inform their possibilities and limitations. The other is to reflect and communicate with others for the possibility of securing the "communicative co-existence with other subjects
beginning with the convocation of the voices."[37] This implies the renun-
ciation of the habit to think about the others and what they have to say
within the paradigm of subject–object. The others are not the "object"
of our reflection and knowledge, but the subjects of their own reflection
and knowledge, who confront and reveal their and our particularities or

"respectivities" in the cultural exchange. We reflect and know with the other subjects.[38]

A third habit for intercultural dialogue is the disposition to take the risk of making proposals for public and critical discussion by the larger community of intercultural and interdiscursive dialogue. This proposal is made as convocation for others to make their assessment and proposals from their perspectives.[39] This implies the negation of the closed and monocultural habit of thinking and defending one's positions in a self-contained, self-sufficient, or self-referential way that pretends to be a distinctive and better alternative, to others. Instead, the proposals and assessments that others make become a crucial element of my way of thinking and knowing.[40]

A fourth habit for intercultural dialogue is the practice of the "inter" space, that is, the disposition to abstain from easy and quick definitions, judgments on the other, or consensus building, given the suspicion that these strategies might be potential forms of domination.[41] It is the habit of giving us the time for listening, appreciating, and understanding one another as subjects who speak our words from our respective cultural locations, practices, and cognitions of history, the world, and "truth."[42]

A fifth habit for intercultural dialogue is to reflect and do research in an interdisciplinary way. The recognition that philosophy happens beyond the Western and European rationalistic method, monographic style, and academic tradition leads Fornet-Betancourt to claim that there are different philosophical voices and traditions in all cultures. The philosophical *logos* appears in a multiplicity of philosophical cultural traditions with their respective sources, methods, concepts, styles, and canons. To be in conversation with these cultural philosophical traditions requires the assistance of other disciplines that allow us to access and understand them dialogically.[43] The awareness of the legitimate presence of multiple disciplines in the academy and of multiple ways of knowing in cultures, along with their limits or finitude, leads Fornet-Betancourt to argue for a nonreductionistic and critical dialogue among these rationalities and epistemic sources.[44] The idea is to become aware of the type of rationality facilitated by the basic discipline we work with, including its limits, and understanding these limits as the "border" or occasion to connect with other types of rationalities practiced in other disciplines.[45]

A sixth habit for intercultural dialogue is the practice of "cultural disobedience."[46] Cultural disobedience refers to the critical attitude and moral disposition to denounce and challenge oppressive cultural practices and patterns in one's own culture in order to change it. It is the ability and duty to critique the stabilized and dominant cultural patterns that claim to be normative and try to hide the cultural conflict through which cultures change and develop.

A seventh habit for intercultural dialogue is to think in solidarity for the sake of liberation. The past and present practices of economic, political, and cultural colonialisms (external and internal), without and within our respective cultures, demand a commitment to the principles of liberation and justice.[47] A just social and cultural order implies the recognition of others in their human and cultural otherness; the appreciation of their human dignity, their quests for freedom; their agency as cultural producers and agents; and the reparation of harms and damages caused by all sorts of oppressions and colonialisms in others and in our own cultures.

In summary, Fornet-Betancourt proposes an intercultural transformation of philosophy that requires new reflective and communicative habits in the midst of the relationships and dialogue among members of different cultural groups in and across countries. The key strategy to promote this transformation is the practice of intercultural dialogue among and within cultures. This dialogue occurs when cultural subjects and agents practice the seven interdiscursive habits I have discussed: (1) the habit of sharing and contrasting; (2) the habit of thinking "respectively"; (3) the habit of making and encouraging others to make and assess proposals; (4) the habit of "inter-space" reasoning; (5) the habit of interdisciplinary inquiry; (6) the habit of "cultural disobedience"; and (7) the habit of thinking in solidarity for liberation.

CONCLUSION

Theological institutions and faculties that do not hire minority theologians, do not include the books of minority scholars in their libraries and in their courses, do not encourage theological teaching and scholarship that engage the work of minority theologians, and do not invite them to be lecturers and administrators are producing monocultural institutions and ethnocentric programs of theological education by fault and default.

Theological education in a multicultural and globalized world and church should contribute to the formation of religious leaders able to develop a Christian praxis, a theological-ethical perspective, and a spirituality that are intercultural in intention, content, and consequences. This requires research, experimentation, and critical reflection with practitioners and theoreticians of intercultural relations, communication, and praxis. Seminaries that are looking to develop a cross- or intercultural model of theological education should explore and learn from the theoretical and practical contributions of minority theologians who are leading the way in defining the contours of intercultural ways of doing theology and, therefore, contributing to the "intercultural transformation" of theology in the United States. The theoretical articulation of models of intercultural theologies and methods is a future task that awaits the reflection and experimentation of their practitioners. Out of their ways of doing and understanding their intercultural theologies, we will be able to discern, articulate, and test concepts and components that will contribute to the development of intercultural models for theological education in the United States.

The notion and practice of the habits for intercultural dialogue that we find implicit in the practice of Latino/a theologians and explicit in the work of Fornet-Betancourt is a potential component to be explored in depth and assessed critically towards the goal of developing a "distinctive and progressive" model of cross-cultural theological education. After all, any theological method and pedagogy requires the discernment of practical and theoretical discursive, reasoning, and hermeneutical habits that will be practiced and promoted in the teaching/learning process and in the theological and spiritual formation of its participants.

NOTES

1. My initial and provisional understanding of interculturality refers to a form of consciousness and praxis that recognizes and affirms cultural diversities, in ways that respect the self-definitions that people claim within and without one's own group, with an open disposition and a political commitment to working together to create spaces and agendas where culturally diverse subjects and groups explore and negotiate, in constructive and participatory ways, the possibility of diverse, inclusive, and just societies.

2. I privilege Raúl Fornet-Betancourt's book *Transformación Intercultural de la Filosofía* (Bilbao, Spain: Desclée de Brouwer, 2001) because it is an anthology that collects his most important essays on the topic of intercultural dialogue. For biography, bibliography, and secondary works on Fornet-Betancourt, go to www.ensayistas.org/filosofos/cuba/fornet/.

3. "Theological Method in U.S. Latino/a Theology: Toward an Intercultural Theology for the Third Millennium," in *From the Heart of the People. Latino/a*

Explorations in Catholic Systematic Theology, ed. Orlando O. Espin and Miguel H. Diaz (Maryknoll, NY: Orbis Books, 1999), 7.

4. Ibid., 24.

5. "Toward the Construction of an Intercultural Theology of Tradition," *Journal of Hispanic/Latino Theology,* 9, no. 3 (2000): 22–59.

6. *Mapping Public Theology: Beyond Culture, Identity, and Difference* (New York: Trinity Press International, 2002).

7. Ibid., xvii.

8. Ibid., xvi.

9. Ibid., 107.

10. José R. Irizarry, "The Religious Educator as Cultural Spec-Actor: Researching Self in Intercultural Pedagogy," *Religious Education* 98, no. 3 (Summer 2003): 365–81.

11. Ibid., 371.

12. Ibid., 375.

13. María Pilar Aquino, Daisy L. Machado, and Jeanette Rodríguez, eds., *A Reader in Latina Feminist Theology: Religion and Justice* (Austin: University of Texas Press, 2002).

14. Ibid., xiii–xiv.

15. Eleazar S. Fernández and Fernando F. Segovia, eds., *A Dream Unfinished: Theological Reflection on America from the Margins* (Maryknoll, NY: Orbis Books, 2001).

16. Ibid., vii.

17. Ibid., viii.

18. Miguel A. De La Torre, ed., *Handbook of U.S. Theologies of Liberation* (St. Louis: Chalice Press, 2004).

19. Ibid., 298.

20. Anthony B. Pinn and Benjamin Valentin, eds., *The Ties That Bind: African American and Hispanic American/Latino/a Theologies in Dialogue* (New York: Continuum, 2001).

21. Ibid., 14.

22. Ibid., 17.

23. Fornet-Betancourt, *Transformación Intercultural de la Filosofía,* 27–110.

24. Ibid., 69.

25. Ibid., 73–76, 81–82.

26. Ibid., 133–64, 235–43.

27. Ibid., 299–382.

28. Ibid., 58.

29. Ibid., 57.

30. Ibid., 60.

31. Ibid., 70.

32. Ibid., 55.

33. The following list is my own reconstruction in content and order of Fornet-Betancourt's lists of habits.

34. Fornet-Betancourt, *Transformación Intercultural de la Filosofía*, 30.

35. Ibid., 40–41, 46.

36. Ibid., 98.

37. Ibid., 99–100.

38. Ibid., 98.

39. Ibid., 54.

40. Ibid., 54–55.

41. Ibid., 51.

42. Ibid., 52.

43. Ibid., 112–13.

44. Ibid., 118–24.

45. Ibid., 124.

46. Ibid., 186–89.

47. Ibid., 264.

CHAPTER 5

Libraries and Multicultural Theological Education: Beyond Nostalgia

Kenneth Sawyer

Enthusiasts speak of multiculturalism as if librarians were new to the issue, but a distinct and substantial chapter of multicultural education is to be found in theological libraries.[1] We need to leave behind the libraries of memory, and instead visit and use contemporary libraries to learn of the multicultural realities and challenges faced by the librarians among us. If we repent of our "biblionostalgia," we may learn how libraries participate in the process of theological formation/education, especially in increasingly multicultural forms.

When asked, many educators will say that the library is the "heart" of their particular school. Can this claim be measured beyond its sentimental resonance?[2] How can the rhetorical commitments to theological librarianship be squared with the marginalization of library programs, through diminished funding and use patterns? The library is rarely noted as a primary site for the struggles of multicultural theological education,[3] but libraries are sites where institutional and individual identities are formed and transformed, and where issues loudly contested elsewhere are engaged by quieter means. Furthermore, theological librarians are often the first to adapt and engage topics, technologies, and trends oriented toward the basic issues of contemporary multiculturalism: diversity, difference, development, and struggle.[4]

OUR CONTEXT

Christianity is growing fastest at its old "margins," while diminishing in its historic "centers." Pressures on theological libraries are shifting the "collecting edge" of collections as collecting communities also change.[5] Globalization, global migrations, and global missions have obliterated older categories, whether of "sending" and "receiving" churches, the hierarchies of "First" and "Second" and "Third" worlds, "developed" and "undeveloped" places of the world. The traditional power of Western Christianity in all its variety is both changing and being changed by new voices, new powers, and new perspectives.

Christianity's shape-shifting ways have rendered some library collections veritably archival, as useful as wax-cylinders or eight-track tapes. Simultaneously, many faith communities flourish without access to or felt need of the inherited memory present in theological libraries. The older East/West conflict has been reframed as the "clash of civilizations."[6] Meanwhile, emerging technologies enable the creation of new ecclesial forms characterized less by locale than by local access to a networked community.[7] Information-use patterns are changing rapidly, as many private users have access to databases well beyond those presented by local libraries, and many have come to consider the Internet their preferred library, with Google as candidate for "favorite librarian."[8]

ATTEMPTING A DESCRIPTION OF MULTICULTURALISM

Multiculturalism articulates a deep truth, that no single *part* of a religious tradition can presume to speak for *all* the tradition.[9] For those within the Christian traditions, this description recognizes that the church has too often lost sight of its diverse origins, its expansive multilingual/multicultural expressions, its worldwide presence and trajectories, and its continuing development. Today's parochialisms suggest what parochialisms always suggest: that things have always been just the way they were before the current changes/challenges upset everything. Multiculturalists have deployed an array of methodological, historiographical, ethical, bibliographical, and theological critiques of present parochialisms and the many cultural captivities of Christian communities.[10] While contemporary multiculturalism can be considered an aspect of the modern era, the values of multiculturalism are also in continuity with varieties of counternarratives of resistance and dissent that run deep within world cultures. Contemporary multiculturalism has provoked a sometimes painful acknowledgment of the sanctioned and selective biases of cultural authority. It is right that theological libraries would also be subject to this analysis, having been willing conscripts in the construction of both the captivity and its narratives.

Contemporary multiculturalism is often mistaken for simple diversity. Diversity is distinct from multiculturalism, though in contested settings the two are often confused or conflated. In current usage, diversity is where you *find* it, while multiculturalism is where you *construct* it. The actual diversity of humanity has not changed, but what has changed is the willingness to see and hear that diversity, even if in commodified forms. If recent decades display more of the "promise of difference" rather than the "problem of difference," the challenge remains of recognizing the "other." If diversity is more about seeing what has always been present, then multiculturalism is more about attempting the construction of a reasonable and generous community that might become worthy of its privilege.

OUR LIBRARIES/OURSELVES: THEOLOGICAL LIBRARIES REFLECT AN AMBIGUOUS PAST

Western theological libraries, and those patterned on them, gladly claim to reflect the commitments and freedoms associated with three distinct movements of the modern era: the Renaissance, the Reformations of the sixteenth century, and the Enlightenment and the secular revolutions (whether in the Americas or Europe). Each of these moments and movements contributed to the form and content of theological libraries and their varied collecting or sponsoring communities or institutions.[11] Theological libraries cannot be adequately understood without an acknowledgment of the cultural biases by which the Western claims to universalism were constructed and experienced, with benefits of "civilization" often withheld from subject populations defined as ignorant, unworthy, or simply "other."

Libraries have never been either value neutral or uncontested. Libraries reflect the values, commitments, and biases of collecting communities. Indeed, the very process of organizing any library in classification and subject heading systems is itself a process of "social construction" that displays the choices, biases, and ideologies of the organizing community. Where we have often allowed a (mis)representation of libraries as "value neutral," we need to acknowledge that libraries are contested territories. All taxonomies require choices, and both classification schedules and subject headings include subjective considerations that display the mind-set of a particular era.[12] For librarians, the power to name and classify has come at a price. Our chief examples lie in the modern period, when the values of the Enlightenment Project issued in claims to universalism in the "taxonomic imperialism" shown in classifying the colonized world. Western science collected, organized, named, and classified all the world from the perspective of Europe as the center, the capital, of the enlightened world. Library classification schemes emerged as reflections of these totalist values, whether in its college, tutorial, or theological seminary forms.[13] If the entire world of information is to be ordered, the resulting employment of ordering hierarchies (both explicit *and* hidden) inevitably carries extensive cultural meanings.[14] With everything to be fit within (Western) universal categories, nonprivileged groups rightly question *whose* orthodoxy or experience is deemed normative.

Libraries and librarians also reflect and frame broader cultural conversations, such that theological libraries serve competing and sometimes conflicting social functions, *whatever* the identity and intent of the collecting community. Libraries serve *and* subvert the values of collecting communities.[15] Because of the self-selection of religious communities, usually drawn along lines of homogeneity, the stratifications of the larger culture are often intensified within religious groups, rendering many religious groups examples of a form of "hyper-segregation." In such settings the library may be the most diverse portion of the collecting community it serves. Theological identity and *bibliographic* identity reinforce one another in both conserving and transgressive forms. Religious communities need boundaries, but theological libraries necessarily look *beyond* those boundaries. Again, libraries are *contested* territories.

If the multiculturalist revival of the category of "hybridity" has again put in play the ambiguities of identity, as R. S. Sugirtharajah and others have noted, it remains to be seen how hybridity can shift definitions of theological identity and community without prompting a reaction against the perceived dangers of syncretism.[16] One example of the promise of hybridity is in the emerging ecclesiologies of intentionally multicultural churches. These ecclesiologies directly challenge the principles of homogeneity and affinity grouping, whether in the name of church growth, missions, parish revitalization, identity conservation, or "niche" ministries. Current discussions of multiculturalism struggle with this conundrum, revisiting the question of self-selection, segregation, and identity, especially among long-silenced or recently recognized groups who may themselves employ strategies of self-segregation. These efforts name and claim multiculturalism not as a predicament, but as promise, and as a response to the segmentation and segregation of communities of faith. Theological libraries/librarians are well placed to provision this discussion between/among competing ecclesiologies.[17] Theological librarians have a particularly important role to play as educators within their communities, in order to contest the central value of homogeneity and the suspicion of hybridity within and among religious traditions.

What is at stake is nothing less than whether *difference* is to be understood as an expression of divine punishment or of divine preference. Insofar as multiculturalism reclaims the multivocality of the Scriptures, the diversity of the early church, and the history of the church beyond its various cultural captivities, all will recognize the rich opportunities for theological libraries/librarians.[18] Wise librarians will support the resurgence of contemporary interdisciplinarity, signaling the lowering of departmental and disciplinary boundaries deemed sacrosanct by previous generations. Interdisciplinarity assists the process of multicultural education, however much it may complicate the librarian's task. The challenges facing theological librarians are those facing all theological educators, as once "exotic" disciplines are enlisted (and occasionally welcomed) for the curriculum.

HOW THEOLOGICAL LIBRARIES EXHIBIT MULTICULTURALIST VALUES

Lending Policies

Lending policies have substantial multicultural effects within schools, since institutional boundaries are defined and reinforced by lending policies (and are further reinforced by interlibrary loan protocols). Since lending policies necessarily follow lines of institutional mission, they (un)intentionally reinforce confessional lines and self-separation, and so blend differences *within* denominations, but sharpen differences *between* denominations or groups. While restricted lending policies seek to protect collections against loss, theft, and so forth, the results are costly in effectively denying access to potential users "outside" a traditional patron base. Naming our lending community is a theological act. *Enlarging* our lending community should be considered an act of faith, and one significant way of serving a broader multicultural project by meeting broader institutional goals beyond narrow constituencies. Restrictive lending policies further stratify lay/clergy distinctions, while more generous lending policies encourage participation of nontraditional patrons.

Acquisitions Policies

Acquisitions policies are expressions of institutional identity and are agents of change *and* servants of the status quo, within the same institution, often within the same budget cycle. The multiple circles of self-fulfilling rhetoric are familiar to librarians, since remarks on the lack of library resources may be linked to faculty searches or enrollment goals. Collection development policies are necessarily narrow as expressions of the focused resources and priorities of collecting communities, but collection development policies are also designed to serve an unsettling and ultimately unachievable goal: to provide the resources for institutions to change. The *process* of book selection is as important as the particular books selected, since the central issues regarding book selection relate to the dynamics of the collecting community. The theological integrity of the acquisitions policy will indicate whether the librarians have successfully enlisted the collecting community, in order to avoid the unhappy task of book selecting on behalf of a disinterested or disengaged community.

TECHNOLOGY AND MULTICULTURALISM

Information technologies are not value neutral. Librarians are rightly suspicious of the "hype" of hypertexts. Nevertheless, the nature of theological communities and their libraries continues to change in response to the development of hypertext sources delivered by broadband networks.[19] The reconfigured intellectual world brings those enjoying access to the Web into new communities of conversation, while those without (stable) access to the Web are presented with diminishing choices.[20] While everyone, on both sides of the digital divide, faces increasing costs in training, staffing, and machinery, the highest costs are borne by those theological libraries unattached to college or universities, and therefore deprived of the benefits of larger systems and support. From the perspective of those who use theological libraries, the value of *access* may be more important than the value of *acquisitions*, rendering the coffee shop/bookstore more attractive, especially if joined with wireless access. Theological libraries serving patrons with previous experience in the corporate sector or in better-funded sectors of education routinely ask these skilled patrons to lay aside their skills when making use of theological collections. For many students, the poorly equipped library, combined with the decline of the research paper in graduate coursework, renders the local theological collection unhelpful. When our libraries fail to provide easy access to text and hypertext materials, when we cede issues of hospitality and comfort to coffee shop/bookstore venues, and when our reduced staff is unable to provide competent reference, we determine a dim future for theological libraries. Some theological libraries continue to provide services best suited for a type of student not seen for thirty years, and some library staff have not been encouraged or rewarded for learning new skills for that same thirty years.

Regarding texts, the unregulated posting of texts on the Internet has not displaced "established" publishing authorities, though patron reliance on unsanctioned texts is increasing. Ownership rights continue to trump all, with fair-use doctrines evolving through case law and selective (but highly publicized) enforcement of copyright. The current climate recognizes the intellectual value and legal prerogatives of the publishing industry, privileging the rights of owners and publishers over the needs of patrons. Meanwhile, ways of reading continue to evolve.[21]

Similarly complex issues have emerged with online text and index services. Librarians know the dangers of mistaking what is indexed for the entire field. As "map is not territory," so also "index is not field." Index services vendors sometimes act as if particular indexes were comprehensive. In truth, indexes themselves display the cultural and theological values, resources, and limitations of the indexers and their sponsoring communities, and display the limiting cultural horizon as well as the limits of what is available/affordable to the indexing agency. Most importantly librarians know that the intellectual tasks have shifted dramatically from *seeking* to *sorting*. Even an inadequate search can produce huge results; so discernment is needed in sorting and evaluation of found materials. Leaving aside the unfortunate term "infobesity," librarians rightly distinguish between information overload, and the broader problem of a lack of discernment among researchers who gather too much of the wrong information.[22]

THEOLOGICAL LIBRARIANS:
NATURAL ALLIES WITH MULTICULTURALISM

Librarians as Agents of Change

The wide array of current demographic, curricular, technological, and "intellectual market" challenges can strengthen existing roles for librarians as agents of creative change within the institutions they serve. To play these roles, theological librarians must themselves do what multiculturalism encourages: become visible and audible within the institutions we serve. Adequate attention to paradigm changes under way in theological anthropology, ecclesiology, and pneumatology can provide exemplary opportunities to join/shape the conversations within institutions, as librarians challenge the monopoly of faculty to speak. Theological librarians are well placed to advance discussions regarding the most prominent issues of our times, whether regarding Islam, the growth of global Pentecostalism, or the current revision of theological anthropology in gender and sexuality issues. Are theological librarians constrained by outmoded models of professionalism? When compared with other forms of religious vocation/ministry, theological librarianship can be as often full of risk and vulnerability, as characterized by risk aversion and protectionism. The slow and sometimes agonizing process of theological change is measured link by link, footnote by footnote, article by article, monograph by monograph, and by the bibliographic instruction for which theological librarians are best suited.

Librarians as Agents of Resistance

Restricting the entry of international students by the current United States government has consequences for theological schools. Well-qualified students are opting for programs in more hospitable countries. The diminishing numbers of international students and the increased stress experienced by international students will change the quality and character of U.S. programs, shown in yet another generation of U.S. students with limited and limiting experience of the world. International students who are granted study visas in the United States face greater scrutiny, heightened bias, and specific restrictions on work prospects.[23] Since theological libraries are key sites for employment for international students, libraries should be centers of welcome, since libraries are as close to the multicultural "frontlines" as any classroom. Theological librarians can enhance this important institutional role by creating or hosting programs specially attentive to the needs of international students and nontraditional students, such as writing programs or language study programs, with the intended purpose of transgressing traditional boundaries while serving the real needs of actual students. Additionally, by recruiting staff from among international students, librarians reframe power relationships within institutions. As theological schools struggle with the issues of multiculturalism, it is a hopeful prospect to consider the place of new voices and views of active library staff.[24]

Staff Diversity as a Theological Value

The staff of theological libraries may well be more diverse, theologically and sociopolitically, than the faculty or student body of the schools they serve. With library staff selection and evaluation following other criteria than those used with faculty or the student body, members of library staffs are *comparatively* freer from some distortions in evaluation of applications by the excess of either political correctness or doctrinal tests, and can sometimes play an interesting role in the multicultural conversation of the schools, depending on openness of the school culture to staff participation. Nevertheless, theological librarians remain subject to the caricatures of administrators and faculty whose understanding of library matters is, at best, outdated. While the *organization* of the library serves a more restrictive interpretive tradition than other parts of the community it serves, the *purpose* of the library serves a more expansive interpretive community. Theological librarians pursue this more expansive, holistic tradition. Rhetoric that portrays librarians as monocultural or antitechnological is offensive on its face, though a common comfort to those unaware of the rigor that characterizes librarianship. Such caricatures continue to impede the work of theological librarians and to delay a useful alliance of the full resources of any theological community, with a multicultural library staff seen as partners in the project of theological education.

CONCLUSION

Are we witness to a "teachable moment" in the current (postmodern) openness to religion? Is this a true chastening of Enlightenment prejudice, or only a false humility caused by a quite temporary uncertainty? If boundaries and prejudices *are* under review and revision, the role of theological libraries/librarians will be crucial to the process of transforming theological education. Because theological librarians are given the power to name, classify, organize, mediate, and transform inherited traditions, librarians *must* be an acknowledged part of the conversation regarding the institutional identities, purposes, and programs they are in the process of constructing. The *promise* of contemporary multiculturalism seeks a wider world and a broader mandate for religion and is thus a good description of much of what active theological librarians currently do. The very *premise* of theological libraries seeks a wider world and a deeper reading of the complexity of religious communities and is thus an expression of many forms of multiculturalism.

We cannot move back in time, yet theological librarians are often asked to reconstitute some imagined "value neutral" space, more an expression of nostalgia than reality. In spite of its limits in cultural formation, in spite of limits in organization, classification, acquisition, and interpretation, libraries are often the most vibrant centers of diversity and resources for multicultural engagement within theological institutions. Wise theological librarians are also adept as critical interpreters of the cultural history of their collections and therefore must be recognized as crucial participants in multicultural theological education. Long before the appearance of the contemporary multiculturalists, theological librarians were in pursuit of the promise of multiculturalism. Long after the disappearance of the current multiculturalists, theological librarians will be presenting and preserving the substance and consequences of this latest multiculturalist moment.

NOTES

1. See Matthew Battles, *Library: An Unquiet History* (New York: W. W. Norton, 2004).

2. See "Panel on the Future of American Higher Education," *Educause Review* 35, no. 1 (January-February 2000): 69–71, at http://www.educause.edu/apps/er/erm00/pp032037.pdf (accessed August 17, 2006).

3. Public libraries are experiencing *greater* municipal support and public use in some cities. Like theological libraries, public libraries are sites of cultural assimilation *and* cultural resistance.

4. For a fuller investigation of these themes, see K. Sawyer, "Multiculturalism Observed," *Journal of Religious and Theological Information* 6, nos. 3–4 (2004) [2005].

5. See Philip Jenkins, *The Next Christendom: The Coming of Global Christianity* (New York: Oxford University Press, 2002); see also Lamin Sanneh, *Whose Christianity Is Christianity? The Gospel beyond the West* (Grand Rapids: Eerdmans, 2003).

6. Samuel Huntington's popularization of the "clash of civilizations" thesis has provoked strong response along both religious and nonreligious lines. For helpful critiques of the essentialism of Huntington and others, see Mahmood Mamdani, *Good Muslim, Bad Muslim: America, the Cold War, and the Roots of Terror* (New York: Pantheon, 2004). See also Olivier Roy, *Globalized Islam: The Search for a New Ummah* (New York: Columbia University Press, 2004).

7. For an introduction to the broader discussion concerning the changing definitions of libraries, see Louis Charles Willard, "Technology and Educational Practices," *Theological Education* 38, no. 1 (2001): 111–16. See also Virginia Massey-Burzio, "Facing the Competition," *College and Research Libraries News* 63, no. 11 (December 2002).

8. See Alane Wilson, ed., *Environmental Scan: Pattern Recognition* (Dublin, OH: OCLC, 2004). See also Kevin Kelly, "Scan This Book!" *New York Times*, May 14, 2006, at http://www.nytimes.com/2006/05/14/magazine/14publishing.html (accessed August 17, 2006).

9. Among the many works on multiculturalism, the following titles have been particularly helpful for this essay: John D. Buenker and Lorman A. Ratner, eds., *Multiculturalism in the United States: A Comparative Guide to Acculturation and Ethnicity* (Westport, CT: Greenwood Press, 1992); David Theo Goldberg, *Multiculturalism: A Critical Reader* (Malden, MA: Blackwell, 1994); Arthur M. Melzer, Jerry Weinberger, and M. Richard Zinman, eds., *Multiculturalism and American Democracy* (Lawrence: University Press of Kansas, 1998); David Hollinger, *Post-Ethnic America: Beyond Multiculturalism* (New York: Basic Books, 1995); Martin E. Marty, *The One and the Many: America's Struggle for the Common Good* (Cambridge, MA: Harvard University Press, 1997); Christian Joppke and Steven Lukes, eds., *Multicultural Questions* (New York: Oxford University Press, 1999). See also Don C. Lock, *Increasing Multicultural Understanding*, 2nd ed. (Thousand Oaks, CA: Sage Publications, 1998).

10. This positive orientation towards change within multiculturalism is referred to by many terms, whether "strong multiculturalism" or "critical multiculturalism" or "constructive multiculturalism" or "interculturalism," with all aware of a mutuality (not necessarily the reciprocity or equality) of interaction and influence. This is a significant way to distinguish "strong" or "transformative" multiculturalism from the "difference multiculturalism" that accounts for a large percentage of the literature and is often the subject of intense criticism for emphasizing difference as an end in itself—diversity for diversity's sake. See Stanley Fish, "Boutique Multiculturalism," in *Multiculturalism and American Democracy*, 69–88.

11. See David Stewart, "Libraries: Western Christian," in *Encyclopedia of Monasticism*, ed. William M. Johnston (Chicago: Fitzroy Dearborn Publishers, 2000), 765–68.

12. For literature relating to classification, see Geoffrey C. Bowker and Susan Leigh Star, *Sorting Things Out: Classification and Its Consequences* (Cambridge, MA: MIT Press, 1999); see also J. Law, *Organizing Modernity* (Oxford: Blackwell, 1994).

13. See Martin Hollis, "Is Universalism Ethnocentric?" in *Multicultural Questions*, 27–43. Barbara Mathe suggests a link between the enthnographic scales of nineteenth-century colonialism and the values Melville Dewey reflected in his classification system. See "Kaleidoscopic Classifications: Redefining Information in a World Cultural Context," paper presented at the 64th IFLA General Conference, August 16–21, 1998, available at http://www.ifla.org/IV/ifla64/109–145c.htm (accessed August 17, 2006). See also Norman J. Kansfield, "'Study the Most Approved Authors': The Role of the Seminary Library in Nineteenth-Century American Protestant Ministerial Education" (PhD diss., University of Chicago, 1981). See also the online essays of the American Theological Library Association section, Theological Libraries: Historical Sources, at http://www.atla.com/sources/index.htm (accessed August 17, 2006).

14. See Mathe, "Kaleidoscopic Classifications." See also the literature on zoological classification, Harriet Ritvo, *The Platypus and the Mermaid and Other Figments of the Classifying Imagination* (Cambridge, MA: Harvard University Press, 1997).

15. See the essays in Martin Hewitt, ed., *Culture Institutions* (Leeds: University of Leeds, 2002).

16. See R. S. Sugirtharajah, *Postcolonial Criticism and Biblical Interpretation* (New York: Oxford University Press, 2002); see also Carl Starkloff, *A Theology of the In-Between: The Value of the Syncretic Process* (Milwaukee: Marquette University Press, 2002). See now Kwame Anthony Appiah, *The Ethics of Identity* (Princeton, NJ: Princeton University Press, 2005).

17. See, for example, Stephen A. Rhodes, *Where the Nations Meet: The Church in a Multicultural World* (Downers Grove, IL: InterVarsity Press, 1998); see also Brian K. Blount and Leonora Tubbs Tisdale, eds., *Making Room at the Table: An Invitation to Multiculutural Worship* (Louisville, KY: Westminster John Knox Press, 2001); see also Curtiss Paul DeYoung, *United by Faith: The Multiracial Congregation as an Answer to the Problem of Race* (New York: Oxford University Press, 2003).

18. While contemporary multiculturalism can be considered an innovation of the modern/postmodern era, multiculturalism is also in continuity with older traditions of resistance and dissent from culturally sheltered or sanctioned bias.

19. See, for example, James J. O'Donnell, *Avatars of the Word: From Papyrus to Cyberspace* (Cambridge, MA: Harvard University Press, 1998); see also Ruth Conway, *The Choices at the Heart of Technology: A Christian Perspective* (Harrisburg, PA: Trinity Press International, 1999).

20. See John Tiffin and Lalita Rajasingham. *The Global Virtual University* (New York: Routledge, 2003). See David G. Brown, ed., *Ubiquitous Computing* (Bolton, MA: Anker Publishing, 2003).

21. See Nancy Kaplan, "Literacy beyond Books: Reading When All the World's a Web," in *The World Wide Web and Contemporary Cultural Theory*, ed. Andrew Herman and Thomas Swiss (New York: Routledge, 2000), 207–34.

22. See James H. Morris, "Tales of Technology: Consider a Cure for Pernicious Infobesity," *Post-Gazette* (Pittsburgh), March 30, 2003, available at http://www.post-gazette.com/pg/03089/169397.stm (accessed August 17, 2006).

23. See Chimamanda Ngozi Adichie, "The Line of No Return," *New York Times*, A 21, November 29, 2004.

24. Public librarians have long questioned an uncritical endorsement of "assimilation." See, for example, Dorte Skot-Hansen, "The Public Library between Integration and Cultural Diversity," *Scandinavian Public Library Quarterly* 35, no. 1 (2002), available at http://www.splq.info/issues/vol35_1/06.htm (accessed August 17, 2006).

CHAPTER 6

From Sideline to Center: Teaching and Learning for a Racially and Culturally Diverse Church

Deborah Flemister Mullen

M ay 17, 2004, marked the fiftieth anniversary of *Brown v. Board of Education*, the landmark United States Supreme Court decision that overturned a legal system of racial preference predicated upon an earlier decision of the highest court in the 1896 case of *Plessy v. Ferguson*. Historian John Hope Franklin reminds us that "when the United States Supreme Court, in the case of *Plessy v. Ferguson*, set forth the 'separate but equal' doctrine in 1896, the decision provided a new stimulus for laws to separate the races and, of course, to discriminate against Negroes. In time, Negroes and whites were separated in the use of schools, churches, cemeteries, drinking fountains, restaurants, and all places of public accommodation and amusement."[1]

Without question *Brown v. Board of Education* stands among the finest moments of modern jurisprudence that contributed to the dethronement of the legal precedents set forth in *Plessy v. Ferguson*. Because of *Brown* the trajectory toward the achievement of equal opportunity education for all Americans, public *and* private, was set for generations to come. *Brown* anticipated an American society that would make slow but steady progress toward becoming more inclusive and appreciative of both cultural *and* racial diversity. *Brown* epitomized an end to America's version of a "color-blind" caste system that divided society into white and black cultural, economic, and political "silos."[2] But what about the *quality* of the educational opportunity guaranteed by *Brown*? Did equal opportunity education imply equal *quality* education as well, or was *Brown* silent on the question of the *quality* of the educational opportunity?

One could argue that, in theory, *Brown* leveled the playing field, making it possible to envision equal opportunity *quality* education as an entitlement of all Americans regardless of race and the color of their skin. I would argue that without *Brown*, this book, *Shaping Beloved Community: Reflections on Multicultural Theological Education*, would be impossible to imagine, much less to be written by a faculty that looks like ours. Concerned for and crusading for the cause of equal opportunity education in the twentieth century, *Brown* set the stage for multicultural theological education of the twenty-first century with its concern and commitment to equal opportunity *quality* education.

With *Brown v. Board of Education* as our springboard, this essay offers a critical reflection on the experiences of one seminary's engagement with multicultural theological education and its intentional efforts to increase racial, ethnic, and cultural diversity as expressions of the progression of equal opportunity *quality* education into the twenty-first century. It serves as a case study, although not strictly in a formal sense, of race and multicultural theological education. It examines some of the ways issues of power, position, and privilege are played out in one seminary's mission to prepare women and men for a church that is racially and culturally diverse. It explores the ways McCormick Theological Seminary has strategically allocated staff and faculty resources to support missional, programmatic, and academic initiatives that serve churches and communities increasingly becoming racially, ethnically, and culturally diverse.

This essay addresses how McCormick Seminary, by moving its so-called racial/ethnic minority [sic] programs from *sideline* to *center*, has sought to be—in its ethos and praxis—"a community of learning and teaching," (1) whose vocation and mission are deeply rooted in its Reformed and Presbyterian traditions, intentionally ecumenical and authentically cross-cultural, and (2) that calls itself to relationships of mutuality and accountability as it exercises its power, position, and privilege to *shape beloved community* within the so-called dominant culture of Anglo-American church and society. Without question, the combination of these commitments, including the tensions that inevitably arise in the midst of such diversity in experience and expectations, makes for an interesting life together on the way to becoming *beloved community*.

McCormick Seminary's commitment to *diversity* has been evolving since the early 1970s, in ways that we continue to affirm in our educational programs, in our service to the church's mission of hospitality and reconciliation, and in our relationships with our closest neighbors and partner constituencies beyond the seminary.[3] Goal One of the most recently adopted mission statement reads, McCormick Theological Seminary will "be a recognized leader in theological education for a distinctive model of collaborative teaching and learning that is Reformed, ecumenical and cross-cultural." This goal reflects what has been a core value for us for some time: to create a seminary culture in which relationships that cross boundaries of race, class, culture, theological orientation, and so forth are *experienced as normative* in preparing leaders for church and in society.

We have made notable progress over the past thirty years on becoming a multicultural community that values diversity as a gift from God to humanity. Still, we have a ways to go before we can claim that by our struggles and strivings we have been fully transformed into a multicultural community of learning and teaching in which issues of power, position, and privilege associated with so-called "dominant" and "minority" cultures no longer strain relations among us. Fortunately, we are not alone in our struggles and strivings. According to *Perspectives on Diversity,* a publication of the Association of Theological Schools (ATS), diversity is one of the greatest challenges facing theological education (and the churches) today. Oddly enough, this acknowledgment of challenge is a hopeful sign that theological education is slowly but surely coming to the awareness that diversity matters!

Jack L. Seymour, former dean at Garrett-Evangelical Theological Seminary, writes: "At its heart, the question of what matters is a theological question. Why does diversity matter? What does it mean? Who decides? For what purpose, for what church, for what ministry? . . . Reflection about diversity begins with exploration of theological visions of the seminary and its education, or more concretely, the responsibility of the seminary to the mission of the church."[4] Julia M. Speller, church historian at Chicago Theological Seminary, writes that the move toward diversity is seen as a "radical move toward positive and transformative change in theological education."[5] The comments of Seymour and Speller are pointed and point theological education in the right direction by raising critical theological questions regarding the nature, purpose, and significance of diversity for seminary education and also for the mission of the church.

If U.S. Census Bureau data are correct in showing that the ratio of nonwhites to whites is increasing at rates heretofore unprecedented in the history of this nation, what does that mean for theological education and the mission of the church? Before the middle of this century, the racial/ethnic population of the United States will likely exceed the current white majority of the nation's population.[6] On a daily basis the media draw our attention to the shifts in demographics that have been taking place since the 1980s. An enormous challenge faces churches today, specifically Protestant churches like the Presbyterian Church (U.S.A.), whose membership continues to be overwhelmingly white, middle class, and aging. The challenge to prepare women and men for ministries of Christian leadership in settings that are more and more racially, ethnically, and culturally diverse does not stop at the door of the churches once considered to be the most influential and well established in America. Churches whose memberships are predominantly or exclusively nonwhite are also preparing their sons and daughters for multicultural ministries in racially, ethnically, and culturally diverse settings in record numbers by sending them to seminary and theological schools.

Given these trends, are today's seminaries and theological schools ready to meet the challenge of a diversity that matters? Is theological education in the United States more attentive than thirty years ago to the "worlds" (the communities and churches) from which racial and ethnic minority students are coming to study for first theological degrees? What can seminaries and theological schools do not only to ensure *excellence* in their graduates as they take on vocations of religious leadership, as pastors, counselors, and educators, in the communities from which they have come, but also to ensure that those same women and men are equipped to lead nonminority and multicultural communities and churches seeking justice, peace, and reconciliation across racial, ethnic, and cultural differences and divisions?

In the space remaining, we will review aspects of McCormick's evolution as a seminary committed to multicultural theological education that prepares men and women to serve the church and God's mission of reconciliation in the world by crossing barriers of race, ethnicity, and culture for the sake of *the beloved community*. We will look closely at McCormick's commitment to three racial/ethnic ministries centers as the *centerpiece* of its self-understanding as a seminary of the Presbyterian Church (U.S.A.) that is Reformed, ecumenical, and cross-cultural. Finally, we will explore what McCormick has learned over the years about multicultural theological education that may be beneficial to others seeking to embrace racial, ethnic, and cultural diversity as gifts of God for *shaping beloved community*.

RESPONDING TO THE CALL:
MCCORMICK'S FIRST MINISTRY PROGRAMS, 1970–2003

Latino Studies Program and Hispanic Ministries

Thirty years ago McCormick Seminary was located north of the Loop in Chicago's Lincoln Park neighborhood. The twenty-six-acre campus sat in the middle of an area of the city where there was a significant Latino presence. As fears of urban renewal (or "removal") and the first wave of gentrification began to pervade the Lincoln Park neighborhood, McCormick was targeted by a number of community organizations, including a Puerto Rican cultural identity group known as the Young Lords. As the story goes, McCormick became a symbol of the dominant culture's greed for land acquisition and economic development while neglecting the needs of local communities and the poor. The Young Lords believed McCormick and other theological institutions in Chicago should be more responsive to the needs of the Latino community and, in particular, pay more attention to the Humboldt Park and West Town areas in which the Latino population was heavily concentrated on the city's North Side.[7]

In a dramatic show of 1970s-style grass-roots community organization and mobilization, the Young Lords took over McCormick's administration building. Long story short: eventually, members of the McCormick community and the Young Lords came together around issues of "justice in their claims" and "to explore ways to serve the Latino community with the formation of leaders for the church." One of the outcomes of the occupation and its aftermath was a commitment in 1973 on the part of the seminary's Board of Directors to form an Advisory Group on Latino Theological Studies at McCormick Seminary. The Advisory Group worked diligently and productively for nearly one year researching and gathering resources for its first public consultation and for its May 1974 report to the board.

The first public event in April 1974 was an ecumenical consultation on Latino Studies. A second consultation, held in February 1975, focused on the theme Dialogo entre Iglesia y Barrio (Dialogue between Church and Community). The apparent success of this second consultation solidified the position and power of the fledgling Latino Studies Program at McCormick in 1976. The consultations opened new possibilities for doing Latino theological education in Chicago, with McCormick Seminary leading the way. While the new partnership with the Chicago Latino community was a major commitment that would shape the seminary's life into the future, it is noteworthy that Latino students have been among those receiving degrees at McCormick since the 1940s.[8]

The seminary's first official racial/ethnic ministry program,[9] the Latino Studies Program, was formed in response to a call from the Chicago Latino community, McCormick's neighbors, to partner with them to develop pastors and community and denominational leaders and to offer graduate theological studies to a community that was historically underserved by theological education. The first years of the program were filled with course development, recruiting Latino/a faculty members to teach in Spanish, community outreach and partnership development, grants development, negotiations with a local college to create a bridge program for non-BA students to begin theological studies, and so forth.[10] The seminary's move to Hyde Park on Chicago's South Side during the first five years of the program would prove over time to place a strain on relationships that had been forged with Chicago Latinos during the seminary's Lincoln Park days.

By the middle of the 1980s the Latino Studies Program was in need of revitalization. Local partnerships that once had been considered "a cornerstone" of the Latino Studies Program had become difficult to maintain. Relationships with national and international programs were not sustained. In one rendering of the history, someone simply writes that "the program became more immersed in the life of the Seminary." At least in the writer's mind the energies of the Latino Studies Program became more inward focused as the seminary focused more attention on its new South Side location, new institutional and community partners, and a new curriculum.[11]

The program took a creative turn in 1987 when McCormick and the Lutheran School of Theology at Chicago (LSTC) joined forces to form a joint Hispanic Ministries Program. This model of cooperation, albeit administratively cumbersome and somewhat labor intensive, lasted three years, with several accomplishments to show for the effort, including "new curricular goals, a concentration in Hispanic Ministries, a community-based Summer Program, and a proposal for a Hispanic field based education experience. Other new development included hosting the Hispanic Summer Program for the first time, and the formation of the first Hispanic D.Min. group in Chicago."[12]

The Office of Hispanic Ministries at McCormick was established in 1993. The next decade would present numerous challenges to the Hispanic Ministry Program around a cluster of issues such as the multicultural, multilingual, multiethnic/racial nature of the program; how to educate and prepare leaders to serve Latino churches; strategies to recruit and retain Latino/a students.[13] The Hispanic Ministries Program at McCormick, for the most part, was a relatively effective model of multicultural theological education. The program offered master's and doctoral students interested in and already serving in Hispanic communities the opportunity to study and prepare for ministry within the familiar context of Latino and multicultural churches. The seminary curriculum offered a number of courses in Spanish each year. Academic advising and support services were increased to meet the needs of students whose primary language was Spanish and whose cultures and ethnic experiences were formed in Hispanic communities across the United States, Puerto Rico, Mexico, and other parts of Latin America.

For all of its efforts, however, the seminary's Hispanic Ministry Program remained on the margins of academic and community life at McCormick. Like other "special" (read: minority) ministry programs at the seminary during that era, much of what went on under the guidance and leadership of the Hispanic Ministry Program amounted to little more than "sideline" events for most students for which the curriculum and educational process centered around preparing predominantly white/Anglo young men and increasing numbers of older white women for ministries in the Presbyterian Church (U.S.A.) and denominations with similar Eurocentric roots.

Korean American Ministries Center

The Korean American Ministries Center was established in 1988 in response to the needs of a rapidly expanding Korean immigrant community in the Midwest. As it has often been noted elsewhere, it is fitting that this initiative to provide leadership training for an emerging Korean American church should come from McCormick Theological Seminary; graduate Samuel A. Moffett, a Presbyterian missionary to Korea in 1890, founded and was the first president of Pyungyang Seminary. McCormick's commitment to develop leaders for Korean immigrant and Korean American churches may likewise be best understood in terms of call and vocation. The Korean American Ministries Center programs focused on leadership formation and language training for pastors and church leaders who sought to be theologically trained to minister in the U.S. context in which recent immigrants and new citizens were dealing with language difficulties and cultural differences.

Like the Hispanic Ministries Program, in the beginning the Korean American Ministries Center operated from a context-oriented community-needs approach to theological education. Such an approach had to be sensitive to the experiences of at least three separate generational cohorts of Koreans that comprised their community: first-generation immigrants; second-generation born in this country; and 1.5-generation born in Korea, proficient in English, and considered in between American and Korean. Then and now the challenges facing the generations are quite different. Among the first generation, challenges revolve around language, values, customs, and the pressure to succeed. Among the second generation, challenges revolve around alienation, acceptance, and being isolated, not fully accepted by either Korean or American society. Among the 1.5 generation, challenges revolve around being seen by the first and second generations as either too Korean or too American.[14]

McCormick's Korean American Ministries Center provided academic and instructional support services through a close relationship with the Language Resource and Writing Center (formerly known as the Language Lab). Working with assigned learning partners, Korean students for whom English proficiency had not been achieved prior to matriculation were enabled to make the best of the seminary's educational programs. In reality, however, with language and cultural barriers to overcome on the part of Koreans and non-Koreans alike, there existed in the seminary a culture that unintentionally nurtured an ethos and mission orientation in which parallel programs for racial/ethnic minorities were assimilated, rationalized, and tolerated. Those were the days when the robust smell of *kimchee*[15] cooking in the 1400 building or wafting through the airways and coursing through the narrow hallways of the Kimbark apartments or being widely shared at mealtime in the common areas of McGaw or McClure would reveal just how nonmulticultural and un-cross-cultural we truly were.

This was not McCormick at her best, nor was it her finest hour in the pursuit of quality multicultural theological education for all. Some of the reasons for this may have been that the ministry programs had become, for both their "constituencies" and for the wider seminary community, self-imposed ghettos and substitutes for engaging the whole seminary experience, because it was too hard to overcome the difficulties with language and differences in cultural understandings.

From its inception as a "special" ministry program center in 1988 until 2003, the Korean American Ministries Center served a target constituency here in Chicago that is reportedly the third largest concentration of Koreans in the United States outside of California and the New York metropolitan area.[16] Korean Christians living in the Midwest tend to come from more socially and theologically conservative churches. Nevertheless, for many, McCormick has been the place to study and learn the ministry skills necessary to be successful in American society with all of its multicultural richness and racial, ethnic, and cultural diversity.

In many ways the Korean American Ministries Center appeared to be the minority leadership development program in which the seminary was most heavily invested both financially, in the allocation of institutional resources including the deployment of faculty and program staff, and missionally. The seminary's historic ties to Korean Christians through Moffett and successive generations of missionaries became a bridge to envision a new relationship paradigm with Korean Presbyterians nearly one hundred years later. In place of traditional patterns of missionary paternalism, McCormick faculty, led by its visionary dean and president, envisioned an empowering teaching and learning partnership in theological education that was focused on language training, leadership formation, and bicultural (not yet multicultural) programs with Korean immigrant churches in the Chicago area.[17] The vision was ambitious; the results were mixed.

Significant among the contributions of the Korean American Ministries Center to the development of multicultural theological education at McCormick, with its concern and crusade for *quality* equal opportunity education in the early days, were:[18]

— Faculty enhancement. Hiring new faculty (including visiting professors and adjuncts) with expertise in Korean American ministry and culture, and offering faculty research and professional development opportunities to non-Korean faculty.

— The promotion of bicultural education and teaching skills formation for pastors and lay leaders. Offering core and elective courses in Korean. Teaching courses in Bible, biblical languages, history, theology, ethics, and ministry in English and from a Korean American cultural perspective.

— Expanding the network of field-based education supervised ministry settings to include a variety of Korean American churches and agencies that will accommodate students from all of the generational cohorts comprising the Korean student population.

— Evaluation of the effectiveness of the Language Resource and Writing Center (LRWC), in support of developing English proficiency in listening, speaking, and writing, for persons whose first language is not English.

— Developing bilingual library resources using Korean *han-gul* characters and including *han-gul* word processing capabilities. Specialization and increased accessibility of Korean bibliographic material within the Jesuit-Krauss-McCormick (JKM) and Regenstein libraries of Hyde Park.

— Developing financial partnerships to fund the development and operation of the Korean American Ministries Center, including substantial annual gifts from the Korean American church community.

— Establishment of a cooperative Doctor of Ministry (DMin) program with the Presbyterian Theological College and Seminary in Seoul.

Next we will turn our attention to the third ministry program center that has most closely symbolically embodied McCormick's commitment to multicultural theological education as equal opportunity *quality* education in keeping with the legacy of *Brown v. Board of Education.*

African American Ministries Program and African American Leadership Partnership (AALP) Program

> There has been an African American presence at McCormick Theological Seminary since close to its founding in 1829. African American students were enrolled at McCormick as early as 1833. William Herbert King served as a professor of preaching for a number of years beginning in 1958. Throughout the years McCormick has welcomed African American students, scholars, lecturers, and partners in ministry.[19]

The above citation from the Report of the African American Ministries Program Review Committee (April 2003) serves as an ideal place to begin our discussion of the last of the three racial/ethnic ministry program centers. In some ways this section is the most difficult for me to write, given my various involvements with the development of the African American Ministries Program at McCormick since joining the faculty in 1989. Unlike the case of the other two racial/ethnic ministry programs, there does not seem to be any written record of an African American ministries program at McCormick prior to 1990. According to oral tradition, however, there was such a program formed by African American students on the old campus in the aftermath of the April 4, 1968, assassination of Dr. Martin Luther King Jr. The idea that something programmatic existed prior to 1990 to address the concerns of African American students and the black church community is both powerful and plausible to entertain, since at the time of Dr. King's assassination black students at predominantly white institutions of higher education throughout the nation seized upon the opportunity to demand changes in two major areas of student life, curriculum and student services.

When the African American Ministries Program was launched in 1990, the vision was for a ministry center that would build on established relationships and develop new ones between African American churches/communities, the Presbyterian Church (U.S.A.), and McCormick Seminary. Initially the program was oriented primarily toward providing student support services for master's level students. During its first years of operation, the program was without a director or office support. There was a student coordinator, and an advisory committee comprised representatives from the administration, the faculty, and the student body. The black student body was small but diverse, drawing on the rich variety of black church traditions located in Chicago and the surrounding region. Program development and curricular concerns, such as developing course offerings with a black church emphasis and finding black faculty to teach adjunct courses at the seminary, were some of the challenges facing the advisory committee in the early years.

Within two years of its start-up, it became evident that if the African American Ministries Program were going to have an institutional impact on the seminary's mission to prepare men and women for ministries in the African American community, it would have to have a voice at the table where strategic missional decisions are made. For all that it modeled in terms of power, position, and privilege for a student coordinator to be the de facto center director, a student coordinator had neither the power, position, nor the privilege of experience to prepare the seminary for the changes that would occur during the next decade. Institutionally the program center needed a director, someone strategically positioned to guide a process of organizational change that few could possibly imagine was about to take place. Rather than hire a program director from outside, as had been the case with the Korean American Ministries Program, the African American Ministries Program named a program director from among the current teaching faculty.

This strategic decision was effective in two ways. First, naming a program director from within the faculty sent a clear signal internally that the ministry centers were as important to the academic mission of the seminary as was teaching. Faculty colleagues would more likely respect and follow a ministry center director who was "one of their own," and generally speaking, administrators and support staff would graciously extend themselves to do everything possible to support the faculty person in his/her programmatic function for the good of the order. Second, naming a faculty director told external constituencies that the seminary was taking seriously its mission to help educate and prepare the next generation of African American church and community leadership by placing the responsibility for directing the ministry center within the primary scope of responsibilities of a respected member of the teaching faculty.

With a grant from the MacArthur Foundation, the African American Leadership Partnership (AALP) was launched in 1993. AALP was the brainchild design of McCormick's only same-year-double-degree graduate.[20] Unlike anything in the seminary's history, AALP would literally change McCormick's understanding of context-based theological education at the master's level. The partnership of African American churches/communities, MacArthur, and the seminary targeted groups (cohorts) of seasoned church leaders from the south and west sides of Chicago, and invited them to undertake a program of graduate theological studies that was designed, as a model of transformational multicultural theological education, to transform churches and communities. In addition to a core curriculum that included Bible, church history, theological methodology, ethics, and pastoral care, AALP course offerings focused on preaching for community transformation, empowerment, and asset-based community development. AALP started as an experimental program under the auspices of the African American Ministries Program, but by its final year it had become a new model for doing multicultural theological education at McCormick.

Despite the original plan envisioned by the creators of the program, only one cohort of AALP students was successfully matriculated directly into the Doctor of Ministry (DMin).[21] However, once AALP opened the door for African American pastors and church leaders from the Chicago area to earn master's and doctoral level degrees while enrolled in context-sensitive courses designed by the McCormick residential faculty and expert adjuncts, multicultural theological education at McCormick would never be the same. Meanwhile conversations were taking place that would eventuate in a new paradigm of African American theological studies offered by seminaries on the South Side. Interestingly two of the three racial/ethnic ministry program centers tried joint programs that were moderately successful but short-lived.[22] The Southside Cluster of Theological Schools, a collaboration of five schools including McCormick, attempted to coordinate course offerings and initiate other academic initiatives under the umbrella of a joint program from 1993 to 1995.

McCormick hired its first full-time director of the African American Ministries Program in 1995. The new director was expected to teach courses related to African American church tradition, develop programs for the ministry center, sponsor workshops, lectures, and discussions on African American history and heritage, and be an outreach worker and liaison between the seminary and the black church community in Chicago and within the Presbyterian Church (U.S.A.). Added to the list was the expectation "that the new director would help shepherd McCormick into making the African American religious experience an active part of McCormick's efforts to be multicultural and cross-cultural."[23]

The African American Ministries Program model of the mid-1990s proved to be a valued addition to seminary life according to the majority of students who sought out the counsel and advice of the director. Students, black and white, benefited from course offerings, events, and mentoring provided by the director. Relationship development with churches and communities was a priority of the program director during this time. Unfortunately, however, the program was not well integrated into the life of the seminary as a whole. Given the expectation that the program would be a central component of the seminary's "efforts to be multicultural and cross-cultural," something needed to change. Plans were under way to strategically move the African American Ministries Programs from its more marginal, sideline position into greater engagement with the rest of seminary life, as a central location for "McCormick's efforts to be multicultural and cross-cultural, when the director's untimely death in summer of 2001 changed everything. Later that fall, McCormick called one of its alumnae to serve as interim program director until such time as a review of the program could be completed and a new strategy developed for how the African American Ministries Program would provide leadership for the seminary in its commitment to diversity and multicultural theological education.

FROM SIDELINE TO CENTER: WHAT HAVE WE LEARNED

In this essay I have attempted to sketch out what it looks like in the life of one seminary to take diversity seriously, as though the very body of Christ depends upon it. Experience is our teacher. We are lifelong learners. Our story is merely one portal through which to enter a space that promises new life though engagement with that which is perceived to be different, unfamiliar, and threatening. The commitment to diversity and to *quality* multicultural theological education is part of a developmental process that has something to do with nurturing a quality of relationships that cut across otherwise formidable racial, ethnic, and cultural boundaries, for the sake of becoming and *shaping beloved community*.

Anne E. Streaty Wimberly of the Interdenominational Theological Center in Atlanta writes:

> Theological education in the twenty-first century increasingly reflects pluralistic cultural contexts. This experience of cultural diversity presents both opportunity and challenge for teaching and learning. Given this context, there is greater opportunity than ever before to embrace and nurture what I call "hospitable kinship." That is, diversity beckons us to enter into a hospitable teaching and learning space that, to use Parker Palmer's words, "makes possible persons' receiving each other, our struggles, our newborn ideas with openness and care."[24]

This work has no ending in sight. The wisdom about which Streaty Wimberly writes beckons us to ask, Is what we are practicing as multicultural theological education fit to be called "hospitable kinship"? If not, we have neither seized the opportunity nor stepped up to the challenge before us. At McCormick we will continue the legacy of *Brown v. Board of Education* "with all deliberate speed" as we go deeper in our commitment and understandings of multicultural theological *quality* education as one way to participate in *shaping beloved community* in church and society.

NOTES

1. John Hope Franklin, *Race and History: Selected Essays 1938–1988* (Baton Rouge: Louisiana State University Press, 1989), 142.

2. I am indebted to my colleague Matthew Ouellett, EdD, University of Massachusetts at Amherst, for his introducing those of us who study multicultural educational theory to this useful term.

3. Dating exactly when the commitment to diversity began is a hard nail to hit squarely on its head, since the discourse of diversity is relatively new, while the seminary's history shows that the first African American students were admitted as early as 1833. In chapter 4 of this volume my colleague Luis Rivera claims that the seminary's commitment to diversity has been ongoing since the 1970s, since the establishment of the first Hispanic Ministries Program. Our ties

to missionary activities among Korean Presbyterians can be traced to the late nineteenth century through McCormick graduate Samuel A. Moffett. As one takes stock of all of the seminary's efforts to attract a diverse student body comprising African Americans, Latinos, and Asians, clearly diversity has been sought after and highly valued for more than 160 years.

4. Jack L. Seymour, "Addressing and Embodying Diversity in Theological Education," *ATS Folio, Diversity in Theological Education, 2003.*

5. Julia M. Speller, "Increasing Diversity in Theological School: A Reflection," *ATS Folio, Diversity in Theological Education, 2003.*

6. *ATS Folio, Diversity in Theological Education, 2003.* Statistics on Race and Ethnicity, 1900–2050.

7. *Hispanic Ministries at McCormick Theological Seminary: 1973–2000.*

8. *Report on the Hispanic Ministries Program,* by Luis R. Rivera and Daniel Rodriguez-Diaz, 2000.

9. The claim that the Latino Studies Program was the first minority student program of its kind at McCormick is under dispute by individual African American alumni, and the matter remains unsettled at this time.

10. *Hispanic Ministries at McCormick Theological Seminary: 1973–2000.*

11. Ibid.

12. Ibid.

13. Ibid.

14. *Second Harvest: A Leadership Development Program in Ministry to the Korean American Community in Chicago and the Upper Midwest,* proposal for support, submitted by McCormick Theological Seminary, 1991.

15. For many non-Koreans, the smell of kimchee, a staple of Korean cuisine, takes some getting used to. An association that comes to mind from my African American social location is the reaction of many non-African Americans to the smell of chitterlings cooking.

16. *Second Harvest.*

17. Ibid.

18. Ibid.

19. Report of the African American Ministries Program Review Committee. April 10, 2003.

20. The Reverend Dr. Leon D. Finney Jr., pastor of the Metropolitan Apostolic Community Church, Chicago, Illinois, holds the distinction of being the only "same year, double degree graduate" in recent memory. Dr. Finney's Doctor of Ministry (DMin) thesis project laid the foundation for the African American Leadership Partnership (AALP) program. AALP holds the distinction of being the most successful African American student recruitment program in the 175-year history of McCormick Seminary.

21. According to the Report of the African American Ministries Program Review Committee (April 2003), "the initial intent of the AALP Program was for students to complete the MATS and then immediately enter into an AALP

D.Min. Program. One group was able to follow this format as an experimental program. However, as McCormick sought to regularize the AALP Program the standards of the Association of Theological Schools caused McCormick to require an M.Div. or its equivalency as well as three years of pastoral experience before students could enroll in the AALP D.Min."

22. The Joint Hispanic Ministries Program with the Lutheran School of Theology at Chicago (LSTC) was the other example previously discussed.

23. Report of the African American Ministries Program Review Committee, April 10, 2003.

24. Anne E. Streaty Wimberly, "Hospitable Kinship in Theological Education: Cross-Cultural Perspectives on Teaching and Learning as Gift Exchange," *Teaching Theology and Religion* 7, no.1 (January 2004).

PART TWO

Biblical and Theological Studies

CHAPTER 7

Of Every Race and People

Cynthia M. Campbell

It is the text that every lay reader (and most ministers) dread reading aloud: "How is it that we hear, each of us, in our own native language? Parthians, Medes, Elamites, and residents of Mesopotamia, Judea and Cappodocia, Pontus and Asia, Phrygia and Pamphylia, Egypt and the parts of Libya belonging to Cyrene, and visitors from Rome, both Jews and proselytes, Cretans and Arabs . . ." (Acts 2:8–11). Every year at Pentecost, this reading takes the church on a geographic and ethnographic tour of virtually the entire world known to Luke and his readers. In so doing, these verses lay the foundation for the theological concept at the heart of the New Testament: that the promise of God, first made known to Israel, is now, through Jesus Christ, God's promise to *all* people.

The fruit of that promise is now a vivid reality: the church of Jesus Christ is present in virtually every nation and culture. Christians worship, read the Bible, and teach the faith in thousands of languages. Christianity today is embedded in such a variety of places as to be called a truly "multicultural" religious tradition. Even though the story of Christianity has often been told from the perspective of Europeans "taking the gospel" to other continents, new historiography calls for a reassessment of this view and a recognition that Christian faith has long been part of many cultures.[1]

It is the conviction of this volume of essays that such a "multicultural" view of Christianity results in a reshaping of American theological education and of the means by which women and men are prepared for ministry in the United States. Some will argue that this approach is a passing fad, a capitulation to a current form of political correctness that has overtaken other parts of higher education. The thesis here is that the foundations for a multicultural approach to understanding Christianity and to theological education are both biblical and theological. The purpose of this essay is to examine those foundations and to explore their claims in light of the opposition to the concept of multiculturalism in contemporary intellectual circles.

Before looking at the biblical and theological resources of this question, some definition of terms is in order. Words such as "culture" and "multicultural" are notoriously difficult to define and are used in widely different ways. In the most basic terms, "culture" denotes all that we humans create and construct that makes human life in community possible. It includes intellectual ideas, moral values, social customs, and ways of organizing life, as well as the artifacts of culture, such as food, clothing, buildings, modes of transportation and communication, and the arts. Looked at from a global perspective, human life has always been multicultural rather than monocultural, in the sense that distinctive cultures have emerged from groups of humans in different locations around the world. When persons from several cultures inhabit the same region, however, or when once-isolated cultures have significant interaction (due to communication, trade, migration, etc.), it is possible to talk about a multicultural society.

BIBLICAL FOUNDATIONS

A theological approach to the question of multiculturality begins with an examination of Scripture. How does the Bible shed light on issues of multiculturalism? Clearly there is no simple answer to that question. Read at face value, the Old Testament presents the view that all humanity is descended from one set of parents who were made in the "image" and "likeness" of God (Gen. 1:26). By the time of Abraham, however, it is clear that the world has many "peoples" or nations (cultures). Indeed, the story of Abraham and Sarah is a saga of migration between and interaction with multiple cultures, even as they become the "ancestor[s] of a multitude of nations" (Gen. 17:5). As one reads the Old Testament, it is possible to draw several conclusions about culture and multiculturality.

First of all, a diversity of cultures and nations is part of the "given" of the biblical narrative: many nations, languages, and cultures exist and interact in a variety of ways, including competition, conflict, and commerce. Second, Israel understands itself to occupy a particular place among the world's peoples as God's "chosen," the "people of the covenant." This puts

Israel in conflict with others in some narratives. The "conquest" of Canaan and the wars for control of territory during the time of David reflect one result of this story of election. On the other hand, Israel is seen as having a "mission" beyond itself (e.g., as "a light to the nations," Isa. 42:6). The story of Jonah is the pointed story of how God's "mission to the nations" will succeed despite the prophet's (or Israel's) reluctance. Eventually, in the eschatological vision, Zion (or Jerusalem) is pictured as the place to which all nations will (eventually) come (e.g., Isa. 55:5 and 56:7). Third, the God of Israel is God of all nations and peoples and uses the actions of others to advance God's purposes (e.g., Isa. 45:1–7).[2]

When this same question, namely, how diversity of culture is portrayed, is asked of the New Testament, the issue is at the heart of the story itself. Christianity began as a movement within first-century Judaism. Jesus and all of his followers were Jews. Crucified and risen from the dead, Jesus was called "the Christ," the Greek translation of "Messiah" or "anointed one." The first critical issue that faced the followers of "the Way" was whether this good news about Jesus was *only* for the Jews or whether Jesus' followers should take the message to Gentiles. The tension between these views can be seen in most of the writings of the New Testament. In Matthew's Gospel, for example, Jesus says (in response to a Canaanite woman who comes seeking healing for her daughter), "I was sent only to the lost sheep of the house of Israel" (Matt. 15:24). By the end of the Gospel, however, a shift in understanding seems to have taken place. Here, Jesus commissions his followers to "go therefore and make disciples of *all nations*" (Matt. 28:19, emphasis added).

Numerous other examples can be observed when one asks the question of where "the other" (or the non-Jew) appears and how those characters are presented. The most obvious examples are the Samaritans: the woman at the well (John 4) and the character in the most famous of Jesus' parables (Luke 10:29–37). Another "outsider" who figures prominently in Jesus' story is the centurion who asks Jesus to heal his servant (Matt. 8:5–13), to whom Jesus says, "in no one in Israel have I found such faith." The *magoi* come to witness Jesus' birth (Matt. 2:1–12), and non-Jewish women (notably Rahab and Ruth) are featured in Jesus' genealogy (Matt. 1:1–16). All of this sets the stage for the theme of the widening of God's promise to include "the others" so that they too are part of God's promise.

The story of this expanding view and the implication that Christian faith and community are open to all people from all cultures is nowhere more obvious than in the Acts of the Apostles. In three pivotal stories, Luke makes it clear that Christian faith is faith for all people and that in

Jesus Christ the promise God made originally to Israel is now open to all through faith.

The first such story concerns Philip and a highly placed court official from Ethiopia (Acts 8:26–40). The official is obviously an "outsider" in many ways. Not only is he not a Jew, but he is presented as one who could never be fully included in the people of Israel because of his physical condition (see Deut. 23:1). And yet when Philip meets him, the official is returning from Jerusalem and reading a scroll of Isaiah. In answer to his questions about the text, Philip interprets the story of Jesus. When the man asks Philip, "What is to prevent me from being baptized?" the first-century reader knows that the answer is, "Any number of things!" The fact that the baptism takes place is a critical turning point in the story of how the Christian church found its mission to the Gentiles.

The second critical story involves Peter and the Roman centurion Cornelius (Acts 10). In a dream, Peter is presented with a variety of "unclean" creatures, and a voice commands him, "Get up, Peter; kill and eat" (10:13). Rejection of unclean food is one of the practices that gives Peter his religious identity as a Jew. But the voice answers each of Peter's refusals with the words: "What God has made clean, you must not call profane" (10:15).

In the next scene, messengers arrive requesting Peter to travel from Joppa to Caesarea to meet a leader of the Roman army. Cornelius is described as "a devout man who feared God with all his household; he gave alms generously to the people and prayed constantly to God" (Acts 10:2). He likewise has had a dream in which he was instructed to send for Peter. After hearing Cornelius describe his dream, Peter begins his presentation with these words: "I truly understand that God shows no partiality, but in every nation anyone who fears him and does what is right is acceptable to him" (10:34–35).

This statement is a critical turning point in the theological development of Christian faith. The God who has chosen (and as Paul argues, continues to choose) Israel to live in a particular covenant relationship *also* extends God's favor or grace to people of all cultures, races, and nations. Peter, Paul, and the other early missionaries do not go to the Gentiles because *they* think it is a good idea. Their mission is the result of seeing evidence of God's presence and activity in the lives of these "others" and *then* proclaiming the good news of Jesus Christ. The clear implication of both these stories is that the "others" hear and receive the message because God is *already* with them and active in their lives. That is to say, God is at work in the cultures and contexts in which these people live.

The third critical story is that of the council of Jerusalem (Acts 15), which follows the description of the work of Paul and Barnabas in Antioch, Cyprus, and southern Turkey. Both Jews and Gentiles have responded to their preaching and are meeting together (and eating together) as worshiping communities. This immediately raises that issue of whether in order to become a Christian, one must first become a Jew and incorporate into one's life all provisions of Jewish law and practice. The critical issues are circumcision for men (the physical sign of the covenant) and observing dietary laws. In this scene, Peter recounts the conversion of Cornelius and his household and reiterates his theological conviction that "in cleansing their hearts by faith [God] has made no distinction between them and us" (15:9).

After the debate, James states the consensus of the assembly regarding requirements for non-Jews. A crucial decision has been made: Christian faith will reach out to include all peoples and nations, because God has chosen to expand the way in which the promises of God are to be understood. Beverly Gaventa underscores the importance of God's initiative in this matter as she comments on verse 7: "a more literal translation would be, 'God chose through my mouth the Gentiles to hear the world of the gospel and believe.' God's selection has here a double object in that God chooses the mouth of Peter and *also* chooses that the Gentiles hear the gospel."[3]

We see this question from another vantage point in the writings of Paul. Especially in Romans and Galatians, we see him wrestle with the implications of the radical grace of the gospel and the historic claims of Israel. Paul has often been misinterpreted as arguing for a "replacement" theology, but his fundamental conclusion is clear: in Jesus Christ (in Christ's body through baptism), "there is no longer Jew or Greek" (Gal. 3:28). This is not so much a statement about enduring cultural difference as it is a statement about the fact that these social and cultural divisions do not restrict God's plan to create a new community grounded in God's love for all.

This brief review of the way in which the Bible looks at the question of multiculturality comes to an end with the vision of Revelation. Gathered around the throne of God and united in praise are both the descendents of the twelve tribes of Israel and "a great multitude that no one could count, from every nation, from all tribes and peoples and languages" (Rev. 7:9). God's promise has opened out to welcome people of all cultures and languages, and all have come (still speaking their own languages!) to the throne of God.

THEOLOGICAL IMPLICATIONS

Many will argue that what has gone before is a highly selective representation of the biblical narrative. It is obvious that both Jews and Christians have told their stories of faith in exclusive ways both religiously and
culturally. The idea of God's election or choice of a covenant people has
often been read in terms of "if A then not B." That is to say, if Jews and/or
Christians are God's chosen people, then all others are *not*. While the
biblical narrative can be read this way, there is good reason to believe
that this is not the only possible or even the best reading. Old Testament
scholar W. Eugene March argues that "there is another, implicit narrative
. . . that has to do with God's ongoing relationship with others beyond
Israel and the church." This other narrative "assumes that all people are
creatures of God and the objects of divine love."[4]

Following March and others such as Clark Pinnock,[5] I want to argue
that several theological affirmations can be drawn from the biblical traditions that undergird the approach to multiculturality found in this
volume of essays. Far from being based on twenty-first-century ideology,
this approach is solidly based on clear implications from the core narrative of Christian faith.

The first theological commitment that underlies an affirmation of
multiculturality is the one most widely shared: namely, that all people
are created in the image of God. This idea is so basic (and appears to be
so obvious) that it is startling to recall how often some Christians have
taught just the opposite, notably with respect to Africans, with respect to
indigenous peoples in the Western Hemisphere, and even in recent
memory with respect to Jews. Precisely the fact that these "others" were
not viewed as being created in the divine image justified slavery and
genocide. But the theological implication of the story of creation is quite
clear: human beings are unique among all the things God made because
humans alone are said to be the image and likeness of the Creator. If (as
the narrative then suggests) all humanity stems from those whom God
first created, it follows that *all* persons, of all races and from every culture, are children of the Creator, sharing together in the image of God.
The most recent confessional statement of the Presbyterian Church
(U.S.A.) puts it this way: "In sovereign love God created the world good
and makes *everyone equally* in God's image, male and female, of every
race and people, to live as one community."[6]

The second theological affirmation follows from the first. Not only are
all human beings created in the divine image, but God is the God of all

people everywhere, whether they acknowledge God or not. God's sovereignty does not depend on human apprehension. This view is clear in the psalms as God's sovereignty is proclaimed over all (e.g., Psalm 33). In the same way, God's providential care of the whole creation is not dependent upon human response (the rain falls on the "just" and "unjust" alike.) God's purpose in human history, the renewal of all creation, is *for* all creation and thus for all people in all cultures (cf. Col. 1:15f).

The third affirmation follows from the first two and has to do with the value of cultural diversity in the one human family. The question can be put this way: is the diversity of culture and language, history and tradition (and even religion), part of God's good creation, or is this diversity one of the marks of the fallen creation? Is diversity, in other words, a sign of how humans have responded to the gifts of freedom and creativity, or is all of this diversity a frustration of a divine plan for the unity and uniformity of humanity? Nowhere in Scripture is there a sense that the unity (or reuniting) of the human family should involve uniformity in the sense of the wiping out cultural difference. The story of Pentecost and the passages cited above from Revelation are critical here. In neither instance is linguistic difference eliminated; it simply ceases to be a problem for communication or praise! Like almost anything else in the creation that God made good, cultural and linguistic difference can be turned to destructive purposes. But that does not mean that the differences and distinctions themselves are sinful or the mark of sin. In fact, if biodiversity and the adaptation of species to the wide variety of habitats on the planet is any example, cultural diversity can be seen as evidence of humans using the very gifts of creativity and ingenuity with which God has blessed us to adapt and thrive.

Fourth, the core message of the gospel is that *all are welcome.* It is impossible to read the story of Jesus without recognizing his consistent pattern of relating to people who would have been outside what was appropriate for an observant Jewish man of his day. Nowhere is this more obvious than in the many times he is described as "eating with tax collectors and sinners," in his conversations with women, and in his touching the ritually unclean lepers. These actions embody the very heart of the good news: that God's love is available to all, that God welcomes all. As noted above, the first "crisis" in living out the implications of this good news came as the Jewish Christians debated whether and how to proclaim it to Gentiles, to the "others." And as we saw above, the view that prevailed was that differences of language, culture, race, gender, and sexual condition are not barriers to the expanse of God's love.

Indeed, the opposite is the case. The disciples are sent "into all the world" and to all people.

Finally, a core theological affirmation that is less frequently recognized as an implication of the study of Acts is critically important for this approach to multiculturality. Not only is the good news of the gospel *for all people*, but as I suggested above, there is in each story an implicit understanding that God was *already at work* in the lives of the Gentiles who came to faith. It was this divine presence and activity that made the Ethiopian and Cornelius and those whom Paul encountered receptive to the gospel when it was presented to them. Thus, the theological claim is that God is present in various ways in the lives of people apart from the explicit proclamation of the Christian gospel. If God is at work in the lives of all (and not just some) people, then it follows that God is also at work in the cultures of all humankind, because individuals cannot be abstracted from the cultures in which they live.

Among the first in the Western world to make this claim were missionaries and missiologists. Based on their experiences among people of many different cultures, some began to question the traditional language of "taking Christ to the nations" as though God was "really absent" before the (Western) Christian missionary arrived. Clearly, the task of the missionary is to tell the story of Jesus Christ, but to claim that the proclamation of the gospel makes *God* known suggests that God is somehow *not* present until Christians arrive with the message of the gospel. Clearly, such a conclusion would contradict the Christian view (and especially the emphasis in Reformed theology) of the sovereignty of God and God's freedom to be and work as God alone wills.

IMPLICATIONS FOR THEOLOGICAL EDUCATION

On the basis of this biblical and theological foundation, we turn to the implications of such a view for the preparation of women and men for leadership in the church. The case I have argued is that Christianity today is a *multicultural faith*: it is not the property of any one cultural tradition, even thought it has been deeply shaped by Greco-Roman traditions and by the culture and intellectual tradition of Western Europe. As a result of the rich ecclesial life and the new theological and biblical work of Christians around the world, Christian life today presents a far wider range of interpretations than ever before. Those who would be leaders of Christian communities today need to know the wealth of theological and ecclesial resources available to them. Congregations likewise are able to reflect on their own context for mission and ministry more effectively when they learn how Christians seek to express and live out the gospel in other settings.

This variety of expressions of Christian faith is a great blessing. It is also a great "relativizer." Hearing the gospel through the cultural expressions of others, one is enriched and at the same time called to examine the ways in which one's own culture shapes and conditions the understanding of the gospel. It will also inevitably lead to a self-critical moment as we reflect on ways that culture has perhaps muted or softened the demands of the gospel. As one member of the McCormick faculty puts it, our goal is to help students learn how to read both *texts* and *contexts*.

One example of this perspective at work in the curriculum is the teaching of theology. In the middle years of the twentieth century, the study of theology at McCormick and other Presbyterian seminaries would have centered around Reformed theologians such as Emil Brunner, H. Richard Niebuhr, Dietrich Bonhoeffer, and Karl Barth. Today, those writers and others from around the world are read in the course on Reformed theology. The introductory course in theology, however, has evolved significantly to reflect McCormick's commitments to both ecumenical and multicultural teaching and learning. The syllabus for this course includes one foundational or core text and a number of other supporting texts from which students are asked to select at least one for in-depth reading. In several years, the core text has been Daniel Migliore's *Faith Seeking Understanding*.[7] This introduction to theology is an example of the way in which a contemporary Reformed theologian incorporates not only voices from other parts of the Christian tradition but also gives careful attention to the ways in which, for example, Latin American liberation theology and feminist thought have reshaped much of the agenda for church and scholarship.

The secondary texts are selected with an eye to the variety of voices currently contributing to reflection on the Christian faith, especially as these reflect various cultural traditions present in McCormick's student body and faculty. Thus, texts such as the following have appeared on the syllabus: *We Have Been Believers: An African-American Systematic Theology* by James H. Evans; *Mañana: Christian Theology from a Hispanic Perspective* by Justo L. González; *Marginality: The Key to Multicultural Theology* by Jung Young Lee; *Struggle to Be the Sun Again* by Hyun Kyung Chung; *Daughters of Anowa: African Women and Patriarchy* by Mercy Amba Oduyoye; *Sexism and God-talk: Toward a Feminist Theology* by Rosemary Radford Ruether; and *The Church in the Round* by Letty Russell.

This course has also attempted to incorporate contemporary debates or conversations in the life of the global church as examples of how theological reflection is carried on and how it affects the life of the church. One unit has often focused on the debate in South Africa over the theological justifications for and critique of apartheid, especially as this was played out in the Dutch Reformed Church, which eventually came to repent of its teaching that apartheid was biblically based. In discussing the Holy Spirit, the class was assigned to read essays produced by the international Reformed-Pentecostal dialogue, in which theologians from both traditions and from at least a dozen countries have come to shared understandings about the person and work of the Holy Spirit and implications for church life today.

A critical component of any study of theology is discussion in which students have the opportunity to question their own views and the views of others, to frame and reframe their convictions, and to learn from one another. At McCormick, we take advantage of the makeup of our student body by setting up small groups that maximize the diversity of denomination, race and ethnicity, and gender. Guidelines that we have adopted over the years provide a structure in which all members of the group are invited to participate and "listened into speech." The goal of both conversation and written work is for students to increase their ability to reflect critically on the diversity of readings, their own experience, and what they hear from lecturers and fellow students as they hone their own theological convictions. Diversity in cultural background is seen as one of the advantages of the classrooms and resources for theological reflection.

CRITICS OF MULTICULTURALITY

As they have been presented, these convictions seem so uncontroversial as to be benign or obvious. It is important to recognize, however, how controversial this question of a multicultural point of view becomes when the venue of the discussion shifts to the public arena. As more American universities have attempted to wrestle with the increased diversity of cultures within American culture, many have come to embrace multicultural education as a strategy for understanding contemporary society and preparing people to work effectively within it.

Among the critics of this development, one of the most prominent is Samuel Huntington, professor of international studies at Harvard University. In his most recent book, *Who Are We? The Challenges to America's National Identity,* Huntington argues that the United States was founded on clear Christian principles that are endorsed by huge majorities of the population as seen in regular polling. Huntington posits that there is a unifying "identity" based on what he (and others he cites) call the "American Creed." The elements of this creed have to do with a belief in the dignity and rights of the individual and with values such as liberty, equality, and opportunity. The origin of this creed, according to Huntington, is "dissenting Protestantism" with its emphasis on freedom of conscience, congregational government, and individual (and social) moral reform. Thus, Huntington concludes, "the American Creed, in short, is Protestantism without God, the secular credo of the nation 'with the soul of a church.'"[8]

What concerns Huntington is the ways in which multiculturalism (which might be defined as the affirmation of varieties of cultures and values existing within one nation or culture simultaneously) is eroding the national identity and creed and thus the unity of American life. In particular, he is critical of the effects of Latino culture and the Spanish language on the United States. He argues that part of the problem is that Latino culture is grounded in another type of Christian faith (namely, Catholicism) whose values clash with the Protestant values at the core of the American Creed.[9]

Whatever one thinks of Huntington's argument regarding the integrity of United States' culture, his argument raises a host of theological questions. The issue is not whether or not sixteenth- and seventeenth-century dissenting Protestantism set the stage for the development of American democracy. The historic case that Huntington makes is not particularly controversial. The issue is whether, as a *Christian*, one can easily come to a rather wholesale preference for one form of Christian life and culture over another. If in fact Christian faith is both theologically and actually multicultural (that is, a religion that can and does find expression in all human cultures), then Christians should be wary when someone attempts to link one particular form of the faith with the national culture as either necessary or normative.

Perhaps Huntington sees the potential "threat" accurately, however. He identifies individualism as central to the American Creed and grounds it in theological values such as "God alone is Lord of the conscience" (to use a phrase from the founding documents of American Presbyterianism). But one could argue that other forms of Christian faith and life have sought to live out the faith more deeply grounded in the values of community and unity, where relationship with others takes precedence over individual expression, and have based their commitments on Paul's description of Christians as members of one another in the body of Christ.

In every age, Christians have asked questions of the Bible and theological tradition based on the problems that have confronted them and the contexts in which they have found themselves. Christians in the United States and in the world today recognize themselves to be living in both a multicultural church and a multicultural world. This vantage point has led us to reread the Bible in the light of these questions. I have attempted to argue that, far from being threatened by cultural diversity, Christian faith provides a lens through which to see the diversity as part of God's gracious providence and as the arena for the fulfillment of God's promise. As far back as the Hebrew poets, we have affirmed that the earth belongs to God, the world and all its peoples. It is because all of us belong to God that we can welcome the variety of peoples and cultures and expect to find in all of them signs of God's presence and insights for our own journey of faith.

NOTES

1. See chapters 15 and 16, by David Daniels and Ogbu Kalu.

2. For a discussion of how the diversity of peoples and cultures is seen as part of God's purposes, see chapter 9, by Theodore Hiebert.

3. Beverly Roberts Gaventa, *The Acts of the Apostles,* Abingdon New Testament Commentaries (Nashville: Abingdon Press, 2003), 215.

4. W. Eugene March, *The Wide, Wide Circle of Divine Love: A Biblical Case for Religious Diversity* (Louisville, KY: Westminster John Knox Press, 2005), x.

5. Clark H. Pinnock, *A Wideness in God's Mercy: The Finality of Jesus Christ in a World of Religions* (Grand Rapids: Zondervan, 1992).

6. Presbyterian Church (U.S.A.), "A Brief Statement of Faith," in *The Book of Confessions* (Louisville, KY: Presbyterian Church (U.S.A.), 1991), lines 29–32 emphasis added.

7. Daniel Migliore, *Faith Seeking Understanding: An Introduction to Christian Theology* (Louisville, KY: Westminster/John Knox Press, 1989).

8. Samuel P. Huntington, *Who Are We? The Challenges to America's National Identity* (New York: Simon & Schuster, 2004), 69. The words quoted in this sentence are those of de Tocqueville.

9. See especially Huntington's chapter "Mexican Immigration and Hispanization," 221–56.

CHAPTER 8

Teaching the Bible in a Global Context

Robert L. Brawley

When I was studying with Bruce Metzger at Princeton Theological Seminary, he told me that Bishop Stephen Neill, missionary to India and New Testament scholar, once confided to him: "I find it tiresome to lecture about something I know nothing about." At the outset of this chapter, I claim kinship with Stephen Neill, although I find the subject at hand far from tiresome. I am deeply intrigued. At the same time I know how audacious it is to discourse on something about which I know so little. The first anomaly is writing about something when I am one of the learners. To be sure, Mikhail Bakhtin suggests that an author is in dialogue with what the author produces, so that one inevitably learns from writing. But beyond that, to raise the subject of teaching the Bible in a global context is to expose myself to a world beyond my comprehension that brings to light what has never yet dawned on me. Further, I consciously use the first-person plural in this chapter not to indicate humanity in general but to indicate that whatever is written to us is written to me.

To be sure, my readings have not been inconsiderable. Further, I lived and taught in Mexico for three years, and I was one of fifty participants in the Hammerskraal Conference on African Biblical Interpretation in South Africa in 1999. Still, any mantle I wear is from a secondhand store. But audacity and secondhand competence aside, I did design and teach a course entitled "Teaching the Bible in a Global Context." Perhaps some dimensions of the rationale for the course, what happened, and the results have some value for replication elsewhere.

For me to undertake the task in the first place required something of a conversion. I relate two personal experiences that were pivotal. 1. In

1965, as I sat in a barber's chair in Río Verde, S.L.P., Mexico, the barber handed me a Mexican magazine. When I read an article attributing the assassination of President John F. Kennedy to Lyndon B. Johnson, I was shocked with incredulity—until I considered that had such an assassination occurred in a Latin American country, I myself would have taken it for granted that the person assuming power was responsible. At that moment I became conscious that I needed to view reality as a citizen of the world beyond my ethnocentrism as a citizen of the United States.

2. It was impossible to study in a seminary when I did my MDiv degree (1962–65) without being profoundly influenced by the civil rights movement. So when I went to Rock Hill, South Carolina, as a pastor in the late 1960s, I immediately joined the Council on Human Relations and became active in race relations. As a result, I got to know Robert Toatley, African American pastor of Mt. Carmel United Presbyterian Church. Robert Toatley happened to be one of the leaders of the first lunch counter sit-ins in South Carolina on February 12, 1960, just eleven days after the sit-ins started in Greensboro, North Carolina. One day a decade later, when Robert Toatley and I played tennis and ate lunch together, I suddenly became aware of how much I enjoyed my association with him. Then I realized that from a patronizing point of view, I had presumed that the reason for relationships across racial barriers was what I and people of my race could do for others. Now I perceived it was the other way around: I needed Robert Toatley for what he added to my life and my social group.

There are a few more steps in my conversion. I did my doctoral studies in the heyday of redaction criticism, which though thoroughly anchored in traditional historical critical methodology, was a shift away from the primacy of historical events to theological interpretations as the locus of the disclosure and experience of God. Due to courses with Hugh George Anderson on "What Is History?" and with George Stroup on "History and the Resurrection" I had adopted a perspectival philosophy of history. In other words, history is mediated through the perspectives of people who passed on memories, and history is understood through the perspectives of modern historians who convey their understandings of the past. But my further conversion was prompted especially by interchanges with colleagues at McCormick over the years: Hun Chun, David Daniels, Deborah Mullen, Homer Ashby, David Cortés Fuentes, Luís Rivera, Ogbu Kalu, and Jae Won Lee. In addition, when I read Michel Foucault, Elisabeth Schüssler Fiorenza, the Bible and Culture Collective, and *The Postmodern History Reader* (ed. Keith Jenkins; London: Routledge, 1997), I began to see how strongly history is written as a rhetorical construct in order to persuade others in power moves, even when participation in the power moves may be unconscious. My conversion was essentially the manner in which my ways of construing reality were disoriented constantly and my life enriched by the reorientations that included areas cultural contribu tions, most especially in the form of personal relationships across cultures. This has significant implications for interpretive methodologies and pedagogical approaches.

RATIONALE

Just as history does not come to us apart from the perspectives of historians, it is a will-o'-the-wisp that biblical interpretation can be fine-tuned by complementary "objective" analyses in succession until interpreters arrive at the "original" meaning. Rather, interpretation is inevitably mediated through particular cultural perspectives. Moreover, interpreters champion their interpretations in their own rhetorical constructs to persuade others for good or for ill.

The same goes for interpreting what "global context" means in the title of this chapter. On the one hand, globalization has meant dropping barriers that have resisted interchanges between people of different cultures, making it possible to achieve mutual enrichment among cultures. On the other hand, dropping barriers to intercultural interchanges works to the advantage of dominant cultures that are most easily able to cross the barriers. In this vein my colleague Jae Won Lee exposes economic globalization as "the transnational and imperial hegemony of Western monetary capitalism."[1] Both of these aspects of globalization were evident in the Hammerskraal Conference on African Biblical Interpretation in 1999. The conference included participants from all over the African continent, but also from Germany, Spain, France, Romania, Australia, New Zealand, the United Kingdom, and the United States. The gathering was possible only because of a certain kind of globalization. But the postmodern *valuing of difference* that was a driving factor in the attendance of many of us from the West was quite strongly resisted by some of the African participants. They perceived that the valuing of difference itself was an imposition from outside their cultures—a new form of colonization. The discourse on difference was itself under the control of dominant cultures in Europe and the United States. Further, the Africans perceived that if one values all differences, then nothing matters. To say this in another way, they believed that they had fundamental (postmodern antifoundationalism notwithstanding) grounds to make challenges and claims on others beyond their local cultures. Thus, if their voices were going to matter, they would have to resist an external force that ironically claimed to value difference in their voices. Further, there were strenuous objections to the influence of U.S. culture in rap music, movies, television, clothing, and the way of construing human sexuality.

Thus on the one hand, the global context is experienced as the opening up of material and human resources for mutual enrichment, whereas on the other hand, the global context is still experienced as domination by economic, cultural, and military powers. Appreciation for cultural diversity is compromised by the ascendancy of some cultures over others.

What does this ambiguous global context have to do with the way we read, interpret, and teach the Bible? I suggest that our global context has implications for methods, hermeneutics, and pedagogy. I turn to each of these in sequence.

Methods

Fernando Segovia's historical accounts of shifts in methodology present diversity in methods in terms of an agonistic struggle.[2] Though he avows that methods are not mutually exclusive, he begins with the presumption of the dominance of historical criticism, with which newer methods enter into battle in order to depose historical criticism from its hegemony. Although I concur that new methods have challenged the hegemony of historical criticism, had Segovia begun his account two centuries earlier, perhaps he would have described historical criticism also in terms of a battle over interpretation. Henning Graf Reventlow has shown how the battle over the authority of the Bible in eighteenth-century England was in partnership with political parties. High-Church Tories used the Bible to support their authority to determine internal affairs of the church independent of the monarchy. Whig ideologues advanced their biblical criticism—with immense sway on the development of modern biblical criticism—in order to repudiate the claims of Tories.[3] The development of historical criticism itself involved an agonistic ideological struggle— evidence in itself that specific social and cultural locations provide lenses for biblical interpretation.

Although Segovia presents biblical methods of interpretation as potentially complementary, he describes them as in competition and in "stable if not actually permanent anomie."[4] On the one hand, if the goal of historical critical studies is to restrict interpretation by an "original meaning," Segovia hits the nail on the head. The new variety of methods not only heightens appreciation for an array of features of texts but also results in a far-reaching diversity of interpretations that resists any trump card which supposedly controls meaning. Further, philosophical presuppositions behind methods may be in conflict. For example, the Enlightenment was strongly dependent on the presumption of a rational universe, the order of which was subject to discovery by observation and human reason, whereas postmodernism presumes that reality is chaotic and achieves order only by constructs arising from the human mind. Thus, the Bible and Culture Collective reproaches biblical interpreters who naively appropriate reader-response criticism without reflecting on the philosophical presuppositions that their interpretations are ideological construals.[5]

On the other hand, I am not as pessimistic about the conflicts among methods as is Segovia. If interpretive methods have any validity in the first place, they must be complementary in some sense. I illustrate this from a glance at literary interpretation, which some interpreters have presumed to be in conflict with historical-critical interpretation. First, just as when I read Segovia, I cannot understand what he writes without comprehending dimensions of his historical context; neither can I understand biblical texts apart from what Wolfgang Iser calls the "repertoire" of the text, which according to Jonathan Culler includes all cultural allusions, social norms, and shared views of reality—in short, everything (modesty to the winds) necessary to understand the text.[6] Historical dimensions of texts are integral to literary dimensions—an illustration of how methods can be complementary.

Further, although Segovia still appeals to the broad range of methodological approaches to biblical studies, he nevertheless associates liberation primarily with cultural studies out of a postmodern perspective that takes all interpretations to be readerly (that is, ideological) constructs. Whereas I share the perspective that all interpretations are constructs, I question whether liberation is more closely associated with cultural studies than with the other approaches. For example, Korean Old Testament scholar Cyrus H. S. Moon looks for a model of liberation by a traditional historical-critical investigation of the exodus, in which he identifies the liberated Hebrews with *habiru* rebels, whom he then takes to be analogous to the Korean *minjung*, that is, oppressed Koreans who act against injustice.[7] What marks Moon's chapter as liberationist is not his historical-critical method per se, but the hermeneutical move he makes by means of the method. Nevertheless, Segovia helpfully demonstrates that postcolonial studies in particular have sensitized biblical interpreters to ideological dimensions of biblical interpretation.

Hermeneutics

It is convenient at this point to turn to a brief discussion of the significance of the global context for hermeneutical moves. My own thinking
on hermeneutics was first strongly influenced by James Sanders, who
advocated a notion of "dynamic analogy."[8] This approach is strongly
predicated on the historical-critical method, because it attempts to look
for analogies between perceptions of God in ancient historical situations
and perceptions of God in present-day historical situations. A major
dimension of the dynamic analogy for Sanders is identification with biblical characters, though Sanders warns against identification only with
heroes. In the name of honesty he encourages identification with all of
the characters.

Identifying only with so-called biblical heroes often conceals the
superimposition of heroic values of our culture onto the biblical characters. In a delightful article on "Biblical Preaching as Divine Wisdom,"
Leander Keck shows that when we make heroes out of biblical characters, we attribute to them idealized values that our culture regards as
heroic.[9] "[The hero] is what we wish we were or strive to be. . . . By definition, the hero cannot challenge the fundamental values of his clien-
tele."[10] Making heroes of biblical characters is the sort of hermeneutical
move that reinforces values lucidly and tangibly, and that has its merits.
But is not the point of the hermeneutical imagination not merely to
reinforce our values but to enable us to envision reality in a new way or
in a way that represents a gain over the quotidian way of construing reality, so that where life is deficient, changes become possible?[11]

There is, however, one type of hermeneutical identification that I
wish to advocate. Rather than identifying with or seeking to imitate a
hero, there are ways in which we so identify with characters in biblical
narratives that we buy into the narrative world. In fact, it seems to me
that Sanders confuses two distinct hermeneutical moves. He takes identification to be a particular form of his dynamic analogy. But identifying
with characters in the sense that I now propose is not merely a way of
drawing analogies between the world of a biblical character and my
world, but a way of buying into the world of the narrative. This is at least
part of what the New Hermeneutic meant by the "word event." Just as
when a bright light aimed through celluloid and focused on a screen can
bring us to participate in a film enough to move us to tears, a biblical
narrative can catch us up into an alternative world where divine reality
invades not only the lives of others but our own lives as well. When this
kind of identification occurs, the world of the biblical text is not so much

shaped by the hearer/reader as the hearer/reader becomes a participant in an alternative world. Instead of demythologizing the distant world of the biblical narrative, we meet ourselves as characters in a story in which all distance vanishes. When I identify with characters in the narrative in this way, what happens in the story happens to me.[12]

At least since the time of Luther, a prominent hermeneutical issue has been the use of a canon within the canon. For Luther himself, this canon within the canon was christological. But with the recognition of ideological constructs embedded in interpretation, we are now faced with the issue of a canon outside the canon. This is in fact a hermeneutical move that is now clearly recognized. For example, on March 1, 2004, Segovia gave a lecture at McCormick Theological Seminary, on the prologue to the Gospel of John, in which he suggested that in John 1:10–11 the Jewish people are negatively stereotyped by a totalizing binary opposition to Jesus. From this he could only recommend that the text could no longer be useful, because it denied difference and was oppressive instead of liberating. In a group conversation after the lecture, I suggested to him that valuing of difference and liberation were external criteria that served as a canon outside the canon, and he was quite willing to allow that my suggestion was correct. I cannot let this comment pass without problematizing liberation along the same lines that Alasdair MacIntyre uses to problematize justice. To say "liberation" or "justice" may presume that that of which we speak is self-evident. But MacIntyre shows that concepts of justice, and by extension I include liberation, depend on what is sought and on the rationale supporting the seeking of it.[13] I refer to this case in order to make the point that a canon outside the canon is not a rare hermeneutical move, and Segovia is quite aware that he is making such a hermeneutical move. In short, the plurality of interpretations in a global context is made more complicated by a plurality of hermeneutical moves.

Pedagogy

For the pedagogical implications of the global context, I turned to two particular sources. First, Paulo Freire has exerted a profound influence on pedagogy as mediating construals of the world through interpersonal interchange.[14] His pedagogy had its origins precisely in the context of oppression in which he advocated a pedagogy for liberation, and he expanded this context to include the global reality.[15] To achieve the great historical task of liberation, he attempted to engender new perceptions of the world ("thematic universe") by naming reality not for the oppressed but along with the oppressed. Here is a case in point from a personal experience. My teacher at the Institut für deutsche Sprache und Kultur at the University of Wittenberg, who was educated under the East German Communist regime, told our class that in the former East Germany, the children of farmers and laborers had priority over others for university education. At that point I said, "O, the children of farmers and laborers had priority over others for receiving an education so that they would not have to be farmers and laborers." She stood dumbfounded. Then she told us that such a way of viewing the reality in which she had lived had never crossed her mind, because she had been educated never to challenge the system. How we name reality can cause us to see reality in an alternative way.

Emphatically, engendering new perceptions of reality is a dialogical process of reflection among peers.[16] From such a dialogical process, Freire advocated interventions arising from the new perceptions of reality. He then expected the interventions themselves to become part of the dialogue in a constant circular relationship with reflection. Solutions for problems are constantly subjected to dialogical evaluation. If teachers and students are peers in this process, however, what happens to the role of the teacher? The teacher's task for Freire is to "re-present" the world to the people who first present it in the dialogical context in terms of posing problems.[17]

The global context inevitably implicates economics, and disciples of Freire have named the reality of the "new capitalism" as intertwined with the interests of the dominant culture.[18] Fellow Brazilian Dermeval Saviani contested Freire's necessary link between education and political realities. He argued that although politics has an educational aspect and education a political aspect, politics is a matter of winning without necessarily convincing, and education is a matter of convincing without necessarily winning.[19] But Michel Foucault has demonstrated persuasively that knowledge inevitably carries with it dimensions of power, and Saviani overlooks the inevitable link between knowledge and power.[20] A necessary association with the politics of global economics, then, is our own experience of participation in the global economy either as oppressors or as oppressed.

Because knowledge is always concretely embodied in each person, Freire's pedagogy resists stereotyping based on matters of social location such as gender, ethnicity, and sexual orientation.[21] Similarly, oppression cannot be reduced to belonging to a certain group, but is personally specific in such terms as class, race, gender, and sexual orientation.[22] Thus one speaks for oneself from his or her own social location and not for others without problematizing speech for others.[23] In summary, dependence upon Freire led to a pedagogy designed to be dialogical but in quite personal terms. To anticipate a bit, the latter is reflected by the place of autobiographical narratives in the course.

For the second source on pedagogical issues, I turned principally to a collection of essays titled *Preparing Teachers for Cultural Diversity.*[24] To my mind five things in particular stand out in this volume 1 Of course the entire volume takes a perspective over against the "cultural deprivation" paradigm of previous generations, which considered non-Western cultures to be deficient and implied the necessity of raising such deficient cultures to Western standards.[25] By contrast, the multiplicity of cultures is taken as a given. Interaction among distinct cultures does anticipate change, but the changes may be mutual rather than the domination of one culture over another.

2. As I indicated at the end of the previous paragraph, emphasis on local and personal (over against universal) ways of construing reality leads to making autobiography prominent in pedagogy. It comes into play in two particular ways. First, autobiographical personal history reflects a stage in which we bring our own constructs of reality to expression. As a part of pedagogy, alternative visions of reality then confront our constructs, producing "disequilibrium." Finally, after reflection on attempts to understand reality anew and to think and act differently, autobiography returns as a means of expressing new construals of reality.[26] This is reminiscent both of Freire's praxis model, in which action and reflection follow each other in a cyclic pattern, and of Paul Ricoeur's notion of the way in which encounters with construals of the world in the Bible disorient hearers/readers from their conventional orientation in a move toward reorientation.[27]

3. For all the emphasis on the individual, an equal emphasis falls on the community. In fact, as Joyce King perceptively claims, true individuality is possible only through participation in community.[28]

4. Because constructs of reality come to expression in the language of a community, language itself is integral to envisioning reality.[29] I digress to note that institutional norms at McCormick Theological Seminary come into play at this point. For fifteen years McCormick has been sensitive to this issue. As a consequence, we do not require proficiency in English for admission. On the other hand, proficiency in English is required for matriculation in courses where English is the language of instruction. In order to deal with this incongruity between admission and matriculation, McCormick has a remarkable language program

developed and implemented by our Language Resource and Writing Center, and we place a high value on bilingual competence as an important factor in the context for ministry.

5. A key to pedagogy in a global context is not merely the conceptual confrontation with how other people construe reality but also interaction with them. Interpersonal interchanges are at the heart of education. In short, this pedagogy follows an interactive model rather than an informational model. A critical component of pedagogy, then, is building relationships of trust.[30] This also reinforces the communal character of pedagogy first mentioned above.

WHAT HAPPENED?

The syllabus presented the course as giving emphasis to dialogical, egalitarian, and communal methods of interpreting and teaching the Bible. Toward this end, the course had two required textbooks: F. Segovia, *Decolonizing Biblical Studies: A View from the Margins* (Maryknoll, NY: Orbis, 2000) and R. Sugirtharajah, *Asian Biblical Hermeneutics and Postcolonialism: Contesting the Interpretation* (Maryknoll, NY: Orbis, 1998). In addition, there were two recommended texts: D. Patte and others, *The Gospel of Matthew: A Contextual Introduction for Group Study* (Nashville: Abingdon, 2003) and M. de la Torre, *Reading the Bible from the Margins* (Maryknoll, NY: Orbis, 2002). In keeping with the emphasis on egalitarian relationships, participants were responsible to grade themselves. In order to assign themselves grades, they were asked to develop the criteria for grading and to evaluate themselves against their own criteria. I did establish two conditions: (1) No grade could be awarded above A (no A+s); (2) I reserved the right to assign a higher grade, but I made the commitment that the final grade would not be lower than the self-evaluation of each participant.

I opened the class with the two biographical incidents in Río Verde, Mexico, and Rock Hill, South Carolina, that I have described above. I then invited the participants to tell similar stories of how they perceived themselves and people of other cultures. This proved to be remarkably rich. Though small, our class had a striking amount of diversity— African American, Latino/a, Asian, and Euro American. One of the Euro Americans was a physician, an epidemiologist, who had extensive experience in Africa and South America in both official and voluntary capacities. He related to us that once in Bolivia, he suggested to some Aymara indigenous people that they needed to change patterns of animal husbandry, grazing, and eating—essentially not to eat produce contaminated with animal feces. The response from an elderly man was, "We were here before the Incas came; we were here before the Spaniards came; and we will still be here after you have come." A woman from Indonesia, a second-generation Christian convert from Islam, told about the loss of contact with her husband's family beyond his father when his father converted to Christianity from Islam, and she described Christian/Muslim conflicts in her homeland. The United States has granted her and her husband asylum because of the dangers they face if they return to Indonesia.

The emphasis on autobiography was a leading thread throughout the course. Participants read Jeffrey Staley's "Reading Myself, Reading the Text,"[31] a delightful interweaving of autobiographical reminiscences of growing up on a Navajo reservation with an interpretation of a text from John. I also had the astounding good fortune to have had the help of a number of colleagues in teaching the course, and they all made their own autobiographical contributions to the discussion. Luís Rivera, associate professor of theology at McCormick, presented his approach to diaspora hermeneutics to the class, which he developed largely from his personal experience of leaving Puerto Rico to study and teach in the United States. Andries van Aarde, professor of New Testament at the University of Pretoria, South Africa, taught a session focused on African hermeneutics and racial, cultural, and religious pluralism in post-apartheid South Africa. He related how he had been an activist for the end of apartheid as a member of the dominant culture in South Africa, for which he has suffered attempted reprisal in the form of a heresy trial in his denomination. David Daniels, professor of church history, made a presentation on African American and Pentecostal biblical interpretation from his background in the Church of God in Christ. R. S. Sugirtharajah, professor of biblical hermeneutics at the University of Birmingham, United Kingdom, meeting with the class while he was at McCormick for a public lecture, related how his present commitment to postcolonial hermeneutics is related to his personal experiences, from his origins in Sri Lanka to his present position in England by way of India. Participants in the class were required to attend his public lecture.

Severino Croatto's "A Reading of the Story of the Tower of Babel from the Perspective of Non-Identity: Genesis 11:1–9 in the Context of Its Production"[32] served as a basis for discussion of canonical and creedal bases for biblical interpretation and teaching. The class read Francisco Garcia Treto's "Crossing the Line: Three Scenes of Divine-Human Engagement in the Hebrew Bible"[33] as a starting point for discussion of *la hermeneútica latina*. Cyrus Moon's article on "A Korean Minjung Perspective" (see n. 7) provided the focus for consideration of Asian interpretation.

The second session of the class was devoted to pedagogy. The spotlight was primarily on Freire, but this was supplemented by materials from *Preparing Teachers for Cultural Diversity*, the collection of essays from Teachers College Press that is mentioned above. In every session we attempted to practice a pedagogy that was dialogical, egalitarian, and communal. As the finale of this course, each participant designed and led a learning event on a biblical text of the participant's own choice.

RESULTS

I mentioned a process of conversion that was prerequisite to my own participation in the course. But I underscore that I was also one of the learners, and as a consequence I must now affirm that the process of conversion is rather constant. This is to say that Luís Rivera's diaspora hermeneutics produced disequilibrium and reorientation for me, so that I now locate myself differently in the story of Jonah.[34] Something similar happened when Andries van Aarde told our class that when apartheid came to an end in South Africa, his struggle for egalitarianism had a remarkable consequence for him and his wife. They had to give up their property and the home they had acquired and now live in a small apartment.

In spite of my claim to have been converted from a patronizing attitude toward African Americans in Rock Hill, South Carolina, I would now caution that there are severe difficulties in avoiding either patronizing other cultures or portraying them as unrealistically exotic. Further, I wonder seriously if it is possible to have cross-cultural interchange without the ascendancy of one culture over another.

Finally, I return to autobiography. I know of little that is more gripping or that better exhibits the concrete embodiment of reality than autobiography. But in the antiheroic mood that I developed above, I suggest that care needs to be taken not to make oneself the hero of the story. The autobiographical mode works best when we are posing problems, as Paulo Freire suggests, or when our construct of reality has been disoriented and we come to see reality with a new orientation.

NOTES

1. Jae Won Lee, "Paul and the Politics of Difference: A Contextual Study of the Jewish-Gentile Difference in Galatians and Romans" (PhD diss., Union Theological Seminary, New York, 2001; Ann Arbor: UMI), 84.

2. F. Segovia, "And They Began to Speak in Other Tongues': Competing Modes of Discourse in Contemporary Biblical Criticism," and "Cultural Studies and Contemporary Biblical Criticism: Ideological Criticism as Mode of Discourse," in *Reading from This Place*, 2 vols., ed. F. Segovia and M. Tolbert (Minneapolis: Fortress Press, 1995), 1:1–32, 2:1–17.

3. H. Reventlow, *The Authority of the Bible and the Rise of the Modern World* (Philadelphia: Fortress Press, 1984), 328–34; J. Barr, *Holy Scripture: Canon, Authority, and Criticism* (Oxford: Clarendon, 1983), 33. With respect to similar struggles during the Middle Ages, see Karpp, *Schrift, Geist und Wort Gottes: Geltung und Wirkung der Bibel in der Geschichte der Kirche: von der Alten Kirche bis zum Ausgang der Reformationszeit* (Darmstadt: Wissenschaftliche Buchgesellschaft, 1992), 66–81.

4. Segovia, "Cultural Studies," 1, see also 7.

5. *The Postmodern Bible*, ed. E. Castelli et al. (New Haven, CT: Yale University Press, 1995), 39–40.

6. W. Iser, *The Act of Reading: A Theory of Aesthetic Response* (Baltimore: Johns Hopkins University Press, 1978), 69; J. Culler, *Structuralist Poetics: Structuralism, Linguistics and the Study of Literature* (Ithaca, NY: Cornell University Press, 1975), 203. See also M. Sternberg, *The Poetics of Biblical Narrative: Ideological Literature and the Drama of Reading* (Bloomington: Indiana University Press, 1985), 6–7. Segovia also recognizes that texts are "socially and historically conditioned" ("Cultural Studies," 8).

7. "A Korean Minjung Perspective: The Hebrews and the Exodus," in *Voices from the Margin: Interpreting the Bible in the Third World*, ed. R. Sugirtharajah (Maryknoll, NY: Orbis, 1995), 228–43.

8. *Canon and Community: A Guide to Canonical Criticism* (Philadelphia: Fortress Press, 1984), xvii–xviii, 70–71.

9. In *A New Look at Preaching*, ed. J. Burke (Wilmington: Glazier, 1983), 137–56, esp. 140–43.

10. Keck, "Biblical Preaching," 142.

11. Walter Brueggemann, following David Bryant, proposes that this hermeneutical imagination is to "take as . . . to assert, claim, and redefine"; *Texts under Negotiation: The Bible and Postmodern Imagination* (Minneapolis: Fortress Press, 1993), 16.

12. See G. Eichholz, *Einführung in die Gleichnisse* (Neukirchen-Vluyn: Neukirchener Verlag, 1963), 26, 31.

13. A. MacIntyre, *Whose Justice? Which Rationality?* (Notre Dame, IN: Notre Dame University Press, 1988).

14. Paulo Freire, *Pedagogy of the Oppressed*, 20th Anniversary Revised Edition (New York: Continuum, 1993), esp. 30–51, 68–69, 77, 109.

15. On the global dimension of Freire's pedagogy, see P. Freire, foreword to *Paulo Freire: A Critical Encounter*, ed. P. McLaren and P. Leonard (Routledge: London, 1993), ix.

16. On critical reflection, see Ira Shor, "Education Is Politics: Paulo Freire's Critical Pedagogy," in *Paulo Freire: A Critical Encounter*, 32.

17. Freire, *Pedagogy*, 90; Shor, "Education Is Politics," 26, 31.

18. P. McLaren and P. Leonard, "Absent Discourses: Paulo Freire and the Dangerous Memories of Liberation," in *Paulo Freire: A Critical Encounter*, 2.

19. Tomaz Tadeu da Silva and Peter McLaren, "Knowledge under Siege: The Brazilian Debate," in *Paulo Freire: A Critical Encounter*, 39–40.

20. Tadeu da Silva and McLaren, "Knowledge under Siege," 42.

21. P. McLaren and Tomaz Tadeu da Silva, "Decentering Pedagogy: Critical Literacy, Resistance and the Politics of Memory," in *Paulo Freire: A Critical Encounter*, 63–65. For a similar view on women's experience, see M. McClintock Fulkerson, *Changing the Subject: Women's Discourses and Feminist Theology* (Minneapolis: Fortress Press, 1994).

22. Paulo Freire and Donaldo Macedo, "A Dialogue with Paul Freire," in *Paulo Freire: A Critical Encounter*, 172.

23. McLaren and Tadeu da Silva, "Decentering Pedagogy," 83.

24. J. King, E. Hollins, and W. Hayman, ed., *Preparing Teachers for Cultural Diversity* (New York: Teachers College Press, 1997).

25. See esp. A. Lin Goodwin, "Historical and Contemporary Perspectives on Multi-Cultural Education: Past Lessons, New Directions," in *Preparing Teachers for Cultural Diversity*, 8.

26. Goodwin, "Historical and Contemporary Perspectives," 17–19; S. Garcia, "Self-narrative Inquiry in Teacher Development: Living and Working in Just Institutions," in *Preparing Teachers for Cultural Diversity*, 147, 151.

27. P. Ricoeur, "Biblical Hermeneutics," *Semeia* 4 (1975): 114–28; P. Ricoeur, *The Rule of Metaphor: Multi-Disciplinary Studies of the Creation of Meaning in Language* (Toronto: University of Toronto Press, 1977), 22, 150, 230–36.

28. "Thank You for Opening Our Minds: On Praxis, Transmutation, and Black Studies in Teacher Development," in *Preparing Teachers for Cultural Diversity*, 162.

29. R. Quintaranar Sarellana, "Culturally Relevant Teacher Preparation and Teachers' Perceptions of the Language and Culture of Linguistic Minority Students," in *Preparing Teachers for Cultural Diversity*, 41–42.

30. See the following in *Preparing Teachers for Cultural Diversity*: S. Melnick and K. Zeichner, "Enhancing the Capacity of Teacher Education Institutions to Address Diversity Issues," 28; V. Ooka Pang, M. Gresham Anderson, V. Martuza, "Removing the Mask of Academia: Institutions Collaborating in the Struggle for Equity," 60; D. York, "Preparing Teachers for Tomorrow's Children: Cross-Cultural Training for Teachers," 81.

31. In *What Is John? Readers and Readings of the Fourth Gospel*, ed. F. Segovia (Atlanta: Scholars Press, 1996), 59–104.

32. In *Teaching the Bible: The Discourses and Politics of Biblical Pedagogy*, ed. F. Segovia and M. Tolbert (Maryknoll, NY: Orbis Books, 1998).

33. In *Teaching the Bible: The Discourses and Politics of Biblical Pedagogy*.

34. See chapter 4.

CHAPTER 9

The Tower of Babel and Cultural Diversity: A Case Study on Engaging Diversity in the Classroom

Theodore Hiebert (Instructor), Jennifer Blandford, Andrew Davis, and Hardy Kim (Students)

One of the temptations inherent in our diversity," as McCormick's *Student Handbook* so well expresses it, "is to adopt the naive assumption that living with one another necessarily means that we understand one another. Unfortunately it is not that easy. The challenge, then, is to explore, intentionally and directly, how we are similar, how we are different, and why?" While we at McCormick have become well aware of our diversity, we are still trying to find better ways of bringing the full resources of our diverse student body and faculty to bear on the experience of learning that goes on in the classroom. It is easy to spend a semester side by side with diverse classmates without ever substantively engaging the differences among us.

In this chapter we want to describe an actual class that was uniquely successful in setting up a genuinely multicultural educational experience. The key to this experience, we believe, was the distinctive goal of the course, a goal that was not actually conceived to engage our diversity. That goal was writing a book together. The course was designed as a collaborative writing project aimed at publishing a book comprising chapters written by the members of the class. Writing a book together, as we came to realize during the course, created a unique kind of learning community in which diverse voices became a more prominent part of the classroom culture, in which critical engagement and dialogue about difference became more substantive, and in which diversity actually raised the bar of excellence for academic study and discourse.

Real obstacles to genuine engagement of our differences often go unnoticed or unspoken in traditional pedagogical practices. It is easy, for example, to set up class processes and content that unintentionally privilege certain voices over others. A traditional course design, with a lecture format and a core textbook, may invite the impression that other perspectives are at the periphery of the learning experience. With the perspectives embedded in the lectures and text assumed as the standard for discourse, an inclusive class culture may be difficult to cultivate. Furthermore, even when a direct attempt is made to engage diversity in class, it is a challenge to set up a safe context for true interaction, genuine dialogue, and critical engagement. It can be difficult to critique the perspectives and opinions of others from different cultures without appearing to disrespect the others' cultures themselves. Finally, it is an unspoken thought of some that to invite all voices into dialogue and to respect all perspectives means accepting all contributions as equally valid, letting discourse weaken to the lowest common denominator, and ultimately lowering the standards of teaching and learning. All of these obstacles stand in the way of real multicultural education, and all, we believe, were overcome in substantial ways by the collaborative writing project we wish to describe.

> One of the reasons many students say they choose to come to McCormick is its attention to and intention in creating a multicultural learning environment. No experience that I have had so far better serves as an example of how McCormick does this than this class. An institution open to not only creating such a diverse classroom but then which encourages dialogue, study, and actual practice of multicultural issues from so many angles is exactly what I was looking for in a seminary experience. This class modeled the kind of ministry that I expect to be engaged in when I leave seminary for a parish in our rapidly diversifying culture. —Jennifer Blandford

DESIGNING A COURSE TO ENGAGE DIVERSITY: THE CONTENT

We believe that an important reason—but not the *most* important reason—for the success of this course in engaging diversity was its subject matter: the course focused squarely on the issue of cultural diversity itself and on perspectives about it in our religious heritage. The course—offered during McCormick's three-week January term—was situated in our curriculum as a course in biblical studies and required practice in the skills of biblical studies that all of our Bible courses do, but it took as its primary concern biblical perspectives on diversity. So diversity and our religious perspectives toward it were at the core of the course content. Entitled "The Tower of Babel and Cultural Diversity," the course aimed to examine the story of the tower of Babel in Genesis 11:1–9 and its interpreters through history, with a particular interest in the ways in which the biblical text and its interpreters viewed cultural diversity. Thus our reading, research, discussion, and writing all invited us to examine perspectives on cultural diversity in our theological traditions and to reexamine our own views in relation to them.

The account of the tower of Babel in Genesis 11:1–9, on which the course was based, is the Bible's classic story of the origins of diversity in the world, so it plays a foundational role in reflections about diversity in Jewish and Christian thought. From the beginning, as we found out in our research, interpreters have almost universally understood the diversity with which the story ends as God's punishment on the human race because of its sin of pride, thus giving diversity a problematic character. By contrast, the instructor and some other scholars have recently argued that the story itself actually presents diversity as God's design for the world after the flood, an interpretation, as we discovered, that was anticipated by a minority of past interpreters. This became the core issue around which our research, discussion, and debates centered: Do this story and its interpreters regard diversity negatively or positively, and why, and what do their perspectives on diversity contribute to our own reflections today?

The research design of the course demanded that we think about diversity at a number of levels. The research goal of each class member—writing a book chapter on one of the tower of Babel's interpreters—required selecting and analyzing a wide variety of biblical readers. They represented a broad range of cultures, historical periods, and theological perspectives. Included among these interpreters were the author of *Jubilees*, the author of the New Testament book of Luke–Acts, the early rabbis, Augustine, Ibn Ezra, John Calvin, John Milton, Dostoevsky, Modupe Oduyoye, Raimundo Panikkar, José Severino Croatto, Jacques Derrida; artistic works including the Salerno Ivories and paintings by Pieter Bruegel and M. C. Escher; and Sunday school curricula and children's Bibles. Each of our book chapters included describing the view of diversity present in our interpreter's reading of the story, examining the cultural background of the interpreter, and considering whether this background and the attitudes toward diversity in it were factors in understanding the interpreter's perspectives. Each chapter also included a brief statement of own view of diversity today and an evaluation of the interpreter's viewpoint on diversity from a contemporary perspective.

DESIGNING A COURSE TO ENGAGE DIVERSITY: THE PROCESS

We believe that the process by which we chose to study diversity had an even greater effect on the engagement of diversity in this class than the course topic itself. No textbook exists for this course topic. Of course, still the instructor could have assembled—as is often done in such cases—a course book, a compilation of primary texts from the Bible and its interpreters, that we would read and discuss together. Instead, we attacked the topic in a more radical way. We set out the aspects of the course topic that we would study as chapters in a book we would compose: an introduction by the instructor on the biblical narrative, followed by chapters by class members on individual interpreters of this story. Then we organized the course to support the reading, research, writing, discussion, and revision that such a volume required. We dedicated the second two weeks of the course to reading and editing each other's drafts of the book's chapters. Rather than building our course around a textbook or a course book, we designed the course to write the book about it. This meant that for this course the book we bought was the book we wrote.

> The idea of designing a class around writing a book goes back ultimately to my interest in planning classes as active learning experiences. My first thought was to set this class up as a traditional seminar, in which each class member would do a research paper on a particular interpreter, make a presentation to the class, and then turn in their completed project for me to read at the end of the term. I was personally interested in the students' research because I had thought about writing a book about the Tower of Babel and its interpretation at some time in the future. Then the thought hit me: why not let the students profit from their collective work as I wanted to do? Why not assemble their work for them to keep? Why not let them write the book? I meant for this book, this collection of student essays, simply to extend the seminar format one step further. What I didn't anticipate was the way working together on an actual publishing project would so significantly change the dynamics of learning in the class and, in particular, the *way we engaged diversity in our theological deliberations.* —Theodore Hiebert

We decided as a class to name the book *Toppling the Tower: Essays on Babel and Diversity.* The name reflects our opinion that the approach to the biblical story of most of its interpreters, which takes the tower as the symbol of humanity's sin of pride and therefore regards cultural diversity as God's punishment, must be challenged. In particular, we wanted to highlight the alternative viewpoint that the story presents cultural diversity as God's design for the repopulated world after the flood, a view that is anticipated by some interpreters and that we came to appreciate. Each of our chapters included, as already mentioned, our own reflections on the value for our society today of the perspectives on diversity found in the interpretations we studied.

At the beginning of the course, we thought about taking our papers to our local Kinko's and letting them duplicate and bind our work. But a few members of the class came up with a better idea. With the advances in printing technology, it is now possible to print a limited number of copies of an attractive volume for a reasonable price. We contracted with Paxton Printing Inc., a local company that publishes our school catalogue, to publish a volume with perfect binding, much like our catalogue. To prepare the copy, one of our class members, James Nelson, did the layout with the Adobe Pagemaker® desktop publishing program. The result was a paperback volume about the size and print quality of an issue of the *Journal of Biblical Literature*. We advertised the volume to the McCormick community and to acquaintances and collected 110 advance orders, bringing the price of our "textbook" down to $13.00 per book.

CREATING AN INCLUSIVE AND CONSTRUCTIVE CLASSROOM CULTURE

One of the most positive results of writing a book together was the experience that the diversity in the classroom had a real and significant impact on learning. By agreeing to engage in a collaborative writing project and entrusting a chapter to each member of the class, we made a conscious decision to value the diverse voices in the class. As a result, we were motivated to learn from each other's diverse backgrounds. Diversity can be a real asset in a classroom, but in a traditional classroom the diversity is rarely sufficiently utilized, because the focus of the class is on one person—the professor. The challenge is to create a diverse classroom where the focus of the class is on each class member, so that everyone has the potential to teach everyone else, and everyone has the opportunity to learn from the diverse group. Our experience can be a guide to creating an inclusive and constructive classroom culture.

In a traditional class, the focus is on the professor's perspectives and on the professor's favorite readings. Students in traditional classes have unique opinions, but students know that the professor, who will be giving a final grade, evaluates these opinions. Students can be tempted to say things in the class that they know will please the professor! Moreover, classroom dialogue is often between professor and students, even when the professor wishes to open up classroom discussion among students. Additionally, in the traditional classroom, there is typically a core text or syllabus that everyone reads. These texts, chosen by the professor, become sources of authority in the classroom. It is difficult for students to introduce ideas supported by other writers into classroom discourse, and the intellectual and theological diversity of the classroom discourse is limited. The diversity is there, but when the focus is on the professor and on the syllabus, this diversity isn't being explored to its full potential.

Our class was remarkably different from the traditional classroom, for the focus was not only on the professor, but was also on every student. This diverse focus allowed the diversity of the classroom to be unlocked and to be a useful tool for learning. The class began in the traditional format, with the professor providing an orientation to the course topic, which got everyone on the same page. This included a tour through the Hebrew text of the Babel story and an introduction to the key issues in its interpretation. After the first week, the focus of the course shifted from the professor to the other class members and their research. We avoided the pitfall of the professor being the focus of the class by making every class member an expert on one interpreter of Genesis 11. Every student was an expert on his or her own interpreter. The resources inherent in our class's matrix of diversity were unlocked and realized. The unique perspectives and backgrounds of our class members had voice and expertise. While the class valued the opinions and research of our professor, his voice was not prized above all other voices. Everyone contributed to the writing of our book, and to the education of all. In a sense, we had not just one professor, but many teachers.

Instead of having a core text or a syllabus chosen by the professor, we created our own text. The text that we read was the text that we wrote. Students were free to choose which interpreter they would study, so the theological possibilities were much larger than they would have been if our professor had assigned interpreters to students. In some cases, students chose interpreters who reflected their own particular backgrounds. Anshi Zachariahi, a student from India, researched Raimundo Panikkar, an interpreter from India. Anshi shared her research with the class and taught us about someone who interested her personally but whom most of us hadn't known prior to her presentation. She taught us that Raimundo Panikkar is an Indian theologian born in Barcelona,

Spain, to a Hindu father and Roman Catholic Spanish mother. As someone with a life rooted in diversity, he articulates a theology that values pluralism as an alternate to monism and dualism. Panikkar interprets Genesis 11 to mean that God opposes empire and all human efforts towards building one culture. Anshi's research, and her reflections on her research in light of her own experiences, was a meaningful contribution to the class that wouldn't have been made if we were all working from one syllabus with our focus on our professor. She was able to share her own cultural expertise with us. The class learned not only about Panikkar, but also about Anshi Zachariahi's political, theological, and cultural world.

Another example is Jorge Betancurt's research on José Severino Croatto. As a Colombian student living in the United States, Jorge helped the class understand the perspective of this Argentinean biblical scholar and theologian. Working with texts in both Spanish and English, Jorge provided a firsthand analysis of the Latin American social context that lay behind Croatto's writing. Croatto, a lay person, interprets Genesis 11 in his context and finds a powerful statement against cultural hegemony and the push towards monolingualism. In his chapter entitled "Tower of Babel and Cultural Diversity: From a Hispanic/Latino Perspective," Jorge observes, "Diversity is God's purpose, God's perfect plan. Therefore, diversity makes stronger people that fight for their rights, their customs and traditions, their beliefs, their languages and culture, without a central power that dominates and subjugates others." He could just as easily have been speaking for the importance of a diverse classroom where each student's voice is valued.

Other students also did research that reflected their particular theological traditions: José Morales, a Pentecostal student, researched the tower of Babel story in light of Acts 2:2–4, the story of Pentecost. Some students chose interpreters who were known by many class members, but the depth of the students' research gave them enough expertise to be our guides to these interpreters. For example, Biju Simon, a member of the Mar Thoma Church of India, studied Augustine, an early North African bishop, and analyzed his interpretation of the Babel story in *City of God*. Sarah Karstens, an undergraduate major in English literature, researched John Milton's interpretation in *Paradise Lost*. We found that reading someone's work taught us more than we already knew, from prior discussions, about that person's own ideas. Although many students knew Beth Hamilton, a Presbyterian student, quite well before this class, we learned much more about her own political philosophy by reading her work on John Calvin in light of his political context, especially her desire to find a middle path between political tyranny and anarchy.

Providing the opportunity for every student to do research on his or her interpreter, and then to share this research in chapter drafts with the class, created an inquisitive classroom culture. Every student was an expert in our classroom, knowing more than anyone else about the interpreter he or she researched. This brought the diversity of the class out into the open, gave it a voice, and granted it an authority that it does not normally have in traditional class structures.

CREATING CRITICAL ENGAGEMENT AND DIALOGUE

As collaborating on a book shifted the class focus from the professor to each member of our class, by making every class member a unique expert on an interpreter, we also created the space for critical engagement and dialogue among students. Creating dialogue among students can be difficult enough, but creating critical engagement in a diverse classroom is daunting. Too often, diverse classrooms treat culture superficially, since people are genuinely afraid of offending each other. It is easier to reduce diversity to differences in dress, language, and customs while avoiding more important issues. Creating an inclusive environment did not complete our work; we needed to engage in critical dialogue.

This class successfully engaged in dialogue that drew heavily upon its diversity. We discovered that working on a common project in which we all took pride and that we wanted to be as good as possible gave us permission to give and take criticism more openly than usual. In this context, reading and editing each other's work allowed us to dialogue with each other in a nonthreatening way. Every student read everyone else's work and helped to edit it. Editing our own book gave permission to class members to critique each other. We corrected each other's grammatical errors, made notes in each other's margins, praised and critiqued each other's work. Editing forced us to slow down and carefully examine not only the spelling, formatting, and grammar, but also the ideas presented. We weren't limited to quick end-of-term student presentations, for we actually helped each other write and therefore had the opportunity to deeply consider each other's research and reflections.

The most critical multicultural dialogue took place in the exchanges after everyone had had an opportunity to read and edit a student's work, when the class gave written and verbal feedback to the author. Students had an opportunity to verbally question each other's research, conclusions, and assumptions. By questioning and critiquing each other's work, we learned more about each other's worldviews. We also learned about ourselves by considering our classmates' editorial criticism. Phrases or ideas that seemed self-explanatory to a student were questioned, and we found that we needed to think carefully about how we wrote. In writing about Dostoevsky's cultural context, Andrew Davis used the phrase "atheistic socialism" in the draft of his chapter he presented to the class. Later he made this observation about the class's discussion of the phrase: "Other students questioned my use of this phrase, especially those students who are Christian socialists. By writing and thinking in a diverse context, I had to think about my own cultural and political background and the assumptions that I carried with me."

Remarkably, there were no heated exchanges in this phase of our class work. Students listened carefully to criticism and questions and responded with respect to each other. Taking the time to read and critique each other's work prevented presumptuous and uninformed attacks on another's position. Working towards a common goal allowed students to be less defensive and more willing to hear critique and to improve our writings. Our class successfully created not only an inclusive environment, but an environment where diversity was engaged, where critique was offered across national, racial, ethnic, and theological differences, and where cultural presumptions and assumptions were questioned by a truly diverse group of students.

DIVERSITY AND THE STANDARD OF ACADEMIC DISCOURSE

Critical engagement between students, as mentioned above, was not a serendipitous byproduct of the diversity found in our classroom. In fact (as many in the McCormick community have come to realize) diversity holds great potential for critical engagement in social, political, and theological discussions, but sometimes it remains just that—potential. The process of editing and feedback by peers—coauthors, really—unleashed the potential for critical engagement that often lies dormant in diverse classrooms, providing us real permission and incentive to be active in learning from and teaching each other. However, another important outcome of this experiment in education in McCormick's multicultural setting deserves extended mention. The diversity represented in the class—when combined with our chosen process of critical engagement, a collaborative writing project—resulted in a much higher standard of academic discourse than we might have otherwise experienced.

Though this result may seem unremarkable, consider it again. While diversity is generally touted as a positive aspect of life in the United States, how is it really viewed in society? Diversity, as a general concept, is accepted as good or perhaps benign—one person's way is as good as another. For from more cynical—and often more deeply rooted—perspectives, diversity is one step away from confusion, absence of common ground, moral relativism, lack of accepted standards, the lowest common denominator. The fear that diversity, or something like it, might undermine our standards, leave us without understanding, and rob us of the very certainties of higher truth has permeated U.S. society ever since our nation's creation. Christian communities have never been immune to these concerns either; Schleiermacher's diatribes against the "cultured despisers" of Christian tradition are evidence that even the foundational thinkers of modern Christianity sensed the problematic nature of creating high moral standards in a world that is increasingly diverse and includes people of many different perspectives. How, then, should McCormick understand the value of diversity in educating future leaders of faith communities? What are we, those engaged in theological education, to do with the confusing combination of diversity and excellence? Is there a better way to engage difficult issues than to say either, "This, alone, is what *we* believe" or "You go your way, I'll go mine"?

At McCormick it is generally accepted that the diversity in the community (in the student body, faculty, and staff) is one of the great strengths of the seminary experience. And while we always value the diversity of viewpoint and experience that differences in race, gender, culture, history, class, or sexual orientation produce in our classroom presentations and discussion, sometimes it is hard to articulate this experience of diversity in a way that is integral to an academically rigorous seminary education, rather than parallel to it. The process we used in the class—a collaborative project where each student was entrusted with the task of creating a chapter in the textbook for the class and helping other students to examine critically their own chapters—allowed us to realize the full benefits of that diversity, rather than see that diversity as a detractor from serious theological work. Thus, "Babel and Diversity"—due both to the participants and the process—was an educational experience where diversity was essential to a high level of academic achievement. This class experience challenges the traditional notion that diversity and high academic standards are opposed or mutually exclusive.

The difficulties that arise when diversity and academic standards meet seem to fall into two general categories. First, diversity often becomes tokenism: viewpoints are easily welcomed, even sought out, solely because they are different or exotic, but they are not taken as serious centers of dialogue. Second, the conflicts produced by real diversity are often avoided through the elevation of relativism: students and instructor are too ready to accept whatever is said by others because (1) they do not want to pass judgment on another's viewpoint, (2) there is no feeling that a different opinion must affect what the hearer believes, and (3) there is no common commitment that creates group ownership of the views expressed by the diverse group.

Solving such problems regarding diversity and education may not have been one of the original aims of our class. However, when we looked back upon our work together and compared it to our experiences in other classes, where attempts were made to include diversity while maintaining a high level of academic discourse, we recognized that our class process effectively addressed these concerns in a number of ways. First, everyone's viewpoint was a serious center of dialogue because we were willing to entrust a chapter to each participant. Second, the real learning that occurred in our class would not have been possible if we had not taken each other's ideas seriously. Third, by committing ourselves to a common book project, we opened up our chapters—and thereby our understanding of God's presence in Scripture as well—to be changed by the viewpoints and questions of others. This engagement in a common process required class participants to display a strong dedication to accepting diversity, and the constant barrage of questions and constructive criticism ensured that this dedication was not the result of setting aside rigorous academic standards.

One of the most important ways for looking at the interaction between diversity and academic standards is to examine the quality of work produced by our class and how that level of work was achieved. As already mentioned, the common goal of writing the book itself changed the learning experience in important ways. In this class the relationship between diversity and high standards was different because (1) instead of discouraging students from cooperating and engaging each other's viewpoints, our collaborative project made cooperation and engagement necessary to success; and (2) instead of causing a diverse body of students to be judged by an arbitrary and monoperspectival standard, the collective, interactive community of the classroom produced the standard by which its members would be evaluated.

Seen another way, real diversity was allowed to operate because different ideas, statements, and chapters were not (whether implicitly or explicitly) being subtly evaluated against an existing standard. The process freed us to take each other's ideas seriously and to reexamine our own positions from the different standpoints of our classmates—while minimizing the notion that we were simply exercising diversity. When we were brought to critical analysis of our own work through the perspectives of others, we had to take the process seriously, because we could not simply discount those perspectives as being outside of the *established standard*.

For example, in a traditional grading system, it doesn't matter to any given student what the student next to her knows or does not know; in fact, it probably makes that student look better if the student next to her knows less than she does. Our collaborative process changed this dynamic, demonstrating to students that their chapters could be made better (not viewed as worse) through the collective knowledge and diverse viewpoints of their peers. We were not competing to look superior in knowledge to others; instead, we relied on the diverse knowledge of those around us. The very fact that others knew things that we did not, and were approaching the discussion from viewpoints we could never imagine, caused us to turn to them for input and guidance in refining our own arguments.

The knowledge of our colleagues was made even more valuable to us by the fact that we could not discard their critiques when they didn't express the singular, monocultural view that might have dominated the class in the form of a textbook or syllabus. This is not to say that there was not a process by which we evaluated each other's work or that there were no standards of excellence behind our engagement. At every point where analyses seemed too simplistic, conclusions unsupported, or connections forced, we challenged each other with vigor. No view was accepted at face value. By questioning each other's views, we were surprised how much we were able to learn about the real values that underlay them. In fact, as we made our presentations to the class regarding our research and writing, each one of our chapters and interpretations underwent this crucible of classroom dialogue. In the end, this trial produced chapters that were clearer about what they were stating and about what logical, cultural, theological, and academic support was important to the arguments they contained. Instead of a process where we simply ignored each other's views because there was no common standard by which to judge them all, our class produced an environment where all perspectives were valued for what they could add to our own and for the unique critical analyses they could provide. Each one of us may have entered the class thinking, theoretically, that diversity was a valuable thing; the process of writing a book together taught us that diversity was a practical, essential component of our common learning experience.

The process of writing a book as a collaborative project revealed that it is not simply enough to say that diversity is important, while still holding blindly to traditional academic values. This will often simply reproduce the conflict where either diversity or traditional academic values suffer. What the "Babel and Diversity" classroom project showed was that valuing diversity and academic standards at the same time can require us to use new educational processes that allow us both to produce intellectually acceptable work and to enjoy the diversity around us. In fact, we are proud to say that our class project, our textbook, was not only good work that represented much of our diversity as a class; it was actually an academically superior end-product *because of the diversity in our class*. We hope that the value of diversity in the McCormick educational experience—exemplified in our class—proves that diversity is not the problem when it comes to academic standards. Rather, academic standards and processes should be judged by how well they allow students to engage in real discourse and critical dialogue, whether they allow us to bring all that we are to the task of learning, and whether they give us the chance to really open up to all that our peers have to teach us.

What this class on "Babel and Diversity" taught us about diversity and standards goes with us beyond the classroom as well. In opening up to sincere but difficult questions from those who were different from ourselves, asking those same questions ourselves—all while coming to see our partners in conversation as valued colleagues—we were privileged enough to experience an engagement with diversity that did not force us to check our opinions at the door, but that did force us to leave aside our certainties. It was important for members of our class to discover that true learning is not about competing for a grade or buying into a dominant understanding of an issue. More importantly for McCormick and the process of theological education, on the other hand, is the broader experience of the relationship between diversity and standards that the participants of our class will take away to their future communities of faith and work. The real knowledge we gained was that valuing diversity does not consist of an "anything goes" attitude; it consists, rather, of a real willingness to engage in a respectful process of mutual transformation that can happen only with those who are from worlds entirely not our own.

IMPLICATIONS FOR MULTICULTURAL THEOLOGICAL EDUCATION

For all of us, students and instructor alike, this experience was a surprise. We expected that the course content, which focused our attention on perspectives toward diversity in the Bible and its interpreters, would compel us to think about diversity. But we did not realize how much this new course goal—a collaborative publishing project—would provide opportunities to embrace and profit from the diversity of the members of the class. Looking back, we believe that the genius behind this book project, which led to this enhanced engagement with our diversity, was shaping the learning experience around our collective contribution to a common goal with a public purpose.

By this single design change, some of the key obstacles to genuine cross-cultural engagement were overcome at once. As chapter authors, the diverse identities and perspectives of class members were brought to the center of the learning experience, not marginalized by a single privileged voice from the professor or the textbook. Direct engagement and genuine critique were possible because they were carried out in the service of a larger common goal: we were trying to make our book as good as possible. And such genuine critique made everyone's work stronger, thus enhancing the quality of our thinking and writing, increasing rather than decreasing the academic standards in our deliberations.

We suspect that these elements of our course might be incorporated into another design and be effective in another format. And we certainly hope there will be a variety of ways of enhancing genuine and constructive engagement with diversity. But we know by experience how powerfully writing a book together supported multicultural theological education. And we recommend this pedagogy to those interested in bringing multicultural learning closer to the center of theological education.

CHAPTER 10

Reading the Bible
from a Postcolonial Perspective

Jae Won Lee

In my practice of reading and teaching the Bible, multicultural reading of the Bible involves at least four levels of cross-cultural experiences. (1) As a Korean feminist committed to a postcolonial *minjung* liberation theology, I help to make reading the Bible in the context of teaching at McCormick Theological Seminary a cross-cultural experience. (2) The students in my classes represent various cultures, and they make our common deliberations a cross-cultural experience. (3) When my students and I read texts from the New Testament, we encounter an ancient culture that is often exceedingly different from our world today. (4) The New Testament itself faces cross-cultural challenges and invests in resolving them. It then becomes a resource for how people in the twenty-first century can work out multicultural relationships.

In this essay I focus on two of these levels. First, I discuss how my feminist and postcolonial *minjung* commitments contribute to a cross-cultural experience in the classroom. Second, I offer my interpretation of the cross-cultural conflicts that Paul faces in dealing with the weak and the strong in Romans 14:1–15:13 and of the politics of difference that he advocates to resolve the conflicts. Although the cross-cultural dimension that diverse students bring to the classroom is an uncontrolled variable, I present my reading of Paul and the politics of difference as an example of reading the Bible in multicultural perspectives.

FEMINIST PERSPECTIVES ON DIFFERENCE

Western thought has disciplined us to think of differences such as gender, class, race, religion, and culture in terms of binary oppositions: male/

female, rich/poor, white/black, Christian/non-Christian, Western/non-Western. This way of construing difference has privileged the first member of each pair as the standard by which the other is judged, with the result that difference means inequality. Binary oppositions sustain hierarchical worldviews by devaluing the second set of terms.[1] Postmodern criticism of foundationalism and essentialism has revealed that viewing difference as "objective" and absolute is indefensible.

On the other hand, postmodernism itself is a Western phenomenon, aspects of which the postcolonial Third World cannot afford, because postmodernism's antifoundationalism diminishes the ability of the Third World to make truth claims. It weakens what is not yet strong. If difference is equated with fragmentation and a lack of coherence, feminists would ultimately lack anything in common to bind them together. Susan Bordo warns that the postmodern "view from nowhere" should not lead to the equally problematic "view from everywhere."[2]

Iris Marion Young distinguishes two understandings of equality: "The assimilationist ideal assumes that equal social status . . . requires treating everyone according to the same . . . standards. A politics of difference argues . . . that equality as the participation and inclusion of all groups requires different treatment for oppressed or disadvantaged groups."[3] In the assimilationist strategy, dominant groups expect those who have been excluded to enter into the mainstream as they define it. Such assimilation devalues the social identity of excluded groups, as the dominant group fails to recognize that it has and perpetrates its own social identity.[4] This means that taking into consideration concrete and multiple situations of oppression, a politics of difference—not the assimilationist ideal—needs to be promoted. Difference now comes to mean not otherness—that is, binary opposition—but specificity, variation, and heterogeneity.

A part of refusing to accept the dichotomy between male and female is to emphasize that gender is a social construction rather than a matter of biological essence. This challenges the social construction whereby male norms are the standard and female difference is reduced to "other." The tendency of universalizing and homogenizing women is the problem of essentialism that ignores differences among women.[5]

POSTCOLONIALISM

My dialogue with postcolonial perspectives centers on: (1) the meaning of difference in postcolonialism, (2) the need to relocate the discourse on difference to specific contexts, and (3) the potential promises of post-colonial criticism for biblical studies.

1. Parallel to my recognition of differences among women in my discussion of feminism, consideration of postcolonialism requires attention to difference and multiplicity among oppressed people, as well as of their commonality in oppression and injustice.[6] Like postmodernism, postcolonialism is committed to unmasking hierarchy and otherness. As in feminist discourse on difference, in postcolonialism difference is first and foremost about a subjectivity denied by colonial/imperial discourses. This calls again for resistance to the complete fragmentation and lack of coherence in a radical deconstruction. Susan Gallagher makes this point clearly: "By questioning colonial authority, post-colonial writers do not necessarily question *all* authority. Rather, they set out to dismantle a specific historically grounded discourse in the hopes of demonstrating that an alternative discourse is possible."[7]

2. Postcolonial theory has highlighted the notion of "hybridity," a term coined by Homi Bhabha to deconstruct "the binary logic through which identities of difference are often constructed—Black/White, Self/Other. . . . [C]ultural hybridity . . . entertains differences without an assumed or imposed hierarchy."[8] Hybridity does not ignore the syncretistic nature of postcolonial societies and stands against "a movement toward nativism, a futile, romantic attempt to return to a pristine, pre-colonial culture."[9] But there is also a critique of hybridity in that postcolonialism, like feminism, should never lose sight of historical specificities and power relations, as well as diverse strategies that respond to different contexts.

3. Specifically in relation to reading the Bible, Musa Dube and Kwok Pui-Lan have introduced postcolonial strategies to resist imperial domination through biblical criticism.[10] It should be acknowledged that the Bible contains not only liberating texts but also imperializing texts. For my concerns, I focus on two points which R. S. Sugirtharajah and Richard Horsley have made clear. The first is the problem of the relationship between Christianity and other faiths. For Sugirtharajah, there is a striking analogy between the "Western construction of the Orient" and "Christianity's relation to other faiths," which establishes "a theological hierarchy with Christianity at the top and other religions placed underneath it as imperfect and inferior."[11] Second, Horsley identifies biblical studies in general as "one of the many products of modern Western imperial culture and its 'orientalism.'"[12] In particular, he proposes a postcolonial reading of Paul that "disrupts the standard, essentialist,

individualistic and depoliticized Augustinian-Lutheran Paul" and "consists in the rediscovery of the anti-imperial stance and program evident in his letter—for those with 'eyes to see.'"[13]

KOREAN MINJUNG THEOLOGY

I turn now to my own context by focusing on *minjung* theology as a Korean Christian movement for transforming Korean society. On the one hand, although I was engaged in *minjung* theology, my social location as an international student in the United States in the 1990s prevented my direct involvement with its development. On the other hand, I have become more conscious of the importance of the reunification of Korea than when I was in Korea. The suffering of Korean *minjung* cannot be understood without taking into account a divided Korea under the imperial power of the United States. How to reunite Korea in spite of differences in ideology and political systems is the most urgent task for the political and cultural identity of Korean *minjung*.

Like liberation theologies in Latin America and South Africa, *minjung*—a Korean liberation theology—emerged as a theology of practice in the crisis of Korean society in the 1970s. *Minjung* theology started as critical theological reflection on sociopolitical and economic oppression among Korean people. As such, *minjung* theology takes the preferential option for the social oppressed and marginalized.

> 'Minjung' is a Korean word, but it is a combination of two Chinese characters 'min' and 'jung.' 'Min' may be translated as 'people' and 'jung' as 'mass.' . . . But when we try to translate it into English, 'mass' is not adequate . . . and 'the people' is politically dangerous in anti-Communist Korea, because it has become a Communist word. Although 'the people of God' may seem to be the most safe and perhaps a neutral expression both in Korean and English, theologically and politically 'minjung' cannot be translated into 'the people of God.'[14]

The *minjung* remained as the "other" to the founders of *minjung* theology before their blindness was changed by the *minjung* of the 1970s. To the majority of Korean Christians and theologians, the *minjung* still remain as "other," because they insist that Christian discourse is about the universal human being rather than particular *minjung* and/or women. For them, difference among *minjung* and/or women does not make any difference for understanding Christian life or reading the Bible as the Word of God.

In the 1970s Ahn Byung Mu investigated the historical Jesus and argued that the "crowd," differentiated from the "people" in Mark, represents the people around Jesus—the so-called tax collectors and sinners.[15] "The crowd" stands in contrast to the ruling class criticized by Jesus and refers to those who were exploited, oppressed, and marginalized. Thus Ahn Byung Mu defined the Jesus event primarily as a *minjung* event in Galilee. Yet he refused to identify *minjung* in terms of dynamics among social classes and concentrated on recovering stories of Jesus living with *minjung*.

Some other theologians tried to express the *minjung* experience by drawing attention to indigenous shamanism in Korea, to traditional *minjung* culture, and to *han*. *Han* denotes an accumulation of suppressed and condensed experiences of oppression rooted in the suffering of the Korean *minjung* and nation, particularly the history in the twentieth century covering colonization, neocolonization, the division of the nation, the pro-U.S. anticommunist dictatorial regime in South Korea, Park Jong Hee's military coup and his long dictatorship, the 5/18 Kwang Ju Massacre, and the Kwang Ju *minjung* struggle.

Enduring invasions, tyranny, Confucianism's imposition of discrimination against women, and hereditary slavery, the *minjung* experience *han* as an overwhelming sense of defeat, acquiescence, and emptiness.[16] On the other hand, *han* is a tenacity for life that comes to weaker beings. According to Suh Nam Dong, the God of the Bible is the one who redeems, atones, and liberates *minjung* from their *han*. While "sin" is the language of the ruling class and Western theology, sin amounts to *han* in the eyes of *minjung*.

Suh Nam Dong developed what he called a "theology of confluence." Confluence is the way two currents of tradition meet together, such as the *minjung* tradition of the Bible and Christianity on the one hand and the political and cultural tradition of Korea on the other. For Suh Nam Dong, the role of theology is to witness to and interpret confluence on the sociopolitical level and on the cultural-religious level.

In the 1980s a second generation of *minjung* theologians adopted the fundamental theological premises of the first generation. But radical change in the social situation in the 1980s presented a new challenge to theologians. The 5/18 Kwang Ju *Minjung* Struggle in 1980, which was Kwang Ju *minjung*'s tenacious resistance against the Kwang Ju Massacre by the Korean government aided by U.S. military intervention, became another watershed in the *minjung* movement. Activists including students, laborers, and farmers were eager to adopt theories of social transformation and praxis. Particularly theories representing eastern European Marxism had great appeal. There was also a growing consciousness that conflicts and contradictions in Korean society were caused not only by the oppressive Korean military dictatorship but also by multilayered oppressive forces of imperialism, neocolonialism, and the world capitalism of the United States into which Korean capitalistic society was incorporated.

The second generation also reappropriated praxis theories. They attempted to elaborate on issues raised in the *minjung* movements such as a theology of *mul* ("material"),[17] the sub-structure of historical revelation,[18] the epistemological revolution with respect to the issues of material and class,[19] and a biblical foundation for *minjung* theology's theory of *minjung*.[20] Simultaneously there was an increasing awareness of the tragedy of our divided nation as a product of U.S. imperial strategy to secure its hegemony over this part of Asia. *Minjung* theologians drew attention to the concept of *minjok* (nation), especially for the praxis of the reunification of Korea. Park Soon Kyung sharply criticized the *minjung* theology of the 1970s for presupposing anti-Communist Christianity and ideals of bourgeois human rights democracy, labeling it as insufficient to interpret Korean history and to envision a new national future, which needed to focus on *minjok-minjung-women*.[21]

In the late 1990s *minjung* theology faced several problems. One problem was that the theories, concepts, and language of theologians of the 1980s were foreign to the majority of the *minjung*. Further, the disintegration of socialist societies of eastern Europe and the ostensible, transient economic growth in Korea caused confusion of theory and praxis. But at the turn of the century the economic situation of Korean society was determined by its subjection to international economic injustice in the name of the International Monetary Fund under the guise of globalization, that is, the transnational hegemony of Western capitalism. In short, Korea faces not only socioeconomic but also cultural-political oppression in the struggle to reclaim the national identity of one Korea by recognizing the nonhierarchical differences between South and North.

PAUL'S POLITICS OF DIFFERENCE

Using the concrete sufferings and struggles of *minjung* as a springboard to reading Paul means for me rejecting individualistic, pietistic, doctrinal, introspective, ahistorical, and apolitical methods of interpreting the Bible that deny historical particularity, including the existentializing hermeneutics of Western scholarship. But Ahn Byung Mu's reconstruction of the historical Jesus reveals a tendency to universalize, in that diverse traditions about the historical Jesus are treated as if they represent a uniform experience of *minjung*, whereas their experiences are concretely particular. This means that when Paul deals with people who are called "weak," the question should be raised whether Paul's inclusivity can be interpreted within the conventional framework of Christian "universalism" over against Jewish "particularism" and "ethnocentrism."

The two options of interpreting Paul, in terms of a defined theology regardless of specific historical situations or in terms of a concrete situation, are reflected in scholarly opinions about Romans. Is Romans a theological treatise containing some of Paul's main ideas that has little to do with the situation of the addressees?[22] Or is Romans, like the other letters Paul wrote, addressed to the concrete situation of the recipients with specific agendas?[23] Increasingly scholars are recognizing Romans 14:1–15:13 as one of the key texts that sheds light on the contingent nature of the letter.

The prevailing opinion identifies the weak in 14:1–15:13 as Jewish Christians and the strong as Gentile Christians. This is grounded especially in Paul's description of the weak as eating only vegetables (Rom. 14:2), observing special days (14:5), and concerned with purity issues (14:14).[24] It is likely that the weak are mostly Jewish Christians, and the strong are mostly Gentile Christians. A significant point, however, is that the problem does not lie in the identification of the weak as Jewish per se, as if the problem is Jewish identity itself. In other words, it is not the practice of Jewish law that is at stake but the *relationship* of the weak to another group who characterizes them as weak. I fully accept Mark Nanos's challenge of the "condescending trap that characterizes almost all interpretations of the 'weak' as their failure to disregard the practice of the Law, as though the practice of the Law demonstrated lack of faith."[25] I do not agree, however, with his further contention that the evidence indicates that the weak were non-Christian Jews.

Did Paul wish to create a single, unified community in which Jewish and Gentile differences were irrelevant? The answer depends on how we understand the dynamics between the two groups, and for that, the immediate context is significant. After dealing with the question of Jewish-Gentile relations in Romans 9–11, Paul was addressing the Gentile Christians in Rome. Given this context, Paul begins chapters 12–13 with an appeal for a pattern of life that does not conform to this world. Christians in Rome should be conformed to this alternative form of life by transforming their minds and bodies (12:1–2). Scholars have neglected to note that in 12:3–8 the oneness of the body is explicitly understood not as sameness ("not all . . . have the same function," 12:4) but as *oneness with difference*. There are different "measures of faith" and different gifts (12:3, 6)—though the meaning of difference is not related to Jewish or Gentile identity in particular. Paul urges the members not to think of themselves more highly than they ought; such an egalitarian mind-set is what makes oneness with difference possible.

This egalitarian mind-set is redefined in 12:9–11 as love. The mutuality of love is highlighted by the emphatic repetition of "one another" (12:5, 10). Loving one another is further redefined in 12:16 as literally "setting up one's mind for others" as opposed to oneself. This is opposed to "upward mobility" that involves dissociation from the lowly. Paul's point is that through the practice of solidarity with/among the lowly, the vertical, hierarchical social relations (haughty-lowly) can be deconstructed and transformed into horizontal, egalitarian social relations toward one another. The statement in 12:16, "Live in harmony with one another; do not be haughty, but associate with the lowly," shows that Paul's rhetorical strategy is to make a tight connection between chapters 9–11 and 14–15. In this context Paul addresses obedience to authorities (13:1–7). Though the interpretation of Romans 13:1–7 is crucial to reassessing the traditional picture of Paul as a social conservative, I leave it aside here to underscore that even the issue of obedience to authorities is framed and determined by Paul's rhetoric of doing "good" (12:21) and "loving one another" (13:8). Paul stresses the priority of loving one another as something that the Romans "owe" and defines it as fulfilling the Jewish law (13:8). It is not accidental that the same terminology for the obligation of the Romans to authorities and to one another (tas opheilas, 13:7; opheilete, 13:8) recurs right at the beginning of 15:1: "We who are strong ought (opheilomen) to bear with the weakness of the weak." This leads to the conclusion that 12:1–13:14 and 14:1–15:13 should be regarded as a unity.

DIFFERENCE BETWEEN THE WEAK AND THE STRONG

Paul gives a simple description of two groups: one believes that they may eat everything; the weak eat only vegetables (14:2). Later the two groups are contrasted on the basis of calendar observance (14:5). What he expects both groups to do is given in 14:3. Those who eat are addressed first; they should not despise those who do not eat; those who do not eat should not judge those who eat.

The weak are characterized as feeling entitled to judge those who follow different eating practices. The judgmental behavior contributes to disputes over opinions (14:1). Paul uses the term "judging" repeatedly in connection with the term "Lord." Further, he uses two pairs of relational terms: servant/master and other/one's own. The first pair represents the relation of subjection/domination and the second the relation of difference/identity.

At first glance it is easy to read "the servant of another" (14:4) as if two masters were implied instead of one. However, according to 14:6, both servants, those who eat and those who abstain, have one and the same master. The relation of servant to master establishes that Jews and Gentiles are different-but-equal servants in the household of the Jewish God. Equality is not incompatible with difference.

In 14:6 Paul moves on to emphasize the christological significance of the coexistence of different practices. "Lord" functions here to integrate differences. Those who eat, do so in honor of the Lord, and those who do not eat, do so in honor of the Lord. Paul does not say that eating or not eating is a matter of indifference. Eating or not eating does matter to those who eat and those who do not eat. Honoring the Lord is common ground—the self-identity of the new community—and yet such an identity does not invalidate the ethnic-cultural differences or absorb one into the other.

Living for oneself stands in contradiction with acting in honor of the Lord (14:6) and with living to the Lord (14:7). Such living is grounded in what Jesus Christ did, that is, Jesus' death and resurrection as a master dying for his servants (14:9). Given the conventional subjection/domination relation between servants and master, the relationship of mutuality that Paul postulates is subversive, for it protests "the one-sided understanding of loyalty which prevailed in contemporary social and political life."[26] All of this indicates that eating for the Lord and not eating for the Lord are not matters of indifference.

Paul assures both Jews and Gentiles that despite their differences, they are integrated in the community of Christ. Certainly a universal perspective is introduced: "For we will all stand before the judgment seat of God" (14:10). But this universalism requires no sacrifice of particularity. In a paradoxical way, both Jews and Gentiles should be accountable for their own difference before God's judgment.

Usually differences among groups stand in unbalanced relationships of power relations. Paul's exhortation in 14:13–18 indicates that differences in the concrete situation in Rome between those who eat and those

who do not eat were leading to an unbalanced relationship. Paul's statement, "I know and am persuaded in the Lord Jesus that nothing is
unclean in itself" (Rom. 14:14), has usually been misleadingly taken as
evidence for freedom from the law.

By first delivering negative imperatives toward Gentile Christians in
14:15–16, Paul affirms their position as Gentiles in Jesus Christ. Then,
from verse 15 on, Paul's exhortation is directed toward the "strong" who
think nothing is unclean in itself. Paul now makes it clear that Jewish
Christians in Rome are in a socially weak position. But Paul stresses that
this is not what love is meant to be among Jews and Gentiles for whom
Christ died. The section in 14:19–23 is directed toward the positive
upbuilding of different groups within the Roman community. The metaphor of edification portrays the community as a household built of both
Jews and Gentiles. Edification is the practice of radical mutuality.

Paul makes it explicit that the strong are responsible for the stumbling
of the weak. They jeopardize unity, which Paul depicts as God's work
(14:20). The strong are instructed to change their behavior, whereas the
weak are not, except in relation to respect and welcome. The accommodation of Gentiles toward Jewish Christians does not require a change of
conviction but a change of ethical behavior. Because "those who have
doubts are condemned if they eat" (14:23) has the weak in view, the weak
are not encouraged to change their conviction. The change of eating
practice is stated, surprisingly, as lack of faith or weakness in faith. This
is a striking reversal of the general interpretation of Paul.

When Paul urges the strong "to bear with the weaknesses of the
weak," he urges them to practice radical mutuality by "holding up" their
weaknesses (15:1). Paul calls for the strong to practice solidarity with the
weak. In 15:3–6 Paul grounds the practice of solidarity with the weak in
the praxis of Christ. The two groups are "to live in harmony with one
another, in accordance with Christ Jesus" (Rom. 15:5). Paul advocates
pluralism of differences grounded on one radical aspect of his Christol-
ogy, that is, Christ's solidarity with the weak.

CONCLUSION

My interpretation of the "weak" and the "strong" in Romans highlights
how different identities of the weak and the strong were being socially constructed within a particular sociohistorical context and how the unequal
relationship between the strong and the weak was shaping the understanding of the marginal cultural identity of the "weak" as "difference," as

"difference" to be disregarded, excluded, and suppressed. Further, my reading of Paul's stance toward the weak and the strong suggests a politics of difference that is to be construed not as mere tolerance of difference, but as radical mutuality based on the practice of solidarity with the weak.

Today's call for multicultural reading of the Bible starts from a critical awareness that many biblical scholars, students, and ordinary readers of the Bible have been implicated in a universalizing reading practice which tends to assimilate and suppress a diversity of reading practices. If such a universalizing interpretation privileges the interests of the dominant culture over against other, marginal cultures, multicultural reading of the Bible needs to problematize, interrogate, and uncover the unequal relationships underlying different readings of the Bible.

Multicultural reading, of course, advocates a diversity of readings, which come from different social locations of races, genders, cultures, and nations. Multicultural reading takes an inclusive stance toward those different readings, denouncing exclusionary practice. Yet the goal of multicultural reading should not be perceived as a multiple/quantitative inclusion of differences. Rather, it is a reading practice that challenges the unequal relationships among different readings of the Bible in both local/national and global/international contexts and promotes the interdependent relationships among different readings through an equal/qualitative inclusion of differences.

NOTES

1. Jacques Derrida, *Margins of Philosophy* (Chicago: University of Chicago Press, 1982), 94.

2. Susan Bordo, "Feminism, Postmodernism, and Gender-Scepticism," in *Feminism/Postmodernism*, ed. L. Nicholson (New York: Routledge, 1990), 133–56. See the reference to similar resistance by Africans to postmodern valuing of difference in chapter 8 of this volume, by Robert Brawley.

3. Iris Marion Young, *Justice and the Politics of Difference* (Princeton, NJ: Princeton University Press, 1990), 158.

4. Ibid., 164.

5. Linda Gordon, "The Trouble with Difference," unpublished paper.

6. Susan Gallagher, *Postcolonial Literature and the Biblical Call for Justice* (Jackson: University Press of Mississippi, 1994), 7–8.

7. Ibid., 14.

8. Homi Bhabha, *The Location of Culture* (New York: Routledge, 1994), 4.

9. Ibid., 32.

10. Musa Dube, "Reading for Decolonization," *Semeia* 75 (1996): 38; Kwok Pui-Lan, "Reponses to the *Semeia* Volume on Postcolonial Criticism," *Semeia* 75 (1996): 212.

11. R. S. Sugirtharajah, "Imperial Critical Commentaries: Christian Discourse and Commentarial Writings in Colonial India," *Journal for the Study of the New Testament* 73 (1999): 88.

12. Richard Horsley, "Submerged Biblical Histories and Imperial Biblical Studies," in *The Postcolonial Bible*, ed. R. Sugirtharajah (Sheffield: Sheffield Academic Press, 1990), 154.

13. Ibid., 167–68.

14. Suh Kwang Sun, "A Biographical Sketch of an Asian Theological Consultation," in *Minjung Theology: People as the Subjects of History*, ed. Commission on Theological Concerns of the Christian Conference of Asia (Maryknoll, NY: Orbis Books, 1983), 16.

15. Ahn Byung Mu, "Jesus and the *Minjung* in the Gospel of Mark," in *Minjung Theology: People as the Subjects of History*, 138–52.

16. Suh Nam Dong, "Toward a Theology of Han," in *Minjung Theology: People as the Subjects of History*, 58. See Andrew Sung Park, *The Wounded Heart of God: The Asian Concept of Han and the Christian Doctrine of Sin* (Nashville: Abingdon, 1993).

17. Kang Won Don, *The Theology of Mul* (Seoul: Han Wool, 1992).

18. Suh Nam Dong, *In Search of Minjung Theology* (Seoul: Hangil, 1984).

19. Ahn Byung Mu, *The Development of the Korean Minjung Theology in the 1980s* (Seoul: The Korea Theological Study Institute, 1990), 348–65.

20. Kim Jin Ho, "*Minjung* as the Subject of History: Reappraisal on '*Minjung*' of *Minjung* Theology," *Theological Thought* 80/1 (1993): 21–47.

21. Park Soon Kyung, "National Reunification and *Minjung* Theology: Toward a New Development of *Minjung* Theology," *Theological Thought* 80 (1993): 56–57.

22. Following G. Bornkamm, Robert Karris and Victor Furnish are leading voices for an affirmative answer to this question. See R. Karris, *The Romans Debate*, ed. K. Donfried (Peabody, MA: Hendricksen, 1991), 65–84; V. Furnish, *The Love Command in the New Testament* (Nashville: Abingdon, 1972).

23. See W. Kümmel, *Introduction to the New Testament* (Nashville: Abingdon, 1975), 305–20; Neil Elliott, *The Rhetoric of Romans: Argumentative Constraint and Strategy and Paul's Dialogue with Judaism* (Sheffield: Sheffield Academic Press, 1990), 9–43.

24. See A. Segal, *Paul the Convert: The Apostolate and Apostasy of Saul the Pharisee* (New Haven, CT: Yale University Press, 1990), 228–33; P. Gooch, *Dangerous Food: 1 Corinthians 8–10 in Its Context* (Waterloo, ON: Wilfrid Laurier University Press, 1993).

25. Mark Nanos, *The Mystery of Romans* (Minneapolis: Fortress Press, 1996), 91. For a similar challenge from a different approach, see P. Tomson, *Paul and the Jewish Law: Halakha in the Letters of the Apostle to the Gentiles* (Minneapolis: Fortress, 1990), 221–81.

26. D. Georgi, *Theocracy in Paul's Praxis and Theology* (Minneapolis: Fortress, 1991), 97.

PART THREE

Ministerial Formation

CHAPTER 11

Teaching Pastoral Care and Counseling in the Cross-Cultural Classroom

Homer U. Ashby Jr.

The McCormick context is marked by diversity in many ways. While McCormick is a seminary of the Presbyterian Church (U.S.A.), the students represent at least a dozen different denominations. Presbyterian students comprise the largest percentage (45 percent), followed next by United Church of Christ (20 percent) and Baptist (10 percent). In addition to the diversity of denominational representation, McCormick is also diverse racially. No one racial-ethnic group is a majority of the student body. Of the students, 38 percent are African American, 39 percent White, 6 percent Latino/a, 4 percent Asian, and 12 percent are international; 55 percent are female and 45 percent male. One-third of the students live on campus, the other two-thirds in the metropolitan Chicago area. Students who come to McCormick seek this multicultural context. Faculty and staff share this desire to live and work in a multicultural context.

MULTICULTURAL AND CROSS-CULTURAL

The multicultural makeup of McCormick generates a number of cross-cultural dynamics. I am making a distinction here between multicultural and cross-cultural. Multicultural refers to the arrangement in which a number of cultures exist side by side with one another. Multicultural is a passive given, in which persons find themselves coexisting in the same space or context. Cross-cultural assumes multiculturality but takes it a step further. Cross-cultural describes the intentional effort to seek to be influenced by other cultures. At its best cross-culturality is the commitment persons make to one another to allow themselves to be transformed by encounter with each other's different cultures. In the cross-cultural context, persons seek change and transformation. They welcome the changes that will occur within them individually and among them as a community. In the multicultural context, there may exist some cross-cultural dynamics. However, the multicultural context does not expect or encourage the kind of transformation expected in the cross-cultural context.

The cross-cultural dynamics of mutual influence and transformation reflect not only a sociological reality at McCormick, but also a commitment McCormick makes out of its understanding of the Christian faith. To be a Christian is to understand one's self as participating in a process of growth and change. Christian formation not only recognizes the need for exposure to others (strangers, outcasts, the poor, enemies) but encourages that those encounters lead to transformed relationships. Strangers are to become neighbors. Enemies are to become friends. Colleagues are to become family. Such transformation is expected for Christian growth and development.

Within the McCormick context, mutual transformation occurs in all aspects of the McCormick community's life, especially in McCormick classrooms. In the acquisition of knowledge, skills, and values, McCormick students experience the dynamics of cross-cultural transformation. Students are encouraged and expected to be open to the cultural outlook of others and in that openness to experience other cultures shaping and reshaping their lives of faith.

CROSS-CULTURAL PASTORAL CARE

In recent years a variety of approaches to cross-cultural pastoral care has emerged. The three that I would like to focus on in this article are: (1) cultural dis-embeddedness; (2) increased cultural competency; and (3) care-receiver-based/caregiver-led pastoral care.

Cultural Dis-embeddedness

One of the chief impediments to cross-cultural pastoral care and counseling is a lack of awareness of one's own spiritual/cultural groundedness. Such cultural groundedness inhibits the caregiver's capacity to hear the pain and distress of the person who has come to him for care. The caregiver's assumptions about the nature of the problem or its solution may be so rooted in her own cultural worldview that she misses altogether what the care-receiver is seeking and would find helpful. I find this particularly the case when students encounter a person from another culture whose expectation is that the caregiving student has an answer for the particular problem he or she is presenting. Working from psychotherapeutic assumptions that the answer lies within the person and that the viewpoints of the counselor should be set aside, the student caregiver often presents a confusing and disappointing response to the request for help by failing to reveal his or her viewpoint on the problem. What the care receiver seeks is someone with authority and expertise to state forthrightly what the problem is and what the care receiver should do. If the caregiver is too embedded in his or her own assumptions, then the care giving will not be helpful to the person from the other culture who, working out of another set of assumptions, is expecting something different in response.

Another element to examine in one's cultural groundedness is biases that exist either about the person or about the person's culture. All of us have grown up in a cultural context where some form of bias or prejudice has been expressed about another culture or the persons from that culture. Although time, education, and horizon-stretching experiences lessen the influence of those biases on us, remnants of those earlier influences may persist. And in the stress and intimacy that often accompany pastoral care situations, the old influences may emerge. Most often in pastoral care giving, these biases will take the form of value judgments about either the person or the person's cultural perspective. Those who provide pastoral care to persons from other cultures should be mindful to withhold judgment about issues such as time, money, closeness or distance in relationships, work, hygiene, and outlook on life and faith until they understand fully the meaning of these themes from the cultural perspective of the care receiver.

Pastoral caregivers should also be aware of how their own previous pastoral care experiences have influenced the care they provide. Those previous pastoral care experiences, both good and bad, certainly influence the nature of the care the pastoral caregiver provides. Pastoral care that is modeled on a good pastoral care experience of one's own, without the caregiver's reflecting on how it may be received by a care seeker from another culture, can be ineffective and perhaps even harmful. Vice versa, a pastoral caregiver's previous experience of a bad pastoral care encounter may be a model of good care from the perspective of the care receiver from another culture.

In the literature[1] self-awareness is identified as a key to effective learning in the helping professions.

> Self-awareness is the key to effective learning. As a practitioner, I am responsible to understand the spiritual and cultural characteristics of life narrative that shape my web of meaning. . . . By placing boundaries around my web of meaning, I am able within the context of a pastoral relationship to recognize the distinctive grounding of another person, the otherness of the human being before me.[2]

Self-awareness enables caregivers to see the assumptions, biases, and previous pastoral care experiences that may interfere with their capacity to move out of the groundedness and effectively enter into the worldview and experiences of persons from another culture.

Cultural Competency

Closely related to self-awareness, cultural competency is identified as a helpful element or approach to cross-cultural pastoral care. The development of cultural competency involves the acquisition of certain capacities in the practice of pastoral care. Anderson has identified five steps (marks) that mark the path for spiritual/cultural competency:

1. The capacity to know and explain one's own "spiritual/cultural set," one's own spiritual/cultural groundedness
2. The capacity to identify experiences and information that are outside of one's own spiritual/cultural references, to identify and learn about "otherness"
3. The capacity to demonstrate multispiritual/cultural attitudes, approaches, and skills leading to effective communication and relating to those with other cultural sets
4. The capacity to identify contextual or relational barriers, as well as one's own limitations, in communication and pastoral practice
5. The capacity to demonstrate respect within and willingness to learn from and evaluate the process of multispiritual/cultural interaction

In Anderson's steps, self-awareness is included as one of the competencies. In other cross-cultural approaches, self-awareness stands more alone as an approach to cross-cultural pastoral care. That is why I identified it as a separate approach. The remaining four steps comprise what I call knowledge and skills necessary for cross-cultural pastoral care. In addition to the knowledge of the cultural self, there is the knowledge of cultural boundaries. The knowledge of cultural boundaries entails the capacity to refrain from cultural imposition, that is, confusing the experience of others with my own and assuming that their experience is the same as mine.

This kind of cultural differentiation also applies across cultural experiences. In the summer of 2004 an African American church group from Chicago attending a denominational conference in Cincinnati, Ohio, lost five of its members who were sucked under and drowned in a downtown fountain. The grief and loss of this group from Chicago should not be compared to the grief and loss of families and friends who lost loved ones in the tsunami that occurred in and around the Indian Ocean. Obviously the difference in the number of lives lost makes for a distinction between the two experiences of loss and grief; however, the cultural factors associated with death, loss, and grief may make for even more profound differences in the way the two different cultures, African American and Southeast Asia, respond to these tragedies and are in need of pastoral care.

Contextual and relational barriers include language, customs, rituals, construction of reality, and trust, to name just a few. Pastoral care providers who wish to care cross-culturally must know what the barriers are, if and how they can be crossed, and whether it is even advisable to attempt to cross them. It might even be better to talk about combining steps 3 and 4, because so much of what makes for effective cross-cultural communication has to do with understanding the limits (or barriers) of such communication, as well as having the sensitivity (or attitudes) to know if, how, and when to attempt cross-cultural communication. It takes great skill to know how to navigate the complicated waters of cross-cultural communication. This is why Anderson's comment regarding step 5 is so accurate, "Ultimately the other person is my teacher." The capacity to demonstrate respect for the cultural realities and sensitivities of others requires a willingness to learn from others. And any evaluation of the process, including how effective we are in the pastoral care we provide, must rely upon accepting the feedback of the other for whom we are attempting to care. More than knowledge and skill, cross-cultural pastoral care competency depends on the willingness of the care provider to be led in how best to bring comfort and care to the other.

While care and comfort are important, a third aspect of cross-cultural pastoral care and counseling is the exercise of the values of passion and advocacy. Fukuyama and Sevig[3] have developed a framework for multicultural competency. Anderson borrowed from their framework when he recommended his five steps for spiritual/cultural competency. In addition to personal (or self) awareness, knowledge, and skills, Fukuyama and Sevig have added passion and action. Passion is defined as a deep personal reason for caring about/doing this work and the ability to articulate this to others. Such passion manifests itself in the caregiver's ability to communicate compassion and empathy; the ability to communicate/share strong feelings of anger, fear, love, excitement, guilt, sorrow, and so on when appropriate; and the ability to lead with heart in addition to head. Action is the ability to behave/act in a manner consistent with awareness, knowledge, skills, passion.

Fukuyama and Sevig want to make sure that the counselor not only has knowledge and skills, but is able to utilize the knowledge and skills in such a way that the counselor's passion and commitment come through. In many cultures the too dispassionate counselor comes across as either untrustworthy or uncaring. If the person receiving care can see the caregiver as a fully human person with deep feelings and personal conviction, then there is more reason to trust and make one's self more available to that caregiver's care. Juan Segundo's excellent treatment of past hidden motives of pastoral action explains why there may be suspicion in some cultures of the motivation of any caregiver from the West.[4] But even though passion might be added to self-awareness, knowledge, and skills, these are not enough according to Fukuyama and Sevig. Pastoral caregivers who come from positions of power and privilege must also be able to recognize the oppression that exists in any given care situation *and* be wiling to take some proactive steps to relieve the oppressive condition. They must be cognizant of the oppressive factors in a given cultural context that may be causing the pain and discomfort the person is feeling. To provide solace is not enough. Such curative approaches may relieve the pain but do nothing to address what may be causing the pain. What is needed is a more preventive intervention that has the possibility to stop the pain from occurring in the first place. The caregivers must look at their own sense of passion and action to determine whether or not their interventions, no matter how noble and well-intended, may be contributing to the discomfort of a particular care situation.

Care-Receiver-Based/Caregiver-Led Pastoral Care

A third approach to cross-cultural pastoral care shifts focus from the work of the caregiver to the perspective of the care receiver. In this care-receiver-based approach, the therapist is led more than leads. This approach expands Anderson's step 5, in which the other person is our teacher. There are two major elements to this approach. The first is that the care receiver has a perspective on his or her problem that can be of use in the care. It would be very important to learn from the care receiver what his or her perception of the problem is, what has been helpful or not helpful in the past, what role and/or action he or she wants the caregiver to take in order to improve the situation. The caregiver may not agree altogether with the perceptions of the care receiver, but it is crucial to have the care receiver's perceptions available to the extent that they help both caregiver and care receiver have the best and most complete information at their disposal. Secondly, the care-receiver-based/caregiver-led approach recognizes that the care receiver has certain assets that can help in the alleviation of pain and empowerment for change. Again, if all of the assets in the situation are seen as residing only in the expertise and action of the caregiver, the insight and energy needed for successful resolution of the situation are severely diminished.

As with all caregiving strategies, there are beneficial and detrimental features to each of the three approaches to cross-cultural pastoral care. Awareness of one's own cultural embeddedness is foundational and is essential to support any of the approaches that have been discussed thus far. Without it, the caregiver can make false assumptions, entertain negative biases, or act on limited experiences. Moreover, the primary agent in this approach is the caregiver. It ignores, in a way, the presence of the person from the other culture. If the caregiver can get it right, then all of the challenges and possibilities of cross-cultural pastoral care can be effectively addressed. Competency and capacity building move in a positive direction toward a better understanding of the other person's culture and the nature of the pastoral care need, but they are focused on the empowerment of the counselor. And if certain capacities are not included in the mix, their absence may thwart or eliminate the effectiveness of those capacities that are employed. The care-receiver-based/caregiver-led approach encourages the care receiver to become more visible in the pastoral care process. The perspectives of the care receiver become more prominent and have the potential to add more insight and energy to the care process. However, what if the caregiver sees problems with the assessment and use of power by the care receiver? How does one challenge without seeming culturally insensitive or unwilling to relinquish power or advocating for the oppressive status quo?

Although there are plusses and minuses associated with each of the three approaches, I think that a more optimal approach is achieved if the pastoral caregiver in a cross-cultural context uses all three approaches. A combination of all three helps to relieve some of the negative fallout, in that some of the approaches exist in order to minimize the problems with one or more of the other approaches. In addition, what is positive in each approach is available, which would not be the case if only one approach was chosen.

This methodological approach is similar to that adopted by John Patton, who identified three paradigms that have defined pastoral care over the ages.[5] The first was the classical paradigm, in which the use of words was prominent in pastoral care. The second paradigm, which began at the start of the twentieth century, he refers to as the clinical paradigm, in which the person of the pastor was the significant element. The third paradigm, which began in the 1960s and '70s, is the communal contextual paradigm, in which the importance of community and context are the chief elements in any pastoral care situation. Patton describes how each of the paradigm shifts was a critique of, and an attempt to improve on, the previous paradigm. However, this does not mean that in our current pastoral care we should diminish the importance of words for pastoral care or forgo clinical insights or the use of the person as an agent for healing. Instead we should use all three paradigms in the optimal healing of the people of God.

CROSS-CULTURAL CLASSROOM EXPERIENCE

In structuring the course I attempt to be sensitive to the different ways in which students learn. Teaching and learning vary across cultures. Moreover, individuals within cultures learn differently. Consequently I offer in the class three different ways of learning and try to integrate them. Each week the class is divided into three parts. Readings are assigned weekly and are the basis for my classroom presentation and whole class discussion. The second part of the class models or provides an example of the theme or topic for that week. I will ask a student to role play a person seeking pastoral care, and I will provide the care. Later in the course, I may have a student provide care for me as I play a role, or have two students play the roles of caregiver and care receiver. The third part of the class is group practice of pastoral care. Students are placed into triads, and the same triad gathers each week. In the triads they rotate among three roles: caregiver, care receiver, and observer. For fifteen minutes the caregiver and care receiver meet while being observed by the third student. After five minutes of feedback and evaluation they switch roles. Twenty minutes later they switch roles again, so that each student has had the opportunity to be a caregiver, a care receiver, and an observer. With this arrangement students have three ways to learn: cognitive reflection, modeling, and practical experience. Because no one learning approach is exclusively used, students from different cultures can learn using their culture's preferred approach, but also learn using a different learning style.

The required readings reflect at least three different cultural perspectives. In the class discussions I point out how cultural differences might apply to a given pastoral care method or approach. I also encourage students to bring their own cultures to bear as a critical lens through which to analyze cases and pastoral care situations.

When I teach pastoral care and counseling, one of the images I use is that of a dance. I tell students that we as caregivers are dancing with the care receiver. As we dance, sometimes the care receiver leads, guiding us in the discussion of his or her hopes, fears, sorrows, and understandings. At other times we as caregivers are leading, guiding the discussion in ways that help to clarify, demonstrate empathy, and encourage reflection, praise, and growth. In this way I introduce students to the care-receiver-based/caregiver-led approach.

In the basic course on pastoral care and counseling I begin my introduction to the dance with a variety of definitions of pastoral care. As we review these ten or so definitions, I try to get students to see that no one definition of pastoral care can do justice to what we do. Moreover, I acknowledge with them that some of the definitions resonate within them and others just leave them cold. Each author came to a definition of pastoral counseling out of his or her own set of knowledge, skills, and values, that is, out of his or her own cultural context. In this sense each of the definitions is an attempt to be a "generic" definition of pastoral care, but each one represents a culturally specific definition. I encourage students to think about the definition of pastoral care they will be creating during the course. They should borrow from the many definitions that feel right to them and set aside the others that do not. I also encourage them to remember that the persons with whom they will meet will all have their own definitions of pastoral care. Some of their care receiver's definitions may in fact be some of the definitions they have set aside. Consequently, the introduction of the definitions is an introduction to the mutual influence associated with cross-cultural pastoral care. Students must be open to the way in which their care receivers desire care, in addition to the ways in which they have come to know how they want to provide care.

In the course I not only try to employ pedagogy of cross-cultural pastoral care that cognitively introduces the subject; I also try to experientially create classroom experiences that embody cross-cultural encounter. As with any dance, partners are chosen and the dancers come close to one another. So I put students together in groups of three for one of the experiential parts of the course. In these triads students will rotate among three roles: caregiver, care receiver, and observer. In putting the groups together, I intentionally seek to provide as much cross-cultural exposure as possible. Groups are mixed culturally, racially, and by gender. It might be easier for a group made up of all African Americans or all Koreans to form trusting relationships, but in the cross-cultural classroom the intentional mixing of cultures fosters cross-culture mutual impact and skill building in how to create trusting relationships across cultures.

I like the dance metaphor for learning and providing pastoral care because persons are forced to embrace one another emotionally. In no other social activity are strangers expected to forgo standard physical distance and bring their bodies together. Similarly, students are expected to share in their small groups about issues or concerns that they ordinarily would keep hidden. Because of the cultural differences around closeness and distance both emotionally and physically, I have students begin the dance slowly and with an embrace with whose emotional and physical distance they feel comfortable. In the first gathering of the small groups, I instruct the students to share with one another an experience where they received good pastoral care and an experience where they received poor pastoral care. One student takes fifteen minutes to share the two experiences while another student listens and the third student observes. After the fifteen minutes of sharing, the observer gives evaluative feedback to the caregiver, and for five minutes all three engage in conversation about what they saw and experienced. Then the students rotate in their roles so that at the end of an hour each student has been a caregiver, a care receiver, and an observer. Beginning with the experiences of good and bad pastoral care, students can begin the dance of opening up and being open to one another without too much emotional vulnerability too soon.

The following week the pace of the dance quickens, but not too quickly. I ask each student to select an issue or a concern in their life at the present moment. The issue or concern should be one that they would feel comfortable in sharing in the group, significant enough that it warrants working on and will take some time to address. Each week students return to their issue or concern in order to receive pastoral care in the triad. I instruct the caregivers to be led by the care receivers. In the dance of pastoral care, the care receivers have the freedom and the power to decide what dance will be danced and to take the lead. Even if the care receiver is not sure what to talk about, the caregiver only makes suggestions of things to talk about and leaves the choice up to the care receiver. The flow of the dance goes back and forth with the care receiver providing primary lead, but at times the caregiver provides the lead, offering suggestions, clarifications, prompts, and advice if asked. Both caregiver and care receiver are transformed in the process as they lead and are led into a dance that reveals to them both new insights and possibilities for faith, life, and witness.

For assessment I do not use exams or term papers. I did so earlier in my teaching career but found them not helpful for two reasons. First, a high score on a test or a well-written term paper did not necessarily translate into the skill delivery of pastoral care. Second, written tests and papers often disadvantaged students for whom English was not their first language. I use two primary assessment tools to avoid those problems. The first is verbatims. Each student presents two verbatims in which they give a word-by-word account of the pastoral care encounter. The verbatims allow me to see how the student is applying the learnings from the course in the actual delivery of pastoral care. The grading of the verbatim is based upon how well the student is able to take the readings, discussion, modeling, and practice in class and apply them to the care of another person. The second assessment instrument is a journal. Students are required to keep a journal and submit its contents three times during the semester. The journal is an integrative exercise in which I ask students to reflect on the various elements of the course and discuss what insights, growth, and development they have experienced as caregivers. While the verbatims show cross-cultural capacities and competencies, the journals reflect the transformation the students have made in their appropriation of the course material and experiences.

The change and growth in cross-cultural pastoral care and counseling apply not only to the students, but also to me. A case example involves a Latino male student, Frank, about fifty-five years old, who pastors a Pentecostal church in Chicago. A parishioner of his had come to him for care around the loss of her husband's job and her anxiety about how the family was going to make it. Frank was short on empathic statements that focused on presence and listening. Rather, he gave her a long sermonette on the need for her to stay strong in her faith, believe that the Lord would look out for her, and pray. For this first verbatim I gave him a barely passing grade and encouraged him to read more in the texts about empathic responses and to practice them in his small group. Frank came up to me after the class in which I returned the verbatim and explained to me what had occurred as result of his pastoral care. After meeting with his parishioner, he had called a number of members of the church and asked them to donate to a fund that would support the parishioner in her time of need. A few days later he met with the parishioner and inquired about his instructions to her to pray and have faith. She indicated that she had done so. Frank then reported to her that the Lord had heard her prayers and gave her a check to cover their expenses for the next month. This was Frank's way of living out the definition of pastoral care made famous by Carroll Wise: Pastoral care is the art of communicating the gospel at the point of a person's need. From the viewpoint of a classical or clinical paradigm, Frank had not provided effective pastoral care. But from a communal/contextual perspective, Frank had offered excellent pastoral care. Drawing upon the resources within the community and operating in line with the contextual expectations of the pastor in this moment of crisis, Frank had effectively responded to the need that this parishioner presented. This was a transformative moment for me. I began to be open to an expanded way of providing care that was more concretely based and saw the pastoral caregiver as an active provider of resources to meet a concrete need. What at first seemed "gimmicky" to me proved to be faithful and effective, given the cultural context within which Frank was ministering. That was six years ago. Since then I have sought to be more open to change in my understanding of pastoral care as different cultural perspectives offer me a broader vision of what it means to care for God's people.

NOTES

1. Robert G. Anderson, "The Search for Spiritual/Cultural Competency in Chaplaincy Practice: Five Steps That Mark the Path," *Journal of Health Care Chaplaincy* 13, no. 2 (2004); David W. Augsburger, *Pastoral Counseling across Cultures* (Louisville, KY: Westminster/John Knox Press, 1986); Valli Kanuha and Beth Ritchie, "Six Steps to Creating and Maintaining Culturally Diverse Social Work Practice" (unpublished manuscript, 1992); Mary Fukuyama and Todd Sevig, "Cultural Diversity in Pastoral Care," *Journal of Health Care Chaplaincy* 13, no. 2 (2004): 25–42; and Paul Pederson, *A Handbook for Developing Multicultural Awareness* (Alexandria, VA: American Counseling Association, 1994).

2. Robert G. Anderson, "The Search for Spiritual/Cultural Competency," 12–13.

3. Mary A. Fukuyama and Todd D. Sevig, *Integrating Spirituality into Multicultural Counseling* (Thousand Oaks, CA: Sage Publications, 1999).

4. Juan Luis Segundo, *The Hidden Motives of Pastoral Action: Latin American Reflections* (Maryknoll, NY: Orbis Books, 1978).

5. John Patton, *Pastoral Care in Context: An Introduction to Pastoral Care* (Louisville, KY: Westminster/John Knox Press, 1993).

CHAPTER 12

"La Gran Encisera":[1] *Barcelona and Education for Interfaith Ministry in the Shadow of Terror*

Robert A. Cathey

Religion is not simply as is generally supposed an inherently virtuous human quest for God. It is merely a final battleground between God and man's self-esteem. In that battle even the most pious practices may be instruments of human pride. . . . The worst form of intolerance is religious intolerance, in which the particular interests of the contestants hide behind religious absolutes. The worst form of self-assertion is religious self-assertion in which under the guise of contrition before God, He is claimed as the exclusive ally of our contingent self. "What goes by the name of 'religion' in the modern world . . . is to a great extent unbridled human self-assertion in religious disguise."

Christianity rightly regards itself as a religion, not so much of man's search for God, in the process of which he may make himself God; but as a religion of revelation in which a holy and loving God is revealed to man as the source and end of all finite existence against whom the self-will of man is shattered and his pride abased. But as soon as the Christian assumes that he is, by virtue of possessing this revelation, more righteous, because more contrite, than other men, he increases the sin of self-righteousness and makes the forms of a religion of contrition the tool of his pride.[2]

WHY BARCELONA?

In the 1980s, as a graduate student at Union Theological Seminary (New York) living in Hoboken, New Jersey, I was a frequent commuter through the World Trade Center. I was horrified at the tragedies that unfolded on September 11, 2001. Part of me disbelieved that the towers were no longer there, for they are so central to my memories and imagination of that great city. Given a change in life circumstances, I knew I could have been a victim myself if such attacks had occurred twenty years prior.

In the months that followed, I found myself asked as a theologian to interpret the tragic events and the global responses. I was torn between the call to understand the complexity of conflicts leading up to 9/11 and the desire for a just defense against further such attacks. I searched for a concrete way to respond to the questions I was hearing from congregations, colleagues, students, our own children, and within myself.

On December 2, 2001, the Chicago Parliament of the World's Religions held an annual fundraiser at the Palmer House Hotel, the site of the 1993 Centennial Parliament. The Rev. Dirk Ficca, executive director, announced that there would be a fourth parliament in 2004 in one of the Parliament's partner cities. At the end of the banquet I approached Dirk with a brief proposal: why not organize a group of theological students and faculty from Hyde Park to attend the Parliament? In the months ahead, this project became my small way of confronting the shadow of terror and complexity of conflicts that 9/11 manifested.

Little did I know that the historic city of Barcelona would be our destination, and that the shadow of terror would fall over Madrid and Spain on March 11, 2004. Two colleagues asked me if it was wise to take students to Barcelona after 3/11, and one student we had selected to go dropped out. But by spring 2004, two years of planning and preparations for attending the Parliament were already behind us. Having visited Barcelona in October 2003, I had fallen under the spell of the city the poet Joan Maragall called *la gran encisera*, "the great enchantress."[3] In fact, attending a parliament of the world's religions for the purposes of dialogue and partnership was a way to witness against one effect of terror: the stereotyping of Muslims and Islam as inherently violent.

The reader may also wonder, What is a Presbyterian theologian doing in the midst of the populist interfaith movement? And what does this have to do with multicultural theological education? I, for one, came kicking and screaming into the interfaith movement. Having grown up in a conservative southern Presbyterian congregation, I was fortunate to be educated by liberal Protestants at Davidson College in North Carolina, who introduced me to philosophy and the comparative study of religion. During my early years in graduate school at Union Theological Seminary, I became convinced that the course of philosophy in the late modern world had undermined the numerous attempts of various religious apologists to demonstrate (based on foundations of certainty) the exclusive truthfulness, moral superiority, and teleological or salvific efficacy of their particular traditions. Working on a dissertation at Duke University, I also was convinced that many Protestant appeals to special revelation (in the gospel, the Bible, proclamation) take the form of arguments or appeals to foundational certainty, and these theories were undermined by the hermeneutical turn in biblical studies since 1945. Therefore, in the marketplace of cultures, the unique and competing claims to truthfulness and wisdom between the world's traditions are leveled epistemologically. Such claims make sense internally to those who practice a faith, but their justifications also are grounded internally, not externally from some tradition-independent point of view. In light of these turns in philosophical theology, conversation and respectful disputation across religious traditions are essential if many religious scholars are to be truthful about where philosophical, biblical, and theological journeys are leading us today.

In 1989, I began teaching undergraduates at Monmouth College in western Illinois, about the same time multiculturalism had become an imperative for North American higher education, in terms of student enrollment, faculty hiring, and curricular reform. I was soon struck with how both multiculturalism and postmodernism in this context included, overtly, the notion that religions are reducible to relative cultural constructs, that is, products of human cultural evolution. The reductive presupposition could be used to equalize the appeals of different cultures and religions to superiority, but it also had the negative effect of cutting the divine or sacred ground out from under the origins and ongoing life of all religions. I had modified my thinking to incorporate a deflation of foundational apologetic claims for a single tradition's uniqueness, but to reduce the faith of others or my own to cultural construction without remainder was to abandon ships that were not sinking. A more faithful reading of the history of religions was that the living God (in the case of Judaism, Christianity, and Islam) or ultimate reality (in the case of Eastern traditions) and human cultural creatures both engage in the construction and reformation of religious traditions over time.

Having retraced these steps, what makes the interfaith movement theologically important is that religious practices and doctrines are being reshaped as the fruit of dialogue and partnership between traditions. In fact, interfaith philosophical theology has recognized that this phenomenon is *as new as* the Middle Ages, when Islamic, Jewish, and Christian scholars heard, read, and responded to each other's appropriations of both scriptural and philosophic traditions.[4] Of course, Spain was one land in the Mediterranean basin where this interchange occurred among the three Western traditions before Christianity came to religious-political hegemony. One reason that makes the interfaith movement important for Protestants and Presbyterians today is that our traditions feel a deep ambivalence about the world's revitalized religions, in part due to the ways they remind us of the Catholic other in our past and present. This ambivalence is exemplified by the quotation from Reinhold Niebuhr and Hendrik Kraemer in my introduction. By learning to come to terms with the religious other from other cultures, we will rediscover the pluralism within our own Christian tradition in new ways that will be fruitful for the ecumenical movement.

BARCELONA AS CONTEXT FOR THEOLOGICAL EDUCATION

Since Spain has enjoyed constitutional religious freedom only since 1978, Barcelona appears a strange place to study interfaith relations, especially if one lives in Chicago.[5] However, one discovery of our engagement with the Parliament was the new Spain and the new Europe. Due to rapid growth in manufacturing jobs in Spain's economy, the nation's population has been growing by 1 percent each year due to immigration. In conjunction with the Parliament, UNESCO sponsored an international forum of cultures in Barcelona through much of 2004 to inform the public about the growing multicultural population of western Europe. Barcelona is just south of France, where now five to ten percent of the population is Muslim.

Although many Spanish citizens are baptized and educated in church-related schools, religious practice in the institutional church is low, as in much of Europe. We heard one estimate that 85 percent of Barcelona's population was nonobservant. Out of this nonobservant population, some are finding their way into meditation, yoga, and other spiritual practices from the East that do not require official affiliation. The young interfaith movement in Barcelona is made up primarily of progressive Catholics who would like to connect with those who have rediscovered spirituality from the East, as well as Jews and Muslims who have struggled to maintain a public presence in Spain for many centuries. As a North American who encountered Barcelona for the first time in preparation for the Parliament, I was struck with the small number of synagogues (two) and mosques (one) open to the public within the central city itself. We never saw or encountered any Protestant church buildings in the city, although the local Protestant council of Catalonia claims one quarter of a million members in congregations or fellowship groups.

In one sense, the global religious pluralism we were going to encounter was created artificially for about a week by the occurrence of the Parliament in Barcelona. In another sense, we were eavesdropping on conversations in Barcelona about how to negotiate a new era of pluralism in Europe itself, with some different political, social, and cultural assumptions from the ones we presuppose in the U.S. context.[6]

THE PARLIAMENT OF THE WORLD'S RELIGIONS
AS CONTEXT FOR THEOLOGICAL EDUCATION

In our first steps, we convened a group of faculty in Hyde Park who teach courses related to world religions and interfaith dialogue. The presence with us of Dirk Ficca and other staff from the Chicago Parliament office provided timely information on how the Barcelona Parliament was evolving as a unique event. Out of those early conversations, we learned that a typical day at the Parliament would include three basic types of events: *intra*religious programs, *inter*religious programs, and engagement programs. Intrareligious programs would focus on

— "basic understanding of religious and spiritual communities, and the teachings, practices, and dynamics of their traditions";
— "resources and rationales *from within* religious and spiritual communities and movements for dialogue, engagement, and cooperation";
— "tools for intrareligious reflection and dialogue."[7]

Interreligious programs would offer

— "structured opportunities for interreligious encounter and dialogue";
— "sharing the convictions and motivations for engaging with each other and the world";
— "innovative methodologies for interreligious encounter, dialogue and cooperation."[8]

Engagement programs would move toward action through

— "building capacity for religious and spiritual people, communities and organizations to collaborate with guiding institutions in service to a peaceful, just and sustainable future";
— "examples of successful programs and best practices that are addressing critical issues around the world";
— "creative approaches and tools for effective dialogue and collaboration."[9]

Given this structure, we decided to focus our pre-Barcelona course on creating a mutually critical conversation between intrafaith and interfaith learnings.

The Parliament not only offered the structure where these kinds of learnings could occur; it also challenged us to think in terms of the multiple intelligences we bring to learning and the ways we are formed in more than cognitive ways. The Parliament included plenary sessions, symposia, performances, exhibits, an art gallery, film-focused programs, morning observances, open space for dialogue, off-site programs, a solidarity fair, and other special programs. For example, morning observances created opportunities for prayer, meditation, worship, movement, song, study of sacred texts, and so forth, so that persons could encounter sacred practices in someone else's tradition or their own.

PREPARING FOR INTERFAITH ENCOUNTER

In spring 2003 we received permission from McCormick Theological Seminary to take a group of Hyde Park students to Barcelona through the seminary's Travel Seminar program. Sarah J. Tanzer, professor of New Testament and early Judaism, and I were asked to lead the seminar. This decision was ideal for our course, since the students encountered an interfaith teaching team, a Jew and a Christian, from their very first application. Making more than one living faith tradition present in the classroom and in the travel-learning process modeled for students before, during, and after the Parliament the kinds of learning that can happen when living traditions encounter each other face to face.

The Travel Seminar was entitled "Religious Pluralism and Ministry in an Interfaith Age." In our course description we identified four learning goals:

> This course is designed as an inquiry into both tradition-based and inter-religious reasons for interfaith ministry. The fourth Parliament for the World's Religions in Barcelona, Spain (July 7–13) provides the occasion for asking how we prepare to do ministry with persons and communities of more than one faith. What does it mean to engage in Christian ministry in a religiously plural world? Both philosophical and practical issues will be explored. The course is focused around four goals:
>
> 1) Exploration of the intra-religious dimensions of this issue, thinking about, e.g., "who am I with respect to religious pluralism?"
>
> 2) Historical/theological and experiential exploration of non-Christian world religions;
>
> 3) The praxis of forging inter-religious partnerships for social action and mutual understanding;

> 4) Preparation so as to best be able to participate in the Parliament of the World's Religions in Barcelona in a way that furthers the first three goals listed here.[10]

From these goals we developed five objectives that were keyed to course projects before, during, and after the Parliament. They included

> — *Course Objective 1:* Work on the Intrareligious focus by thinking and writing about "Where am I on the map of religious pluralism?" and considering, in general: What happens when we (I, my local faith community, and my denomination) bump up against others? Where is my local worshiping community in relationship to what the denomination says about religious pluralism?

This objective required students to research their own denomination or congregation to discover statements (theological, policy, or documents on missionary activity, evangelism, church growth, or sermons) in which non-Christian religions were recognized. Then they prepared a handout for our first class session in which they were asked to do the following:

> — Describe the key affirmations or policy statements from these documents.
> — Analyze these statements in terms of their presuppositions/attitudes toward interreligious dialogue. Consider also (to the best of your experience/knowledge), does your denomination practice what is stated in the documents?
> — Provide your own honest reflection on where you stand in relationship to these documents.

The course included three Presbyterians, two Pentecostals, two Lutherans, and one United Church of Christ student. This ecumenical diversity was ideal, for they encountered parts of the internal pluralism of their own Christian tradition before encountering the global pluralism of religions in Barcelona. In class discussion there were also moments of insight and honesty around whether they thought their denomination practiced what it proclaims, and where they stood as individuals in relation to institutional statements or expectations. One helpful distinction that Sarah Tanzer introduced into the discussion was that denominations as institutions are required to speak up for their own tradition in all its particularity. What an individual thinks or believes may not be identical with the denominational position or practice. Part of theological inquiry is learning to assess where one stands in relation to the tradition and its institutions and practices. We considered this part of the course crucial to working with students preparing for ministry in particular denominations. Knowing who or what one represents, and exploring how one thinks about and relates oneself to public positions taken by one's denomination or congregation, are a necessary form of self understanding for integrity in interfaith ministry.

> — *Course Objective 2:* Begin an exploration of the Comparative World Religions focus by (a) reading (in an assigned textbook) about at least three world religions other than your own and (b) selecting one to focus on at the Parliament and then reading one other book (chosen from a list) about it prior to the Parliament. Teach a session on your world religion to the rest of the class. At the Parliament spend a large portion of your time in sessions involving that other world religion.

In this part of the course all of us became learners. It is an Hegelian task to survey all the major faith traditions of the world, and neither Sarah Tanzer nor I is a global comparativist by training. However, one can always take first steps in getting to know another tradition, and this allowed students to become teachers among us.[11] Each one was required to make

> An in-class presentation of 30 minutes, followed by 15 minutes of discussion on the world religion you have been assigned or have chosen. This should include introductions to teachings, practices, sacred texts, rituals, etc., and should select 7 key things you think we should be exposed to in order to begin to experience and comprehend what is central to this religious tradition. You are encouraged to engage us on more than the cognitive level. Your fellow students will have read the appropriate scripture texts in preparation for the presentation.[12]

The traditions chosen by our students included Islam, the Sikhs, Hinduism (two presentations), Buddhism (three presentations), and the Yoruba. Our course design was that students at the Parliament would shadow representatives and presentations focusing on the tradition they had summarized. In some cases, like our student who chose the Sikhs who were very present at the Parliament, this worked well. In other cases, students found their chosen tradition limited their options or that the plurality within their tradition required further choices about whom and what to shadow.

> — *Course Objective 3:* Begin observation of and participation in Interreligious Dialogue at Barcelona, as you encounter the

issues talked about in a global forum, as you see seasoned inter-faith leaders interact and consider how this works/doesn't work and why it is significant.

One of the crucial assignments of this course was a daily journal to be kept by each student during the Parliament. They were asked to note

> the questions that are generated and what has been confirmed or disconfirmed. What are you learning about yourself and your comfort level as you explore other religious traditions? What has been reinforced in your understandings of your assigned world religion? What has been startling or new in your under-standing of your world religion? Edit and produce a typed edi-tion of the journal with a post-Barcelona concluding entry.

This self-reflective piece provided some very interesting reading at the end of the course.

We used two aphorisms in the pre-Barcelona part of the course:

> "Map is not territory."[13]
> "Don't look for you in the other."[14]

The pre-Barcelona course did supply some maps. We spent quite a bit of time discussing and arguing with Paul Knitter's four models of Christian interfaith relations:[15]

— The replacement model claims there is "only one true religion" and Christianity is it. Both total and partial variations on this model are surveyed. Karl Barth is made one of the exemplars of this type.
— The fulfillment model claims "the one [religion] fulfills the many" and Christianity is it. Vatican II is made the exemplar.
— The mutuality model claims "many true religions [are] called to dialogue." Raimon Panikkar, John Hick, and some liberation theologians are among the exemplars.
— The acceptance model claims there are "many true religions: so be it." Francis X. Clooney and some postliberals exemplify this type.

Within our class, students could identify themselves and their own com-munities with one or more of these models. They could also see the rela-tive strengths and weaknesses of each type as we problematized Knitter's choice of some of the exemplars with class handouts for discussion.

How did these maps match up with the territory in Barcelona? None of our students observed other Christians engaged in verbal evangelism or proselytism of persons of other faiths at the Parliament. However, they did encounter representatives of new religious movements in the exhibits who were openly proclaiming the virtues of their path. This experience of being "evangelized" by some religious others at the Parliament was an unexpected surprise. It led back to the intrafaith question: Are there appropriate ways within one's own tradition to engage in proclamation, to witness to the claims and values of one's own faith, especially in a setting like the Parliament or any multicultural neighborhood or workplace today?

For our group, the Sikhs of Birmingham, England, were the best witnesses to their tradition in Barcelona. Each day from noon to 3:00 p.m., they served *Langar* ("blessed vegetarian food") to thousands of Parliament participants free of charge in a large tent set up on the Mediterranean beach. Discretely adjoining the dining area were displays about their history, scripture, and practices. We were invited to remove our shoes and wear a head covering during *Langar*. Some members of our group asked if they could help prepare the meal and were invited into the kitchen to participate in chanting and cooking. One student was invited to *Amrit Sanchar*, a ceremony in which a Sikh takes on more responsibilities within the faith. The Sikh spirit of hospitality was overwhelming and made a lasting impression on everyone.

In student reflections on *Langar*, analogies to the Christian Eucharist were quickly drawn. Sarah Tanzer pointed out that, as sacred meals today, *Langar* and Eucharist serve different functions in the two traditions. *Langar* is an intentional shared meal open to all regardless of creed. Eucharist is a meal by which the Christian community identifies its particularity in the world. Some celebrations of Eucharist are only open to members of a specific tradition; others are open to all baptized Christians; but few churches celebrate eucharist for just anyone who happens to come in, the way *Langar* is celebrated. Distinguishing a meal of indiscriminate hospitality from a meal of community identity and formation is important to avoid projecting "you" into "the other."

— *Course Objective 4:* Develop an initial strategy for communicating intrareligious and interreligious learnings from Hyde Park and Barcelona in your own community after the Parliament.

The final project for our course was a "reflective, critical and integrative essay" for sharing what was learned "back at home." It concluded with a "detailed outline or plan for" one of the following:

— Curriculum for an adult or youth study series, Bible study, or focus group for your worshiping community (plan for four sessions);

— Plan for a retreat on a specific topic for your worshiping community or a specified group within it;

— Design for interfaith prayer or liturgy in worship, specifying the setting in which you would like to use it;

— Revision or articulation of your personal faith statement in light of your response to religious pluralism and in the context of your own community's standards and expectations for ordination;

— Program for social action or witness in (interreligious) partnership with persons and communities of your own community and other traditions;

— Strategy for ministry in an interreligious or intrareligious setting: such as on a campus, in a hospital, in a prison, as part of a CPE program;

— A program for self-directed study and action undertaken to grow in interreligious awareness.

This was perhaps the most difficult assignment, since it was fulfilled after the Parliament was over, when students were back in Chicago for the summer. However, at least one student in our group developed a curriculum of three sessions for an adult education class in a local church that she taught with some presentations by me. One surprise we had in this teaching experience was that the presentation of different models of Christian interfaith relations (see above) did not elicit as much concern as the presentation of the challenges raised by the Barcelona Parliament to the crisis of debt among some developing nations. Interfaith relations on the level of belief was acceptable to discuss, but the practical implications of interfaith partnership to address global problems was more stress-producing for some in the class.

— *Course Objective 5:* Prepare for/participate in/and debrief the Barcelona experience.

In preparing our class to attend the Parliament, we showed the video "Peace Like a River," which was made to document the 1993 centennial Parliament in Chicago. As we discussed the video, I recall saying to the students that attending a Parliament was more like going to Woodstock than going to the American Academy of Religion. By design the Parliaments are populist events for a very broad public. They attract many persons who are activists in their own contexts, engaged with a variety of social issues. When you bring together in one place and time so many deeply committed people, and bring them into dialogue with the possibility of future partnership, the rhetoric can become optimistic, idealistic, utopian. The daily experiences of the Parliament range from new information and transformative encounters to a feeling of being jaded and overloaded. Further, we tried to prepare our students for such daily experiences by inviting a colleague from another institution to talk about his experiences with students at the 1999 Parliament in Cape Town, South Africa.

Perhaps we did not emphasize enough the idealism of the Parliament. For a Christian experiencing a Parliament for the first time, there were moments when I said to myself, Is this not a foretaste of the new heaven and new earth? But for some students, the repetition of themes like "peace, love, and harmony" in some programs they attended failed to address the roots of violence, hatred, and injustice that fuel both political and religious conflicts in our age. Our students were asking for a more realistic assessment on the part of the interfaith movement of what it can do to overcome complex global problems that have dimensions beyond religious differences per se.

THE PARLIAMENT OUR LABORATORY

Although we had prepared our students to encounter other religions at the Parliament, we had not prepared them to encounter Spanish Catholic Christianity on the ground. In the middle of the Parliament, the offer came to spend a day visiting Montserrat, the monastic city on top of a mountain thirty-one miles west of Barcelona. Independently we all signed up to go and found ourselves traveling by bus to the most sacred site in that region of Spain. The views atop Montserrat were breathtaking, but some in our group were not prepared to meet pilgrims bringing flowers to place before the shrine of the Black Madonna and kissing her image. One couple found a room in the monastery near the shrine full of wheelchairs, crutches, and canes, and then realized these had been left behind by pilgrims who came seeking healing. From Montserrat we traveled to the village of Olesa at the base of the mountain, where the local community presented an abbreviated version of their annual Passion Play, performed every year during Lent since 1540. On the bus on the way back to Barcelona, the students crowded around Sarah

Tanzer to hear her comments on *La Passió d'Olesa* and its representation of the Gospel narratives. Here was a rich opportunity for interfaith reflection.

With these experiences and the omnipresence of Catholic churches in Barcelona, including Antonio Gaudí's Sagrada Familia (Temple of the Holy Family), our students found their own Christian tradition defamiliarized in a new cultural setting. This suggested to me that one way to introduce interfaith relations with Protestant seminarians is to ask how they have experienced Catholic Christians in their own lives. For some, to recognize the Catholic other as Christian other (the same yet different) is already to incorporate some degree of pluralism into one's own notion of Christian identity.

We were surprised at how much time we spent during the Parliament debriefing our experiences as a group. Our first notion was that, once the Parliament began, we would not see most of the students for a week. But the group kept finding ways to convene over late evening meals to compare experiences. This kind of daily opportunity for sharing, interpreting, and questioning each other's experiences and our own happens less frequently in our other classes.

One difficulty our students faced was finding the religious other "out of context" in brief episodes of encounter. Because many of us were short-term travelers to Barcelona, with a crowded schedule of presentations, panel discussions, and so forth, and the challenge of communicating in a multilinguistic setting, some felt that opportunities for true dialogue were too few. Often one could watch dialogue happening among members of a panel presentation in English, Spanish, Catalan, or French, but issues of translation limited the responses of the audience. The questions and answers tended to be between panel members and a few individuals in attendance, but not with each other. Thus many sessions facilitated presentation of new information and ideas but were less successful in building a short-term community of persons who could walk out in dialogue.

DEBRIEFING ENCOUNTERS IN SPAIN

After the Parliament was over and we had returned to Chicago by our different paths, we reconvened for a final debriefing session. Some of the student observations and suggestions show the need for revisions in how theological educators think about and prepare students for interaction with the interfaith movement today:

— Better preparation is needed for encountering new religious movements that do not fit into the categories of the classic traditions and that are experienced as cults.[16]
— Although precourse work helped a lot, students needed more background on religions they had not covered in their research (e.g., Judaism, Zoroastrianism, the Jains).
 Sessions they attended where Islam was the focus were disappointing. For example, a session entitled "The Headscarf Debate: Religious Dress and Secular Fundamentalism" was a presentation of arguments for *hijab*, the Islamic headscarf, not a debate between different points of view. Understanding between Muslims and Christians in the world after 9/11 and 3/11 needs greater attention.[17]
— Sessions should grapple more deeply with religious differences as well as similarities.
— Paul Knitter's acceptance model of Christian interfaith relations can be more fruitfully explored in seminaries. Students are taught how to read biblical texts closely in Hebrew and Greek, using various critical methods. To add other sacred texts would be a step toward linking biblical studies with interfaith dialogue.[18]

Theological education has a vital role to play vis-à-vis the interfaith movement in the world today. Whereas organizations like the Parliament are capable of staging mass public events that gain attention from the media and people in all walks of life, institutions of theological education have the resources and calling to raise the harder questions of interfaith differences and conflicts that go beyond "peace, love, and harmony." If we can find ways to help our students recognize and maintain the value of many particular differences between religious traditions and continue to be in dialogue with others, then there will be spinoffs as they face intrafaith differences among members of their own tradition and community.

As theological educators, many of us could reflect on why interfaith relations and coalitions are sometimes not as risky for us as encountering the more conservative or progressive members of our own traditions. The interfaith journey that some have made with other traditions now seems to require some intrafaith journeys if we are to open interfaith education to a wider public. In our case, encountering the theological differences within our own group was a helpful preparation for the Parliament and taught us how much we already have in common as members of a theological institution with an ecumenical vision.

TEACHING FOR INTERFAITH PARTNERSHIP AS MEANS
OF INTRARELIGIOUS RENEWAL

In this new century and millennium, our Protestant ecumenical seminaries often find ourselves eclipsed by the growth of evangelical, Pentecostal, and non-Christian movements in North America. Likewise, in politics, economics, and other issues of social justice, mainline Protestants seemed to have lost the cutting edge enjoyed during the heady days when Reinhold Niebuhr and other Christian realists could impact the public debate about issues of policy and principle. As is often the case, the way forward is not to circle up the wagons and declare our moral and theological superiority to both conservative Christian and non-Christian others. The way forward lies in part through a new engagement with the religious pluralism that God has willed for our species, and a rediscovery of the pluralism within our own traditions, communities, and seminaries. Tools for dialogue, partnership, and respectful disagreement are needed if students and teachers are to negotiate the boundaries between traditions and the minefields within their own traditions' internal conflicts. Since Christians trace our roots to a Prince of Peace whose own pilgrimage of faithfulness led him and his followers into conflict with political-religious authorities, we witness to the way of faithfulness when we teach our students the tools for more peaceful, honest, and fruitful relations with our religious others in a time of terror, when overwhelming lethal force seems to many our only sure defense.

NOTES

1. The title is in Catalan, the indigenous language of that region of Spain and parts of southern France, not in Español. It means "the great enchantress."

2. Reinhold Niebuhr, *The Nature and Destiny of Man: A Christian Interpretation* (New York: Charles Scribner's Sons, 1941, 1964), 1:200–201. Quoted material is from Hendrik Kraemer, *The Christian Message in a Non-Christian World* (Grand Rapids: Kregel Pub., 1938, 1963), 212, which reads: "what goes by the name of 'religion' in the world is to a great extent unbridled human self-assertion in religious disguise."

3. Robert Hughes, *Barcelona the Great Enchantress* (Washington, DC: National Geographic, 2004), 19. For much greater detail, see Robert Hughes, *Barcelona* (New York: Random House, 1992).

4. E.g., see three works by David B. Burrell, CSC: *Knowing the Unknowable God: Ibn-Sina, Maimonides, Aquinas* (Notre Dame, IN: University of Notre

Dame Press, 1986); *Freedom and Creation in Three Traditions* (Notre Dame, IN: University of Notre Dame Press, 1993); *Faith and Freedom: An Interfaith Perspective* (Malden, MA: Blackwell Publishing, 2004).

5. John Hooper, "A Dwindling Flock: Religion and the Church," chap. 9 in *The New Spaniards*, rev. ed. (New York: Penguin Putnam, 1986, 1987, 1995), 127.

6. E.g., see Jean Paul Alduy, Javier Otaola, et al., *Secularism, Spiritualities in the City* (Perpignan, France: Ville de Perpignan, 2004). Also available on the city's Web site at: http://www.mairie-perpignan.fr/pdf/Anglais.pdf.

7. *Pathways to Peace: The Wisdom of Listening, the Power of Commitment* (Barcelona: Parliament of the World's Religions, 2004), 24, emphasis added.

8. Ibid.

9. Ibid.

10. Sarah Tanzer authored the course description and syllabus quotations that follow.

11. As survey textbooks, we used Willard G. Oxtoby, ed., *World Religions: Eastern Traditions* and *World Religions: Western Traditions*, 2nd ed. (Toronto: Oxford University Press, 2002). As an overview source, we used Joel Beversluis, ed., *Sourcebook of the World's Religions: An Interfaith Guide to Religion and Spirituality* (Novato, CA: New World Library, 2000).

12. Philip Novak, *The World's Wisdom: Sacred Texts of the World's Religions* (New York: HarperCollins, 1994). Students could substitute Robert E. Van Voorst, *Anthology of World Scriptures* (Toronto: Wadsworth, 2000), a more extensive anthology.

13. From Jonathan Z. Smith, *Map Is Not Territory: Studies in the History of Religions* (Chicago: University of Chicago Press, 1993; Leiden: E. J. Brill, 1978).

14. From a presentation for our pre-Barcelona course on June 21, 2004, by Scott C. Alexander, associate professor of Islam, Catholic Theological Union, on "What It Means to Be a Converted Outsider."

15. Paul F. Knitter, *Introducing Theologies of Religions* (Maryknoll, NY: Orbis Books, 2002).

16. E.g., Ted Peters, *The Cosmic Self: A Penetrating Look at Today's New Age Movements* (New York: HarperCollins, 1991).

17. E.g., see John L. Esposito, *Unholy War: Terror in the Name of Islam* (New York: Oxford University Press, 2002).

18. See Francis X. Clooney, SJ, "Reading the World in Christ: From Comparison to Inclusivism," chap. 5 in Gavin D'Costa, ed. *Christian Uniqueness Reconsidered: The Myth of a Pluralistic Theology of Religions*, Faith Meets Faith series (Maryknoll, NY: Orbis Books, 1990).

CHAPTER 13

Open Worship: Strategies of Hospitality and Questions of Power

Gary Rand

The other day I was eating at my local mall's food court. As I looked around, I began to think, "What if my church reflected the cultural and ethnic diversity represented at the tables around me?" People from the middle class, working class, old people, the disabled, kids, teenagers, Latinos, African Americans, Asians, white folks like me—we were all gathered together, drawn by the power of place, by friends to hang out with and by an inexpensive meal.

The food court in my neighborhood seems to find a way to meet a wide variety of needs for a wide diversity of people. How is that possible? How is it that the people of my neighborhood have turned the mall, a typical beachhead for consumerism and dominant culture, into a place of multicultural community? These are good questions. They remind me of questions we often ask about worship in the halls and classrooms of McCormick Theological Seminary. How is it that our weekly gatherings for worship invite a variety of experiences, or conversely, how is it that our worship gatherings sometime seem exclusive or closed off to certain people? We take these questions seriously at McCormick. It is often in our community worship itself that we find the best opportunities to both ask and respond, to explore and discover. In worship we find opportunities to try things out, believing worship that embraces the depth and wonder of our diverse humanity will not only enrich the life of praise and prayer, ministry and mission at this seminary, but will also provide a rich formative experience in the lives of students who will go out to serve in our increasingly multicultural church.

This brings me back to my experience at the mall. Maybe what goes on at my food court can be of some help to us as we think about multicultural worship.

CONSUMING CULTURE

Of course, not everyone is a fan of the food court at the mall. Many critics rightly argue that the food court can be viewed as an example of white European culture once again plundering other peoples for cultural objects to satisfy its curiosity and fascination with novelty. Building on this perspective, Mark Bangert gives a warning about multicultural worship. He writes, "If going about multicultural worship begins to look like a liturgical version of a world food court," we are acting as nothing more than privileged consumers.[1]

I understand what Bangert is saying, but my experience at my local food court makes me wonder if it is always true. His statement did remind me, however, of my experience at Walt Disney World. Visiting Florida a few years ago, I was fascinated by the Epcot Center and its world village. Many countries of the world are represented in an environment that is clean, safe, and shopping-friendly. I was struck by the fact that aside from an occasional parade, dance, or drama, every country is basically reduced to the two same elements—a restaurant and a gift shop, distinguished only by their characteristic decoration.

If my nearby food court feels to me like a living, breathing, multicultural gathering place, by contrast, Epcot Center felt empty, an elaborate masquerade of impressive facades. To me, Epcot seemed filled with representations expertly crafted but lacking substance—lacking the spirit, the messiness, the complexity—missing the cultural density of actual life. Epcot seemed narrowly conceived to represent the world in such a way that everywhere was essentially the same, save for the decorations, the seasonings, and the choreography.

Think of an Epcot Center approach to multicultural worship. This is a vision that must fuel Mark Bangert's worst fears. Bangert's concern is that rich Westerners take the artifacts of diverse cultures and make them into commodities to be consumed. Epcot gathers in the art, architecture, food, and music of a culture and repackages it, usually in plastic, for American consumption. Decontextualized from their original cultural referents, these exotic cultural symbols become mere products, while their makers are either romanticized or ignored.

Bangert's concern is not unwarranted. This is just what happens, sometimes, in our attempts at multicultural worship. Our new hymnbooks are full of music from around the world, arranged and repackaged for American tastes. In the same way that wicker chairs and exotic textiles from Pier One decorate our homes, these songs give us the pleasure of diversity without having to actually experience it. It only takes a moment of listening to a Caribbean setting of "Halleluja" played on the pipe organ to realize how another culture's music has been decontextualized and re-presented.

POWER

I think the Epcot approach to worship would also frighten Princeton Seminary professor Richard Fenn, but for another reason. Fenn argues persuasively that introducing multicultural diversity has historically been a form of social control. The designers of the Epcot Center, for example, offer us a new world of peace and harmony, made possible not as the result of toleration, mutual respect, or painstaking cross-cultural work, but simply because of the belief that deep down, despite all the diversity, we are all the same—white, middle-class Americans. Likewise, when the American church consumes cultural artifacts from around the world, we are also asserting our own primary position in a hierarchy of value. We like music from around the world in our worship, but not before it is scrubbed up and made presentable. Fenn warns, "Most groups would be well advised to see the movement to achieve diversity within the liturgy as an attempt to incorporate and neutralize smaller, distinct, and diverse groups within a larger institution or community."[2]

The fundamental issue here is one of power. Cultural theorists talk of these power relationships in terms of hegemony—the dominance of one group over others. Epcot Center and the type of worship I have just described have the "look" of multicultural but maintain the hegemony of the dominant group. The usual response among the other groups—whether they be youth, African Americans, Mexicans, Asians, or any number of others—is to attempt assimilation or resistance.

CULTURAL PARTNERSHIPS

Michael Hawn is one of many who argue for a different kind of multicultural worship, one in which there is a true cultural partnership, where "no clear majority dominates and culturally diverse members reflect the surrounding neighborhood and work together in a shared Christian community."[3] Yet this kind of "cultural partnership" does not come easy.

As much as the food court in my neighborhood may foster multicultural community, it is still not an example of the kind of cultural equality Hawn envisions. Fundamentally, the food court is a restaurant, with the goal of making profit from the sale of food. On this point, the mall, with its diversity of food choices, is the equivalent of the Epcot Center. What does make it different, however, is the greater opportunity it provides, not for food choices, but for the making of meanings and the experiencing of pleasures. Epcot is a tightly controlled environment. The location of each venue, the flow of the day's activities, the traffic patterns, the limits of diversity are all carefully conceived and maintained. In contrast, the mall is much more informal—some might say chaotic. The main decorative feature of my food court, for example, is a group of large living palm trees. While exotic and novel in a suburb of Chicago, the palm trees don't seem to be part of any totalizing design scheme. Are we supposed to imagine ourselves in California, Mexico, or Florida? It's hard to say. Each person who arrives at the mall has the opportunity to make this meaning for himself or herself. Where do you want to be? In a similar way, each small restaurant around the food court is competing for attention, struggling to create a winning identity. These attempts, however, can never be completely successful. People make their own choices; they make up their own dining worlds. There are times in the food court, for example, when I find myself reliving memories of a Mexican zócalo, eating tamales and watching Spanish-speaking families enjoying an afternoon together. At other times, I am reliving my youthful exuberance downing fish burgers with buddies at the local fast food stand. The point is not what meanings I make; the point is that the food court allows me to make them. There are many meanings to be found here, and the mall succeeds by allowing their possibility.

Success itself, of course, has various meanings. The owners of the food court allow and promote diversity only in so much as it increases their profits. The mall is a corporate enterprise. If the food court does not make money, it will be changed or eliminated. But regardless of the motivation, diversity is welcomed, at least for now. That's a start. And to my mind, the key element at the food court—what sets it apart from Epcot—is that there is a structural openness to the enterprise which encourages people to make use of what is given to them and to make it personally meaningful. I think this is the most important lesson the food court has to teach to those who plan worship.

You may ask why this lesson can help us if the food court itself is not an example of a cultural partnership. My answer is that this is exactly why the example of the food court is relevant. We may agree that full cultural partnership is a goal to be achieved, but the reality is that very few local churches can serve as an illustration. The example of the food court suggests that strategies of openness in worship can help congregations experience multicultural community in situations where a full cultural partnership may still not exist. In these churches, a more open structure for worship can provide hospitality to a diversity of meanings, even as these meanings are still in some level of resistance and negotiation with a dominant viewpoint.

STRUCTURAL OPENNESS

It is time to take a deeper and more comprehensive look at the concept of "structural openness." The idea that a work can be open to a variety of interpretations is not a new one, but recent literary, media, and cultural theorists have been very interested in the idea. Though they may use slightly different terminology, many of these scholars are asking the same questions that my experience at the food court raised—the same questions we are asking about gatherings for worship.

There has been a significant turning in critical theory from concerns about finding the "right" meaning—of a novel, for example—to investigations of "possible" meanings offered by a work. This approach has led, in turn, to a new appreciation of the role of readers in the act of interpretation. Researchers have discovered that readers often resist and negotiate the meanings offered by a work. Discovering these strategies of resistance and locating their "intertextual" contexts has been a rewarding area of study for many contemporary scholars.[4]

For many of these theorists, cultural works like a TV show, a film, or a gathering for worship are understood as battlegrounds, as sites for a struggle of meaning. In other words, at the moment when a work is read or experienced, the work and the reader engage in a battle. The objective of this struggle is the right to control what meanings will be produced. For its part, the work may take an aggressive position, using strategies to enforce its authority, struggling to close down the possibility of "wrong" interpretations. On the other hand, the work may take a more conciliatory position by opening itself up to be understood in a variety of ways and from a variety of perspectives. In any case, the reader's task is to open up the work to meanings and pleasures that are to his or her benefit and interest. With some works this is easy; with others it is much more difficult. Theorist and novelist Umberto Eco was one who described these two types of works as "open" and "closed."[5]

I hope this all sounds familiar. The Epcot Center is a cultural work that attempts to limit and control the possible meanings available. My neighborhood food court is more open to varieties of meanings and pleasures. What this theoretical perspective now makes clear, however, is that works do not have total control over the meanings and pleasures they offer. No matter how closed a work may appear, there is still some opportunity for readers to make it their own. This means, for example, that more may be going on at the Epcot Center than we realized in our first analysis. This is not to deny our observation that the food court is more structurally open; it is only to affirm that what is going on between the Epcot Center and its visitors is a dynamic and complex interaction in which both parties participate. What comes of this interaction is not always easy to predict. It is not impossible for someone to make an authentic, cross-cultural connection at Epcot. However, it will still be easier to do this at my local food court.

This last fact is my focus here. *A work can be structured in certain ways to allow for more active participation by those who engage with it.* Recent research shows that it is not possible to know for sure what meanings or pleasures will be experienced by specific people in a gathering for worship. But planners of worship gatherings have the choice of either trying to control the experience and the meanings which come from it or opening up the experience to diversity. I believe that true multicultural worship depends on a structure of openness.

READERLY AND WRITERLY TEXTS

French theorist Roland Barthes developed his own terminology to describe this. Barthes proposed that a common characteristic of a closed work (or text) is a structure which presents the text as "real" and "natural," disguising its origin as a constructed work with a definite point of view. Because these texts are so full of "common sense," they read easily. Barthes called them "readerly" texts. Texts that do not follow a "realistic" or linear logic, texts that require the reader to help "write" the work by providing links, connections, and social/cultural experience, Barthes labeled "writerly" texts.[6]

A helpful example of Barthes's concept is presented by Susan Leigh Foster in her dissertation, *Reading Dancing*.[7] She develops a discussion,

originally presented by Barthes, on the differences between Western realist theater and the Bunraku puppet theater of Japan. According to
Barthes, Western realist theater is a prime example of a "readerly" text.
The actor/dancer performs on a stage, framed by a proscenium that dis-
guises the means of production. The actor/dancer expresses an intentional meaning, and the reader/audience, in the dark and intently
focused on the world represented on stage, engages in an interpretive
process to gather it up.

In the Bunraku puppet theater, however, the experience is much different. The puppets are large and the puppeteers are in full view. The
"voices" of the puppets come from someone standing to the side, sepa-
rating the "voices" from the puppet "bodies." The hall for the performance is well lit, and there is no stage or proscenium to make a distinction
between audience and actor.

Susan Foster writes, "When the rhetoric of a unique, intended message presides . . . viewers' responses as to what it means are hierarchically
classified in terms of their accuracy. The Bunraku, in contrast, supports
infinite interpretations. Viewers watch their favorite parts and ignore the
rest. Each response is valid and only different from others. The Bunraku
is reinvented or authored by each of its viewers."[8]

Christian liturgical practice also offers examples of readerly and
writerly texts. One example is evident in the contrast worship scholar
Frank Senn sees between Western Christian worship and the liturgical
practice of the Eastern church. He writes, "Our [Western Church] paradigm of liturgy is the classroom. We sit in straight rows facing in one
direction and do what we are told. . . . [In the Eastern liturgy] each person contributes at his or her own level to the total event. At times wor-
shipers are doing their own thing—lighting candles or kissing icons—at
other times they come together for common things—for example, to
hear the Gospel, to receive Holy Communion."[9]

Reformed worship, particularly in the eighteenth and nineteenth centuries, was clearly a closed, "readerly" text. In general, gatherings for worship were dominated by long sermons and pastoral prayers delivered by
a male clergy in stark rooms with no crosses or liturgical symbols. Congregational participation was limited to singing unaccompanied psalms.
Like Senn, ritual scholar Catherine Bell draws a connection between this
type of gathering and the classroom. She writes, "The sermon is the center of their ritual life, and it is primarily a teaching commentary on
scripture."[10] Similarly, Leonel Mitchell, an Anglican liturgical scholar,
suggests that "post-Reformation worship has tended to reduce ritual to a

collection of audio-visual aids to make the meaning of the spoken word clearer."[11]

Surprisingly perhaps, this description of Reformed worship is not too different from how one might describe "contemporary worship" today. In many contemporary gatherings for worship, the focus is a long teaching sermon, often with audio-visuals, delivered in a school (or school-like) auditorium, with few crosses or liturgical symbols, everyone looking forward, with a minimum of ritual and with congregational participation often limited to singing. Like traditional Reformed worship, contemporary worship gatherings make "common sense" to the cultural community who attend. Christianity is "naturalized" to seem completely comfortable with a particular cultural system. This is a "readerly" text as Barthes described it. Incongruities, ambiguities, or varieties of interpretation are not encouraged.

These brief descriptions of worship gatherings, admittedly too general to be definitive, suggest a picture of closed worship. By helping us to see what open worship is not, they lead us finally to a most basic and practical question: What is open worship? How is it structured? I'd like to suggest three characteristics that I think are present in an "open" gathering for worship: participation, multiple means of expression, and density.

OPEN WORSHIP: PARTICIPATION

Barthes uses the word "writerly" to describe an open text because he believes one of its characteristics is that readers actively participate in writing the work, rather than passively trying to figure out what the work is saying. According to Susan Leigh Foster, in the Bunraku theater, each member of the audience authors his or her own version of the story. They are active in picking and choosing what they will see and hear. Frank Senn's depiction of Eastern liturgy draws attention to the same idea—each person contributes to the total event at his or her level.

Participation is not a new idea for Christian worship. Worship is an action; liturgy is the work of the people. In practice, however, gatherings for worship have often closed off certain avenues for participation. At various times this has been done by privileging the clergy in the performance of ritual and sacrament, by removing symbols and signs from the space, by allowing only authorized prayers and litanies, and by carefully regulating the use of music and the arts. While not exhaustive, this list makes clear a pattern of reducing most people's participation and giving control to a few.

A structure that encourages participation is a strategy of openness. There are many ways to do this. Most obvious, perhaps, is to invite physical participation in rituals and processions, dances and songs, prayers and sacraments. Sometimes this means creating a welcoming space for participation. Fixed seating, narrow aisles, high pulpits, and bad acoustics all discourage participation. Structures that encourage participation reduce the spotlight on clergy, music leaders, and choirs and raise the light on the people.

Another way to invite participation is to move the structure of worship gatherings away from linear, rationally ordered presentations, to more organic, associative forms of organization. For theorists like Barthes, linear structures disguise an underlying point of view, making one perspective appear as "common sense" truth for all. A structure that allows associations or connections to be made in several directions at once helps to open up the experience to other points of view, making it possible for different people to make different meanings at the same time, each equally truthful. Lutheran Frank Senn is one who has complained about attempts to give worship a more unified flow. He writes, "We are infected with the notion that the liturgy must have a certain rational progression. So we tend to force it in certain directions by means of commentaries and explanations—all of which tend to turn the liturgy into a rather dull and inefficient sermon and render the congregation correspondingly passive."[12] Evangelical author Dan Kimball notices a nonlinear approach in what he describes as "emerging" churches. He says that "emerging generations have grown uncomfortable with the boxed-in feel of many contemporary worship services. . . . Emerging worship moves in an organic flow. . . . [This] means a weaving of many things throughout a meeting that people can participate in. It is much more than sitting. It is also more than a couple of ways of worshiping."[13]

In the gatherings Kimball describes, people are given the opportunity to move around the room. This is another structural strategy that invites participation, quite similar to the structure of the Eastern church or of the Bunraku theater. Kimball writes that "having the freedom to move about at appropriate times during the worship gathering is a very freeing and beautiful thing in emerging worship. . . . During a gathering some people may sit still, and some people will move about quite a bit. The point is, there is freedom."[14] This freedom invites participation from within one's own experience and culture.

OPEN WORSHIP: MULTIPLE MEANS OF EXPRESSION

Another characteristic of open worship is what I call "multiple means of expression." With this term I group together a variety of activities (for example, standing, singing, meditating), communication strategies (for example, rhetoric, narrative, the arts, media), and sensory experiences (for example, smell, taste, touch) that are both the means by which we understand and enter into worship experiences and the means by which we express our experience. Since no one means of expression is equally suited to the cognitive style or cultural competencies of each unique person, structures that offer a wide variety of expressive means are strategies of openness. In the Bunraku theater, dance, dialogue, color and pageantry, puppets, and music work in relationship, offering up a wide assortment of possible meanings in a variety of forms of expression. Similarly, there are times and places in Christian worship, past and present, where a mix of music, sculpture, incense, candles, painting, ritual, and rhetoric work together as means of expression. In contrast, however, some gatherings for worship, which have depended substantially on certain verbal competencies or musical styles, have closed down meaningful participation to all but the select group who can make sense of things in the privileged way.

When Frank Senn compares Western worship patterns to a classroom of students listening to a lecture, his reference point is a model for education that is gradually losing its dominance. Educators are recognizing that students are not all alike, that people learn differently, and that the extent of people's knowledge cannot always be measured on standardized tests. Educator Howard Gardner is well known for his theory of multiple intelligences. Believing "that people have different cognitive strengths and contrasting cognitive styles,"[15] he is a strong advocate for teaching with a diversity of approaches. He also suggests an additional benefit: "The adoption of a family of stances toward a phenomenon encourages the student to come to know that phenomenon in more than one way, to develop multiple representations and seek to relate these representations to one another."[16] In other words, multiple means of expression not only offer the opportunity for people to learn and to express themselves within their personal strengths and cultural competencies; they also offer them a multidimensional experience that is potentially rich with the possibility for deeper and more interconnected meanings.

OPEN WORSHIP: DENSITY

Multicultural worship—open worship—creates the possibility for deeply interconnected meanings and pleasures. It also creates the possibility for incongruities and contradictions. Incongruities, contradictions, and ambiguities are common characteristics of open or "writerly" texts as described by Eco and Barthes and others. For some in the church, this may be the most difficult characteristic of open worship to imagine. Old Testament scholar Walter Brueggemann, however, argues that to avoid incongruities and contradictions is to "thin down" our knowledge of God. He writes that in the Bible, God is "endlessly quixotic and enigmatic, filled with contradictions, always present, but distressingly absent at the dangerous times; all knowing, but sometimes wondering, questioning, testing, unsure; all powerful, but clearly not master of the evil that is still loose among us." Brueggemann urges that the stories of the Bible be told and retold—"tales of grace and rage, of presence and absence, of honor and shame, of forgetting and remembering, of noticing and ignoring—tales of our lived life, tales in which God is endlessly embedded, wild and beyond domestication."[17]

Brueggemann uses the term "density" to describe these qualities of ambiguity, mystery, and depth. It is a good label for the third characteristic of open worship. Brueggemann adapts the word from the anthropological term "thickness," most familiar in the work of Clifford Geertz, which refers to webs of connections, codes, and symbols that make up a culture. Fully known only to those on the inside, outsiders generally have a hard time negotiating these thick webs of meaning.[18] Outsider representations of cultures—Epcot Center, for example—are often considerably thinned down. Brueggemann's term "density" is more expansive than "thickness," however. He uses the word not only as a way to describe cultural thickness, but also as a way to describe God, people's lives, and the Bible. In this regard, he points to a history of thinning down the text of the Bible to singular meanings and reducing our understanding of God to a set of propositions. He calls instead for "practices of density," arguing, for example, that the sermon's purpose is not to lecture on the one true (thin) meaning of the text; but rather, it is to bring to life a "convergence of dense text, dense people, and dense God."[19]

The "practice of density" is a strategy of openness. We thin down cultures, people, and God in order to close down the possibilities for surprise. We thin down in order to gain control. Affirming density is to let go of control. Practices of density include listening without knowing what answer will come, speaking in languages we don't understand, dancing when it seems too awkward, sharing bread and wine without knowing the precise theology, and praying when we are without hope. Practices of density affirm the presence of the unknown and the unknowable; they affirm the presence of complexities and ambiguities and multiple meanings.

As Brueggemann describes it, the practice of density opens us to the depth and mystery present in everyday experience at the same time that it affirms our deep rootedness with our own Christian community: "Our density is not simply because we are *Homo sapiens*, but because we are baptized, committed, beloved, commanded persons with all the complexities that accompany passionate commitment and unconditional grace."[20] This is the fundamental experience that makes multicultural worship possible. It is this dense experience of God—more than we can describe in thin language—that calls us to baptism and commitment, that calls us to worship. Though expressed and understood in many ways—full of contradictions, ambiguities, and mystery—it is this experience of God that holds us together. To hear Brueggemann is to recognize that open worship is not simply a multicultural imperative, but a theological one as well.

STRUCTURES OF OPENNESS, STRATEGIES OF HOSPITALITY

I think most of the folks who come to my local food court feel welcome. They bring their kids; they stretch out; they talk in their own language; they eat. Somehow there is an openness to the space that invites them to be themselves. Strategies of openness can extend a welcome to people. In our gatherings for worship, greater opportunities for participation, multiple means of expression, and the affirmation and practice of density will help us welcome people in all their diversity as equal partners in the worship of God. What we learn from my neighborhood food court is far from being the whole story of multicultural worship. But what we learn can help us.

NOTES

1. Mark Bangert, "How Does One Go About Multicultural Worship?" in *What Does "Multicultural" Worship Look Like?* ed. Gordon Lathrop (Minneapolis: Augsburg Fortress, 1996), 27.

2. Richard Fenn, "Diversity and Power: Cracking the Code," in *Making Room at the Table*, ed. Brian K. Blount and Leonora Tubbs Tisdale (Louisville, KY: Westminster John Knox Press, 2001), 67.

3. Michael C. Hawn, *One Bread, One Body: Exploring Cultural Diversity in Worship* (Bethesda, MD: Alban Institute, 2003), 8.

4. See, for example, Tony Bennett and Janet Woollacott, *Bond and Beyond: The Political Career of a Popular Hero* (New York: Methuen, 1987).

5. Umberto Eco, *The Role of the Reader: Explorations in the Semiotics of Texts* (Bloomington and London: Indiana University Press, 1979), 8–10.

6. Roland Barthes, *S/Z*, trans. Richard Howard (New York: Hill & Wang, 1974).

7. Susan Leigh Foster, *Reading Dancing: Gestures towards a Semiotics of Dance* (PhD diss., University of California, Santa Cruz, 1982), 76–77, 202–9.

8. Ibid., 77.

9. Frank Senn, *Christian Worship and Its Cultural Setting* (Philadelphia: Fortress Press, 1983), 68.

10. Catherine Bell, *Ritual: Perspectives and Dimensions* (New York and Oxford: Oxford University Press, 1997), 189.

11. Leonel L. Mitchell, *The Meaning of Ritual* (Wilton, CT: Morehouse-Barlow, 1977), 109.

12. Senn, *Christian Worship and Its Cultural Setting*, 69.

13. Dan Kimball, *Emerging Worship: Creating Worship Gatherings for New Generations* (Grand Rapids, Zondervan, 2004), 76–77.

14. Ibid., 90.

15. Howard Gardner, *Multiple Intelligences* (New York: Basic Books, 1993), 6.

16. Ibid., 204.

17. Walter Brueggemann, *Cadences of Home: Preaching among Exiles* (Louisville, KY: Westminster John Knox Press, 1997), 76.

18. Ibid., 73–74.

19. Ibid., 25, 76.

20. Ibid., 75.

CHAPTER 14

The Formation of Ministerial Authority and Identity:
Cross Cultural Experiential Education

Joanne Lindstrom

W hat changes a person from someone merely knowledgeable about Bible content, theology, sacraments, pastoral care, church administration, and religious education into a pastor or minister—someone who is a leader, secure in personal identity, acting with appropriate authority, living out vocation with passion and integrity? The making of a minister requires the integration of theory and practice, skill and wisdom, *being* and *doing*. The primary matrix for this integration is an experiential education program, a place where students can minister as they become ministers—a process of maturation and transformation.

Experiential education is also the place where students move into new contexts of learning and ministry. Ideally, these contexts are different from those the students are most familiar with, so that students come to a deeper understanding of their own gifts in different settings for ministry. If students are open to new learnings in these different contexts, then students can be formed and transformed into ministers and pastors prepared for ministry in any number of contexts.

In *The Courage to Teach: Exploring the Inner Landscape of a Teacher's Life*, Parker Palmer posits that teaching flows from the teacher's soul. The state of one's soul depends on self-knowledge—the ability to look into the mirror and not run! Self-examination, Palmer suggests, requires engaging the subject at the deepest levels of embodied, personal meaning. This is no less true for those called to ministry. Integrity in ministry requires continuing theological reflection on life and vocation so that ministers can be, as Palmer says, at home in their own souls.

Self-examination is especially crucial for students in multi/cross-cultural placements. Relevant ministry with persons from different racial/cultural backgrounds requires that one be at home in his or her own soul. To be at home in one's soul, one must know who they are, how they were shaped and formed, what values and prejudices they still harbor, what biases and entitlements they still believe are due them, what they believe about those different from them. This kind of self-examination dares to look at all that can be celebrated in one's life and history, all that can be mourned, and all that must be redeemed. Self-examination and being at home in our own souls are what makes true multi/cross-cultural ministry possible, what allows us to move beyond food and fiesta to interact with one another at deeper levels.

In this chapter I will (1) review the goals of experiential education as a discipline in the context of multi/cross-cultural education; (2) provide working definitions for authority and identity while examining the challenges presented by different cultural understandings of authority and identity; and (3) delineate the respective roles of the supervisor/mentor, the community, the student, and the seminary in the process of transformation in a multi/cross-cultural context.

THE DISCIPLINE OF EXPERIENTIAL EDUCATION

Experiential education (field studies, field education, supervised ministry) is a contextual learning process with the student at the center. It is a preparation process providing students with opportunities to explore relationships between theology and experience, between private convictions and public actions, and doing so while actually engaged in the practice of ministry under supervision. Students develop general ministry skills: preaching, teaching, pastoral care, public witness, and administration, reflecting on those skills formally with an on-site supervisor. Through this process of theological reflection, ministry activities become educative. In multicultural education, this skill development is filtered through the particular contexts of the ministry site and the seminary setting. Students become ministers in new ways as they interface with communities and supervisors who bring very different perspectives to the learning/teaching process. Students are challenged to integrate ministry practice and academic knowledge in ways that deepen and broaden both.

Experiential education addresses various dimensions of the preparation for ministry: theological reflection, personal/spiritual formation, professional formation, and ministerial skill development. These dimensions of preparation work in concert as students are transformed into thoughtful practitioners, skilled in reflective discipline that integrates theological, experiential, and contextual information.

Through *theological reflection* students integrate classroom learning with ministry experience. Study and reflection in community help them discern what constitutes ministry and how gifts of God's spirit are evidenced in the ongoing discernment of call. In *personal/spiritual formation* students endeavor to understand and exegete their own experience in continuing exploration of their own personal faith journey as shaped by their faith tradition and by the theological disciplines in which they are receiving instruction. In *professional formation* students explore issues of personal integrity: a healthy sense of self and healthy relationships with others—relationships ethically appropriate, respectful of boundaries, and built on a well-nurtured relationship with God in a continuing faith journey. Students crossing racial and cultural boundaries are challenged in new and different ways to develop and maintain integrity in relationships. In *ministerial skill development* students learn the importance of holistic and comprehensive leadership, exercise their gifts for the building up of the body of Christ, cultivate traits necessary for various ministry situations, and develop ongoing assessment processes utilizing self-evaluation and feedback from others. Cross/multi-cultural skill development for different ministry settings can be unsettling for students at times when self-evaluation and feedback include racialized perspectives.

Students struggle and are enriched by these processes regardless of the ministry context. The unique strength of multicultural education as the place in which students become ministers is the way in which the experiences of the students are brought into theological education, further pushing theological education to expand its capacity to educate students in a multi/cross-cultural context. Pastors and leaders who are educated in these contexts in turn provide a challenge to the churches and other institutions they serve. Multi/cross-cultural field placements may change the expectations that students have of their ministry sites upon graduation. Students are also better prepared to cross cultures in their future ministries.

WORKING DEFINITIONS OF *AUTHORITY* AND *IDENTITY*

Authority can be a most difficult issue to address during a student's placement at a church or community agency. Part of the difficulty comes from not knowing exactly what authority is: who has it, how to use it.

Many students shy away from it. In *As One with Authority: Reflective Leadership in Ministry*, Jackson Carroll comments on the relationship of authority and power. He suggests that *power* is a resource allowing goals or purposes to be accomplished with or without the consent of others who are affected by its use. But *authority*, he says, is power that has the consent of the group. "When a pastor or lay leader exercises power legitimately—that is, acts with authority—he or she does so by directing, influencing, coordinating, or otherwise guiding the thought or behavior of others in the congregation in ways that they acknowledge as right."[1]

Students may see their authority grow over the course of their placement year because of its relational quality. However, there will still be some ambiguity. The student is, after all, a student with a limited tenure and under the supervision of a senior pastor or agency director.

For students in multi/cross-cultural settings, the issue of authority may be more confusing if they are unfamiliar with the different ways that authority is understood and if they are unfamiliar with different expectations. This presents an opportunity for transformation for both the student and the community the student is serving. Students from the dominant culture may feel particularly sensitive about their authority in a ministry setting that is a nondominant culture. Students coming from more casual, consensual leadership styles will be challenged to engage the more formal, hierarchical styles.

As creatures fashioned by God, our identities are a mix of our genetic makeup, our family history, culture, and upbringing, our experiences— all that has gone into making us unique persons. Closely intertwined with our identity is integrity. Parker Palmer helpfully connects these two: "*Identity* lies in the intersection of the diverse forces that make up my life, and *integrity* lies in relating to those forces in ways that bring me wholeness and life rather than fragmentation and death."[2]

Students in experiential education may struggle to differentiate between personal identity and pastoral/ministerial identity—an understanding of self and relationships so that one is clear at any given time about vocational call and appropriate relationship. Authority questions get wound up in identity as well. This was clearly evident in one student's conflict at her Missionary Baptist Church field site. The church insisted on calling her Reverend Sally, even though she was an intern and not ordained. The student was extremely resistant to this. *Just call me Sally.*

A number of issues were at play in this situation. Sally had the consent of the group to exercise authority. This was evidenced by their acknowledgment of her set-apart role among them, even as they recognized the fact that she was a student. Even in her student status, they respected the pastoral role for which she was preparing. In that particular context, if you serve in the pulpit, are in formal training for ministry, are preaching and teaching, and/or have been licensed to preach, you are accorded the title "Reverend."

Another issue is that Sally found herself in a cultural context different from her own. While she had come from the black church experience and now in her field studies placement was learning and serving in another black church, the contexts were very different. The differences ranged from denominational identity, theology, class/economic/ educational status of the membership to church size. Cross/multicultural education is not always about moving between and among different racial, ethnic, or language groups, but about moving into a context different from one's own experience—however those differences might be defined.

Sally's field context raised a mixture of issues: growing into her call, seeing herself as "Reverend Sally," differentiating between her personal identity and her pastoral/ministerial identity. This was complicated for her by the very different cultural context in which she found herself— the different traditions, different rituals, different theologies. Sally found herself in deep reflection as she sorted through these questions. She was better able to articulate the nuances of her own tradition and her own theology as she became more comfortable in relating to a church community with a different understanding of her role. From the point of view of the seminary, this is what multicultural educational contexts are meant to provide.

THE ROLE OF THE SUPERVISOR/MENTOR

Supervisors/mentors play a crucial role in the transformation process for students. If ministry is anything, it is relational. The relationship between student and supervisor/mentor, for good or for ill, will be influential. Students observe their supervisors/mentors engaging in ministry tasks. They see the triumphs and the disappointments of their supervisors, their senses of certitude and their questions. Students see the Spirit of God working through a minister with feet of clay. In order for this experience to be integrative for the student, the supervisor/mentor must be ready to invest time and energy and to understand the mentoring and training of new leaders as part of his or her vocation of ministry. Basic supervisory gifts or traits include

— availability—physical, emotional and spiritual presence;
— ability to confront, to ask good questions, to listen carefully to what is and is not said;
— capacity to see what the student cannot see—gifts and graces, fears and limitations;
— willingness to share appropriately their own faith journey;
— commitment to consistent supervisory meetings and theological reflection;
— maturity and commitment to the supervisor's own growth;
— capacity to lead in the midst of changing ministry contexts.

Supervisors/mentors make space for a student—physical space, emotional space, spiritual space, holy space. Supervisors/mentors make space for a student's life story to emerge and converge with new skills and gifts—with all the attendant insecurities and surprises that entails. Supervisors/mentors walk with students as they get used to being called Reverend or Pastor. Supervisors are there as students fuss with clerical collars or tug at robes on Sunday morning, trying to get comfortable—trying to figure out whose reflection they see in the mirror. Supervisors respectfully help students probe deeply into the mysteries of vocation and preparation for ministry—indeed, holy space.

Supervisors working with students from different racial/ethnic/cultural backgrounds find themselves growing in supervisory skills. If there are language issues (e.g., the student's speech is heavily accented), then the supervisor is called to work with both the student and the congregation. One supervisor asked the student to prepare a written manuscript when he preached for the first time. Prior to the preaching event, the supervisor practiced with the student, helping him to slow down. The manuscript was printed in the church bulletin so that the congregation could follow along with the student. The supervisor also made it clear that language was not solely an issue of the student's speaking but also an issue of the congregation's listening.

Supervisors may find themselves learning in depth about another culture and trying to find ways to bridge the two worlds in which the student finds her/himself. For one Korean student serving in a Japanese American congregation, it was unheard of to say no to an elder (not an ecclesial term). Consequently, the student found himself saying yes to every request and unable to fulfill each commitment, which led to a terrible sense of shame. This supervisor, along with a wise older member of the lay ministry support team who understood his cultural context, began to teach him how to say no and to set appropriate boundaries as a student pastor. As the Euro American supervising pastor serving this Japanese American congregation with an affiliated Indo-Pakastani congregation and a Korean intern, she also was in the unique position of hearing the student's pain of the Japanese occupation and creating space for healing conversation with this third- and fourth-generation congregation.

THE ROLE OF THE COMMUNITY

Ministry does not occur in a vacuum. Churches and agencies are not mere buildings but living organisms made up of wonderfully wacky, diverse, gifted, grouchy, creative, resourceful, cantankerous people. The other partner in experiential education is the community in which the student serves. Traditionally students completed their experiential education requirements in congregational settings; now many students also opt for settings in community, health, or social-service agencies.

While the supervisor provides understanding of mission and ministry from the perspective of a pastoral leader, the community provides an understanding of mission and ministry of the church from a lay perspective. While the mission and ministry themselves are the same, supervisors and communities offer different perspectives based on role and function. The community also helps the student understand ministry context and history. In some cases community members have been around longer than the pastor/director and may outlast that leader. Basic traits of a healthy community include

— understanding the training of leaders as part of its ministry;
— willingness of members to share their faith journeys with the student;
— welcome of the student (and any family members) into the ministry site;
— ability to articulate the ministry and mission of the community and to interpret history and vision to the student;
— capacity to affirm the student, accept mistakes, and celebrate new growth.

The community provides physical space, emotional space, spiritual space, holy space for the student. As they make space for a student to learn the arts and skills of preaching or teaching, to organize a community meeting, or to present a hospice case at a staffing, they make room for the next generation of leaders. They offer a gift of trust and collegiality.

Throughout the process, they walk with the student, offering support, feedback, and evaluation with sensitivity and honesty—holy space, indeed.

The community is shaped and formed by language, culture, class, race—all that has gone into making this community the unique creation that it is. As the community shares its own faith journey, both communally and as individuals, it rehearses how God lives, moves, and has God's being in their lives. As they share their life with the student, they are entrusting a precious gift—the story of their life. As a student in turn shares her or his life, he or she is also entrusting a precious gift. However, life experiences may differ greatly and painfully. It is the commitment to God, to the church, and to the training of leaders that keeps communities of faith committed. Their task is to help interpret to the student the community—its mission and ministry, history, and vision for the future—so that the student might more appropriately and fully minister in that context. This includes tradition, ritual, family connections, why things are done a certain way, sacred space and symbols, as well as culture, race, and ethnicity.

The community—particularly the small group of individuals assigned to work with the student—provides a safety net. This is the only time in a minister/pastor's life when there is any kind of safety net. In the future, when a pastor/minister makes a mistake, he will bear full responsibility for the mistake. But for this short time, if the student makes a mistake, the community picks her up, dusts her off, and starts her back on her way.

Transformation also happens for the faith community through its interaction with the student. Accepting the student as a leader entails an openness to being changed by a student. The depth of this change varies, given the short-term nature of a particular student's tenure there. The learning is reciprocal. The community may be taking a risk by taking on a student from a different cultural or racial context, and congregational life is affected.

THE ROLE OF THE STUDENT

Today's students are amazingly diverse. In recent years McCormick students have brought a wide range of experiences and expectations to theological education. Ranging from twenty-one to sixty-plus years in age, they are female and male, from various racial and ethnic backgrounds. They represent many faith traditions, cultures, and nations;

they are single, married, and partnered, with and without children. They come from careers in business, education, science, technology, from public and private sectors. Some are homemakers and community volunteers. We can no longer assume they have grown up in the church or know the Bible. Students may come with years of lay leadership experience or with as little as two or three years in the church.

A student comes to field education shaped by countless life experiences that inform their openness to the field education process. Some students believe they have nothing to learn; others believe that they have everything to learn. Some students worry about knowing more than their supervisors; some worry about looking stupid. Some students believe their years of lay leadership will automatically transfer into ordained leadership without a hiccup.

Regardless of the conceptions/misconceptions, the role of the student is ultimately that of a learner, regardless of what gifts and graces he/she brings to a ministry site. The primary objective of the student engaged in ministry under supervision is to grow and develop in ministry. This is a very personalized process designed to strengthen already-identified gifts during the discovery of new ones, all the while discerning and celebrating the ongoing presence of God. This is a time when the work of head, heart, and hands comes together; when the student seeks to listen as God calls out the one God has truly created.

One Euro American student serving in an African American church wondered how he could serve a people who had such a different experience from his own. He also questioned why God sent a country boy to the urban church. And yet, through this experience he was able to stretch beyond the world he knew to include a world he could not have imagined. This world included not only his experience in an urban, African American congregation solely because of its racial ethnic reality, but also his own growth as a minister in this safe place of exploration and reflection.

Students sometimes have hard transitions or find themselves in situations that they do not understand from their own cultural context. A business meeting at a Euro American congregation was very troubling for a Korean student. How the business was conducted and the role of the pastor in the business meeting stirred up many feelings—some of which were quite protective of the pastor in what the student perceived to be a less than friendly environment. The student had to learn a different way of doing business in a new context and learn also that it did not translate into a hostile environment for the pastor.

For students who risk great vulnerability by choosing a placement in a context exceedingly unfamiliar, the reward is great. They are pushed to think and experience ministry more broadly, to question and discern their motives for and understandings about ministry, and they come face to face with unknown biases and prejudices that need to be acknowledged and forgiven. It can be an extraordinarily grace-filled year of growth.

THE ROLE OF THE SEMINARY

Experiential education is designed for discernment and growth. It is a time for students to examine and explore, to struggle and to test their call. It is important for students to move into situations beyond what previous experience has afforded. If we are preparing women and men for leadership in a racially and culturally diverse world, it is the seminary's responsibility to offer placement sites that prepare the leaders we say the world needs. John Fish in *Liberating Education* writes: "Our primary task is to place students in new situations where they experience a new demand and are thereby impelled to ask new questions, see new realities, and think new thoughts."[3] This means we cannot place students where they might feel most comfortable; rather, we provide sites that can provoke the kinds of questions and struggles that will shape and form the thoughtful, moral, compassionate, active leaders the church and world so need.

This creates a number of challenges. We need to find ways to bridge cultures, cultivate a quality of dialogue that is consonant with goals of the program yet honors the community context and culture. As a multicultural institution, the seminary needs to struggle with the variety of ways experiential education is put into practice in many different faith traditions. For example, African American students often come through a mentoring process in the black church and do not wish to leave that process for placements elsewhere. Not only do the students find it disruptive to their mentoring process; they can also find it detrimental to future ministry possibilities. Nonetheless, these students also need the opportunity of a new experience where they are "impelled to ask new questions, see new realities, and think new thoughts."

Other issues that the seminary must attend to include language, culture, judicatory requirements, and geography. Requiring a new situation for experiential education is quite complex. The challenge before the seminary is to provide quality multi/cross/intercultural placement. While encouraging and promoting this value, the seminary must also continue to be in dialogue with other faith traditions with in-house mentoring systems as well as first-language ministries. For students who complete their experiential education requirement in their home congregation/agency, the seminary must be clear about requirements that provide students the unique learning experience leading them to see new realities and think new thoughts.

As the seminary continues to prepare women and men for ministry, the whole seminary community is part of the transformation process. Students in multi/cross-cultural placements are challenged at their core as they are formed as leaders and pastors and, ideally, bring those struggles into the classroom and into the community. The process by which ministers are made is one in which classes and community life play an important role in helping to expand the boundaries through the facilitation of multi/cross-cultural learning throughout the rest of their seminary career. When both faculty and class members model integrity in multi/cross-cultural encounters, students learn how they might best navigate across cultures in their field placements. As students become more adept in doing so, they in turn contribute to the classroom setting.

FINAL THOUGHTS

Whom are we preparing for ministry? Are we preparing Euro Americans to serve Euro American communities? Latino/Latinas to serve Hispanic communities? African Americans to serve African American communities? Or are we preparing women and men for ministry in any church? The answer is yes. It is both/and. The reality is that the majority of students will end up serving churches of their own racial ethnic background. However, some will not. And we are preparing ministers and pastors for the exception and for the church *that we cannot yet see.* And those students who will serve congregations that look like themselves, if they have been shaped and formed by multi/cross-cultural experiences and education, will be more fully aware of the variety of ways that God may express God's presence in this world. They will also have a broader sense of concerns that may affect communities other than their own. They will be more adept at reading their own ministry context—what works and why or why not. They will have experienced education and ministry through another's eyes and been companions, allies, and sojourners having their own faith journey enriched and expanded in the process.

Each member of the partnership is indispensable. If supervisors/ mentors do not fulfill their sacred responsibility, the learning is largely abstract, with limited personal formation and growth. If the community leaders do not fully engage the student entrusted to their care, learning is largely individualistic, with limited wisdom gained about the impact of context on one's practices. If the seminary defaults on its responsibility, learning is largely cloistered, with limited challenges to grow beyond areas of comfort. If students regard field education as nothing but a hurdle to graduation, learning becomes compartmentalized, with limited integration of Christian tradition with pastoral practices. Experience, in and of itself, is a limited teacher. A far better teacher is praxis—a process in which one's acts of ministry are subject to theological reflection and are integrated into new ways of being and doing.

However, the indispensable partner is this mystery of identity and formation is the Spirit. When openness to the Spirit is central to the process, with an accompanying vulnerability, then the whole team—student, supervisor/mentor, community, and field educator—can address, with integrity, the multiple and layered issues of growth toward formation and identity. At the end of this particular, formal, educational process, each member of the partnership will have done everything possible to ensure the student's preparation for ministry, and the rest is left to the Spirit.

With gratitude to my colleagues and conversation partners,
Presbyterian Field Educators, Laura Mariko Cheifetz,
David J. Schlafer, and Joseph Tortorici, OP

NOTES

1. Jackson Carroll, *As One with Authority: Reflection Leadership in Ministry* (Louisville, KY: Westminster/John Knox Press, 1991), 37.

2. Parker Palmer, *The Courage to Teach: Exploring the Inner Landscape of a Teacher's Life* (San Francisco: Jossey-Bass, 1998), 13.

3. John H. Fish, "Liberating Education," in *Liberation and Ethics: Essays in Religious Social Ethics in Honor of Gibson Winter*, ed. Alvin W. Pitcher and Charles Amjad-Ali (Chicago: Center for the Scientific Study of Religion, 1985), 20.

CHAPTER 15

Teaching Afresh the History of Global Christianity

David D. Daniels III

Teaching the history of global Christianity implies a future for theological education in which the global reality of Christianity is presented critically and imaginatively. The contemporary global church will provide material in the construction of the identities of Christians and churches around the world. And if a new identity for church is constructed out of the reality of global Christianity, Christians might recognize each other across the divide that separates Christians and create new forms of solidarity and common witness. In order to make such a shift in teaching and identity, a globalized narrative of Christianity needs to be developed.

In this chapter, I propose a multicontinental approach to teaching the history of Christianity. I discuss how this approach is best construed and explore the compatibility of various models of church history with this approach, along with how the issue of periodization could be addressed. Then I conclude with some reflections about pedagogy.

THE IMPACT OF A WIDER LENS

When we teach history, we often tell a story. A story of how an era is formed. A story of how contrasting events distinguish two historical periods. A story of how ideas or events take similar or dissimilar paths in different societies or even denominations. While there are historians who resist the idea, many historians employ a narrative structure to organize and teach survey courses on the history of Christianity. While Catholic, Protestant, and Orthodox variations of this narrative do exist, the basic structure of these courses remains intact. Williston Walker's *The History of Christianity* and Justo González's *The Story of Christianity* are widely read versions of this narrative.

An increasing number of survey texts examine the history of Christianity on various continents, and general surveys increasingly include chapters offering material from these regions. This regional or continental approach includes the works of Adrian Hastings, Elizabeth Isichei, Enrique Dussel, and Samuel Hugh Moffett. The general surveys include texts by González, Adrian Hastings, John McManners, and Spickard and Cragg. The texts by McManners and Spickard and Cragg remain bound by the dominant narrative. Of the nineteen chapters in McManner's edited history of Christianity, only five chapters significantly explore Christianity outside of the West. But for the most part the authors focus on South America, Asia, and Africa and ignore the role of the church on these continents in the formation of Christianity worldwide. Spickard and Cragg adapt the dominant master narrative also, committing five chapters out of seventeen to Christianity outside the West. In other chapters they explore the global dimension of Christianity prior to 1500, with brief discussions of Christianity in West Asia, the Indian subcontinent, North and East Africa, and China; Christianity beyond Europe between 1500 and 1800 under the rubric of European expansion; mission also under the terms of expansion; the features of Christianity in various countries on different continents; and the major challenges facing Christianity around the world.[1]

The surveys by González, McManners, and others have erased the line between mission history and general church history. History has become the rubric for all historical topics; all historical documents are deemed worthy of study. Consequently, the documents of mission history have become as significant as the documents related to the history of Christian institutions or doctrine, and nineteenth-century documents from Burma are as important as seventeenth-century British documents. The challenge is that mission history and general church history have pursued different historical questions and developed different basic narratives. Thus merely consolidating the texts and their respective historical questions is inadequate. Clear advancements have been made. The growing list of regional histories provides new information and interpretations. The merging of mission and general church historical documents expand the corpus of material. Yet attempts to incorporate these advancements into general surveys have been flawed. A revamping of the whole historical enterprise is needed.[2]

In order to revamp the historical enterprise, we must account for the change in our historical context. The new context has prompted historians to design new course surveys that recognize the collapse of the basic narrative structure and incorporate the erasure of differences. In addition to the erasure of difference, there has also been a shift to a wider geographic focus; instead of portraying the history of Western Christianity as central, this wider lens presents the history of Christianity on continents and in regions outside of Europe. The resulting course titles include *The History of Christianity in Asia, The History of the Church in Africa, The History of Christianity in Southern Africa, The History of Latin American Christianity, The History of Christianity in Oceania.* All of these developments are informed by the emerging global reality. Regional histories have given students fresh ways to explore the history of Christianity.

SEEING WITH WIDER LENSES

Regional histories are the product of a new historical moment shaped by three factors: demographics, postmodernity, and a millennial perspective.

1. The current demography of Christianity reflects the presence of Christian congregations across the globe and the shift in the Christian majority from Europe and the North to the Two-thirds World and the South. Included in these demographics is the emergence of Pentecostalism as a Christian family on a par with Roman Catholicism, Eastern Orthodoxy, and Protestantism itself. These demographics suggest a reconfiguration of Christianity.

2. The new moment is further defined by postmodernity as a historical moment, with its challenge to metanarratives and historical objectivity. Significantly, postmodernity values a variety of worldviews, rather than the primacy of the modern or Enlightenment world. Postmodernity has undermined the hierarchy of the races, especially through its deconstruction of the concept of race itself, and so deprivileged Europe and the European diaspora and promoted the equality of people and of churches across the races and continents.

3. The new moment is also defined by the entry of Christianity into its third millennium, which offers a wider historical angle. A long view allows us to localize the Reformation, which looms so large in Protestant-oriented courses, and create space to explore other topics, such as the emergence of Christianity in the South Atlantic world of Africa and the Americas.[3]

How we utilize regional histories in courses prompts a set of key questions that we need to probe: *Whose history?* Whose history are we telling?

Regarding the course, who constitutes the audience? Who are the students? The answers to these questions will inform the course objectives and pedagogical strategies. For instance, I teach at a Protestant seminary located in a North American city with a multiracial student body affiliated with Presbyterian, Methodist, Baptist, and Pentecostal congregations. The students are white American, African American, Latino/a, and Asian American, as well as citizens from countries such as Korea, Indonesia, Taiwan, Germany, Cameroon, Kenya, Brazil, and Mexico. Whose history will I design the course to tell? Recognizing the shift from a confessional focus to a geographic focus, do I try to illumine the history of Christianity in the geographic locations represented by the students in my class?[4]

Identifying the community that will be represented in a course does not, however, exhaust the questions of representation. Other issues remain: What are the challenges of representation? How are primary texts produced and interpreted? How are multiple viewpoints and voices represented in the course? Even though there might exist clear commitments to particular stories of Christianity, the politics of representation makes the task of teaching these stories daunting.[5]

In an era defined by identity politics, we must avoid too glibly answering the question, Whose history? A pivotal insight in the identity politics debate is that all identities—whether national, ethnic, racial, or gender—are socially constructed; none are biologically inherited. Thus identity of the Asian or African or North American churches discussed in the course must also be recognized as a socially constructed entity. In some sense, geographic focus creates regional entities that are also contrived. Yet if we recognize the limits of regional histories due to identity politics, they are currently a good approach to teaching the history of Christianity.

MODELS OF HISTORY WITHIN REGIONAL HISTORIES OF CHRISTIANITY

At least five models of church history are employed in regional histories of Christianity: evolution, expansion, eruption, emergence, and encounter. In most cases the models are paired; rarely is a model used alone. Conceptually the models incorporate metaphors from biology, geology, botany, the military, and politics; each model engages a multicontinental approach, with varying degrees of success.

The *evolutionary model*, the dominant one used in teaching church history, has been shaped by the key question, How did Europe become a

Christian civilization? In this story, the church evolves out of Judaism, by differentiating itself from Judaism. From there, it evolved out of its Semitic form/context, by being contextualizing into a Greek and Latin identity. Williston Walker employed this model.[6]

The limitation of the evolutionary model is its enmeshment with Eurocentricism. It is as if the infancy phase of Christianity was its Semitic form, the toddler and adolescent phase was its Greek and early Latin form, and the adult phase was its Roman Catholic form and, for Protestants, certain forms of Reformation Protestantism. In either the Roman Catholic or Protestant scenario, the churches on other continents become the younger relatives of mature European Christianity, either adolescents or young adults, but never mature. This approach retards the development of teaching Christianity in a global perspective, for it is always weighted towards European Christianity and interpreted through Eurocentric lenses or even prejudiced by Eurocentric categories and experience. The evolutionary model also universalizes, so that the genius of Christianity becomes its European embodiment. Closely aligned in the historical rendering is its enmeshment with European civilization and culture. The evolutionary model uses the biology metaphor and implicit survival-of-the-fittest rhetoric. I wonder, Could the evolutionary model tell a broader story? First, what would be the central question? Could it be, How does Christianity become a global phenomenon? Could the evolutionary model carry this question, even though it downplays the multicontinental reality of Christianity across time and space?

The *expansion model* is probably the best recognized alternative to the evolutionary model. This model, made credible by Kenneth Latourette, adopts the military metaphor of invasion and spotlights the growth or extension of Christianity into new areas/territories or among new people. Its key question is, How did Christianity enter new territories? The expansion model clearly highlights the missionary impulse within Christianity, focusing on how it extends to a new territory or among new people. The history of missionary activity and stories from the missionary's perspective are prominent in this model. In this model, what precedes the arrival of Christianity is inconsequential to the narrative, because the focus is on the arrival, not the reception, of Christianity. While this model recognizes the multicontinental reality of Christianity, it fails to spotlight the cross-cultural exchanges.[7]

The *eruption model* accents how Christianity arises suddenly in a place and asks, What particulars in a society make it possible for Christianity to erupt in that society? The eruption model adopts the geyser metaphor; its focus is on the suddenness of the outbreak, on pent-up religious energies or frustration, or ruptures in the society, that create space for Christianity. Christianity is described as political or oppositional. This model tends to keep the regional histories separate.

The *emergence model* stresses both the dynamics in the local context that make its people potentially interested in Christianity and the local agents who nurture this interest, in addition to interpreting and translating the Christian message and practice into local languages, customs, and cultural idioms. The key question is, What are the local agents and conditions that make it possible for Christianity to take root in a culture or among a people? The emergence model privileges local contexts. It stresses the local themes, issues, and social developments that shape the context in which Christianity takes root. The emergence model adopts the garden metaphor with an accent on growth. This model also tends to keep the regional histories distinct.[8]

The *encounter model* stresses the creative interplay between insiders and outsiders. It borrows from the emergence model by spotlighting local agents and potential interest by providing insight into how a particular worldview and culture interpreted the Christianity that it received and accented particular themes that resonated in the culture. Attention is also paid to the themes that lack resonance or created dissonance in the culture. The key question is, How is Christianity produced in an area out of the encounter between two cultures? Conceptually, the encounter model must display more than contact and must explore mutuality. To switch to a botany metaphor, it must illustrate cross-fertilization, cross-pollination, that is, how through the encounter communities in both regions are changed. This model has the greatest conceptual capacity to engage a multiregional approach.

AN EXAMPLE OF REGIONAL HISTORY

Most of these models have the conceptual capacity to carry the teaching of regional histories, yet each one's limitations will affect teaching adversely. We must ask, In order to take local context/local histories or contextualization seriously, is the global history of Christianity best taught in terms of regional histories placed in a multiregional or continental framework? Regional histories allow for local stories to be heard rather than be drowned out by the dominant local stories of the West, and a multicontinental approach grants regional histories scope and depth.

Within a regional history of African Christianity, for example, a focus on Calvinism in South Africa illustrates some of the issues discussed above about models of history. Is the history best presented under an evolution, expansion, eruption, emergence, or encounter model? Which segments of the history are best employed by different models? South Africa serves as a good case study because of the various distinct communities involved in the construction of Christianity within that country.

Within South African society there are three major racial groups: Africans, Europeans, and Asians. The Africans belong to various ethnic groups such as Zulu and Xhosa. The Europeans consist of basically two white ethnic groups: Afrikaners who are descendants of the Dutch, who arrived first in 1652, and the English, the descendants of the British, who first came in 1795. The Afrikaners were primarily responsible for introducing Calvinism in South Africa. Prior to 1910, white colonies and black African kingdoms coexisted within the boundaries of contemporary South Africa. In 1910 the four white-ruled colonies united to form the Union of South Africa, and the white-ruled government dominated or colonized the black majority. The descendants of the British dominated the Union until 1948, when Afrikaners took over the government.[9]

Johann Kinghorn has employed an emergence model to study the social conditions that made it possible for Calvinism in South Africa to embrace apartheid by examining the impact of urbanization on Afrikaner churches between 1925 and 1950. Within this time period, the Afrikaner churches and communities shifted from being mainly rural, with members who were farmers and landowners, to being mainly urban, with members who were manual laborers and poor. In response to the social dislocation caused by urbanization, Afrikaner churches created programs to serve poor Afrikaners, whose impoverishment forced them, as poor whites, to compete with poor blacks (the Africans) for jobs and housing.

In response to the increasing competition between poor whites and blacks, and to the fear of interracial marriage among Afrikaners, some Afrikaner church leaders advocated segregation in employment, housing, churches, and social life. In 1948 this pattern of segregation, called "apartheid," became law when the political party of the Afrikaners, the National Party, took power. The new government passed the Prohibition of Mixed Marriages Act, the Immorality Act against interracial sexual relations, and the Group Areas Act, which legalized housing segregation. Each law reflected apartheid, the racial policy of Afrikaner Christianity.

Kinghorn traces the roots of apartheid to nineteenth-century neo-Calvinism, nationalism, and racism. Nation became the concept used to define the sociopolitical dimension of ethnicity. Theologically, only in and through a nation could individuals become fully human, and Christians were called to serve and love their nation as part of their calling to serve and love God. Ethically, it was argued, there exists a hierarchy of nations, and higher nations should not mix with lower nations. Pastorally, segregation defined all religious relations.

Afrikaners established separate denominations for whites, blacks, and mixed race peoples (so-called Coloreds). The black and Colored denominations were mission churches of the different Afrikaner (white) denominations.

While the emergence model provides Kinghorn with a framework to examine an aspect of Afrikaner Calvinism, other historical trajectories could also be studied, especially through the encounter model. The various developments associated with the relationship between Afrikaner Calvinism and other Christian traditions in South Africa itself could be the topic. There is also the wider inter- or multicontinental approach that would ask, What are the relationships between the developments in Calvinism in Holland and South Africa? What are the relationships between the developments within Calvinism among Afrikaners and black Africans? What are the relationships between the developments of other Afrikaner Christian communities such as the Pentecostalism of the Apostolic Faith Mission and Pentecostalism in Europe or North America?

FROM A REGIONAL TO A MULTICONTINENTAL VIEW

Moving beyond the approach of regional history presents many challenges. Because the expansion model has shaped the dominant historical narrative for church history, adopting other models of histories requires new images of the development of Christianity, as well as new methodologies. Borrowing from the French philosophers Gilles Deleuze and Felix Guattari to grasp the multiplicity of voices and the plurality of origins that construct the Christian tradition, Dale Irvin suggests rhizomes as a new image. Rhizomes are "plants with subterranean, horizontal root systems, growing below and above ground in multiple directions at once." Irvin contrasts rhizomes with trees to describe the interlocking character of Christian tradition.

> A tradition . . . is not like a tree, organized with a major trunk and smaller (or minor) branches, and drawing primarily from a single, dominant taproot that likewise grows in one direction. A

tradition is more like a rhizome, agglomerating and stabilizing at times around common experiences or locations, but then branching off and spreading rapidly at other times, in several directions at once. It is a decentered, or multicentered, system flowing across multiple material and subjective fields.[10]

This image provides a new way to visualize the relationship between Christianity on various continents, capturing the multiple ways in which the churches on these continents are intertwined historically.

Roger Bastide's sociological concept of the interpenetration of civilizations offers another way to go beyond the expansion model. "Continent" could be substituted for Bastide's term "civilization" in order to contend that a regional history must be interpreted as the intersection of continents. The resulting multicontinent approach would resist teaching the history of Christianity in Latin America as a mere extension of Portuguese and Spanish Catholicism. Instead Latin American Christianity would be studied as the product of the encounter between Native American, African, and Latin European civilizations, which created a cluster of religious expressions, ranging from varieties of Catholicisms to Neo-Yoruban religions such as Candomble. The accent would be on intercontinental and religious interaction, and in American Christianity would be historically reconstructed within a multicontinental approach that highlights the impact of non-Western cosmologies, cultures, and politics on the development of Christianity, while acknowledging the role of Latin European Catholicism.[11]

While we might engage in the process of historical reconstruction of regional histories, utilizing Bastide's concept of the interpenetration of civilizations, we must ponder, How employable is civilization as a construct? We cannot deny that a range of regional and diasporic identities do exist. On the one hand, there are societies or civilizations where continuous cultures and traditions do exist and offer good cases to study Bastide's approach. On the other hand, many societies can no longer presuppose continuities in cultures or traditions because of the impact of colonialism, postcolonialism, the market economy, nation making, and globalization. How do we illustrate the dynamic interaction in these societies with Bastide's approach? Scholars such as James Clifford may provide help. Clifford proposes developing a conception of culture that takes seriously both (1) the apparent disintegration of various cultures around the world as a result of the acid of modernity and (2) the integrity of the culture exhibited in its inventiveness. Continuity is not the only trait that indicates cultural vitality; inventiveness is a sure sign of cultural vigor. "Many traditions, practices, cosmologies, and values," according to Clifford, have been lost, and "some literally murdered; but much has simultaneously been invented and revived in complex, oppositional contexts." The challenge is to teach students to recognize the inventive nature of Korean Presbyterianism or Nigerian Anglicanism or Brazilian Pentecostalism.[12]

At its extreme, Clifford's project strives to interpret a postcolonial and postmodern culture, broadly defined, which appears to have no essential or distinctive features of "language, religion, land, economics, nor any other key institution or custom." By definition, culture is always acculturating. For Clifford, though, the key question is, "How much historical mix-and-match would be permissible before a certain organic unity is lost? Is the criterion a quantitative one? Or is there a reliable qualitative method for judging a culture's identity?" For our discussion, a couple of dynamics are at work. Let's use Korean Presbyterianism as an example. First, there's the inventiveness of Korean Presbyterianism. Second, there's the multicontinental interaction of which Korean Presbyterianism is a production.[13]

Another task of historical reconstruction is to recognize the dynamic nature of the interpenetration of civilizations. We can glean some insights about this from W. E. B. DuBois's concept of double consciousness, which has been employed by scholars to describe how African American Christianity embodies a dual religious heritage, African and European. We could widen DuBois's double consciousness into triple or quadruple consciousness, reflecting one's faith, gender, ethnicity/nationality, and culture so that under the rubric of Asian Christianity, the triple or quadruple consciousness of Tamil Christians would be distinguished from that of Maori Christians and Korean Christians. This option encapsulates the multiple paths a culture may use in strategies of cultural change, appropriation, resistance, subversion, masking, compromise, translation, invention, and revival. People utilize these paths as they confront the realities of dread, despair, depression, dis-ease, and death, as well as the realities of belonging, friendship, hope, love, and life, in addition to liberty and oppression. In the case of Korean Presbyterianism, for example, there exist multiple ways in which it can produce and reproduce itself. In developing a more complex concept of culture, we must be careful how we participate in the politics of difference. The politics of difference demonstrated the role of the Other in historical and contemporary ventures. For instance, Jean Danielou sketched early Christianity as three distinct realities: Jewish Christianity, Hellenistic Christianity, and Latin Christianity. He noted difference within the same era, yet ignored the cross-cultural exchanges and the broader commonalities. Currently, the politics of difference informs the historiography of studies in southern African church history, African American church history, Korean church history, and Filipino church history. How do we benefit pedagogically by pursuing this strategy? We do gain a sense of the particularity of different Christian communities. What do we lose pedagogically? We could lose a sense of the commonalities. A multicontinental approach would require attention be given to the cross-cultural exchanges as well as other interactions.[14]

THE MULTICONTINENTAL APPROACH, CHALLENGES OF PERIODIZATION, AND GLOBAL IDENTITY

Even after identifying the encounter model as the best and a multicontinental approach as ideal, there remains the issue of the ordering of the subject matter related to the history of Christianity. Ordering the material thematically without attention to chronology is an option, but most historians prefer wrestling with the challenge of periodization. Of course, periodization imposes artificial divisions, since the movement of history resembles a rushing river more than a cultivated field. Clearly the dominant scheme of periodization—the pre- and post-Nicene era, medieval era, Reformation and modern era, and post-Christendom era—privileges Western Christianity, fails to illuminate the history of Eastern Orthodoxy, and ranks the expressions of Christianity in the Two-thirds World as lesser movements.

While a new periodization that orders the global history of Christianity has yet to emerge, there are a couple of frameworks that could be employed as we wait. Justo González, for example, recommends a course on the origins and development of global Christianity. He begins the course with an analysis and characterization of the current reality of global Christianity. The course objective would be to answer the question, How did this come about? How was the current reality of global Christianity constructed? The history professor would arrange the subject matter of the history of global Christianity into various major sections and during the introduction of each major section would inquire how the events, discourses/worldviews, and people in a particular historical section participated in the construction of global Christianity. Attention would also be given to the events, discourses/worldviews, and people that contributed to alternative historical paths or trajectories.[15]

Another framework adopts a slightly different tactic. In addition to clustering the subject matter into eras or periods, the professor would offer a comparative discussion of the events, discourses, and people within these eras across the regions or continents where Christianity was practiced. The focus here is more on the multicontinental reality of Christianity and its continuities and discontinuities over time and space, rather than on the origins and development of global Christianity. The continuities and discontinuities of the multicontinental reality of Christianity would be studied within each major era as well as between eras. Thus connections would be drawn between Christianity on various continents during an era, in addition to connections between Christianity in different eras.

History is critical to the construction of the global identity of the church. I suspect most students still carry within their minds local or, at most, regional images of the church. How we teach history is partly to blame for this. Constructing a global identity of Christianity is complicated and must progress in a particular way. We must first construct and tell the local history of a student. That local history must be placed in a wider historical context of a region. The region should be situated in a multicontinental context. The dynamic interplay between these contexts must be highlighted, both within eras and between eras. Students should come to realize how churches on various continents within their era and the preceding era contributed to their Christian identity. They should also come to recognize the church in its multicontinental diversity and unity.

A multicontinental approach has much to offer in teaching the history of global Christianity. The small but growing selection of regional histories provides teachers with good material to draw upon. The course must be more than the reading of a string of regional histories from different continents; it must also highlight the interactions and exchanges between and within regions. As I have noted, the existence of regional histories does not eliminate for the teacher the difficulties of employing compatible models of history and schemas of periodizations. When they are crafted, the professor will advance the teaching and representation of global Christianity.

OTHER PEDAGOGICAL MUSINGS

How does a professor utilize texts whose models clash with the model reflected in her lectures and her pedagogical objectives? Clearly the professor should instruct the students in how to critique historical texts and models. While this is educational, the effort might better be expended on other topics. And there are other pedagogical issues. What are the best cognitive strategies for students? Should linear thinking or spiral thinking shape the lectures and discussions? Or should both be at play? Which cultural values should be operative? Should communal values become the norm, or should individualism be prized? How do the dynamics of honor and shame function? Do we incorporate pluriformity or uniformity in how the class operates? Is a polycentric and multivocal view embedded in the course, or is a monocentric and univocal view upheld? How do we honor and hear local stories? How do they relate to the other narratives of the course?

CONCLUSION

The global reality of Christianity can be presented critically and imaginatively in the classroom. It will require new interpretive images, such as rhizomes, and new interpretive approaches, such as the interpenetration of civilizations. These approaches can provide material to construct the local and regional identities of Christians and churches around the world. And with these identities, Christians will be able to recognize each other as Christians regardless of historical differences.

Pivotal to this new history is the construction of a globalized narrative. The narrative will be tentative because of the challenge of engaging multiple voices and viewpoints. In the classroom, the tentativeness of a globalized narrative can be accented, illustrating the difficulty of teaching in this new way. While there exists a growing collection of excellent surveys and monographs that explore regional histories, there remains the pedagogical task of illustrating how and where these fine regional histories interrelate.

NOTES

1. Adrian Hastings, *The Church in Africa 1450–1950* (Oxford and New York: Oxford University Press, 1994); Adrian Hastings, *A History of African Christianity 1950–1975* (1979); Elizabeth Isichei, *A History of Christianity in Africa* (Grand Rapids: Eerdmans, 1995); Enrique Dussel, *A History of the Church in Latin America*, trans. Alan Neely (Grand Rapids: Eerdmans, 1981); Samuel Hugh Moffett, *A History of Christianity in Asia*, vol. 1, *Beginnings to 1500* (San Francisco: HarperCollins, 1992); Justo L. González, *The Story of Christianity*, 2 vols. (San Francisco: Harper & Row, 1985); John McManners, ed., *The Oxford*

Illustrated History of Christianity (Oxford and New York: Oxford University Press, 1993); Adrian Hastings, ed., *A World History of Christianity* (Grand Rapids: Eerdmans, 1999); Paul R. Spickard and Kevin M. Cragg, *A Global History of Christians: How Everyday Believers Experienced Their World* (Grand Rapids: Baker Academic, 1994).

2. Frederic Jameson, "Postmodern and the Consumer Society," in Hal Foster, ed., *Anti-Aesthetic* (Port Washington, NY: Bay Press, 1983), 112.

3. See Robert F. Berkhofer Jr., *Beyond the Great Story: History as Text and Discourse* (Cambridge: Belknap Press of Harvard University Press, 1995).

4. Joyce Appleby, Lynn Hunt, and Margaret Jacob, *Telling the Truth about History* (New York: Norton, 1994).

5. Berkhofer, 138–76.

6. See Williston Walker, *The History of the Christian Church* (New York: Scribners, 1985).

7. See Kenneth Scott Latourette, *History of the Expansion of Christianity* (New York: Harper & Bros., 1937–1945).

8. See Ogbu Kalu, *The Embattled Gods: Christianization of Igboland, 1841–1991* (London and Lagos: Minaj Publishers, 1996).

9. Johann Kinghorn, "Modernization and Apartheid: The Afrikaner Churches," in *Christianity in South Africa: A Political, Social, and Cultural History*, ed. Richard Elphick and Rodney Davenport (Berkeley: University of California Press, 1997).

10. Dale T. Irvin, *Christian Histories, Christian Traditioning: Rendering Accounts* (Maryknoll, NY: Orbis Books, 1998), 47.

11. Roger Bastide, *The African Religions of Brazil: Toward a Sociology of the Interpenetration of Civilizations* (Baltimore: Johns Hopkins University Press, 1978).

12. James Clifford, *The Predicament of Culture: Twentieth-Century Ethnography, Literature, and Art* (Cambridge: Harvard University Press, 1988), 16.

13. Ibid., 323.

14. See W. E. B. DuBois, *The Souls of Black Folk* (1903; New York: Penguin Press, 1982); J. Danielou and H. I. Marrou, *The Christian Centuries, I* (London, 1964).

15. Justo L. González, "Globalization in the Teaching of Church History," *Theological Education* (Spring 1993), 67.

CHAPTER 16

Multicultural Theological Education in a Non-Western Context:

Africa, 1975-2000

Ogbu U. Kalu

CONSTRUCTING A MULTICULTURAL DISCOURSE

The concept of multiculturalism has become ambiguous. In the North American context, it conjures images related to the culture wars or serves as a code word for race, socioeconomic class, gender, language, sexual preferences, or disability. It may even be used as a term of derision regarding ethnic differences. From a simple literary perspective, it moves beyond the presence of many cultures in one context to the dynamics of their interaction, the potential for an emergent culture, and the unavoidable competition that results amid various efforts to dominate the environment and formulate "a competing definition of the social world that corresponds to a particular social, political and economic interest."[1]

Multiculturalism is a power concept because it refers to the cultural hegemony that orders access to resources and defines the fortunes of those who are powerless due to race, gender, and class. It describes the power dynamics that emerge when differences are encountered in the public space. It turns attention to the problem of social justice in the face of efforts by the powerful to protect their vested interests by installing a monoculture, consensus, and common culture in which they determine the boundaries and composition. It has been symbolized by concepts such as the melting pot or assimilation policy (sometimes modified along liberal lines) and by the rainbow or pluralistic model that creates a sanitized social space where each culture is acknowledged and the social justice implications of the power of the dominant group are blurred. Without valorizing the concept of multiculturalism to include conflicts over political, economic, and social justice, it could be weakened, and already many prefer cross-culturality or even transculturality as an alternative concept.

At the heart of multiculturalism lie the understandings that in culture contact, (1) hegemonic forces compel the assertion of local identities, (2) the weak create infrapolitical zones of resistance and appropriation, and (3) the weak design an epicenter where deep interests are retained while the interaction occurs at the periphery. Thus, those who are powerless retain agency and could eventually challenge domination systems. The challenge of multiculturalism becomes crucial when it is applied first to education and specifically to theological education. It compels both a strategy of teaching and learning that affirms the full humanity of the other person, and reflection upon and practice of the rulership of God in such a manner that love of God and love of neighbor are affirmed in a beloved community.

The Lucan account of the council of Jerusalem shows clearly that the Jewish definition of the Gentiles as goyim and their claim that salvation belonged first to Jews soon produced the demand that converts live as if they were proselytes. The first debate in the new Jesus movement was over multicultural theology. Former proselytes and God-fearers appropriated the gospel in a new way and challenged the cultural hegemony mounted by the Jews.

A similar debate was repeated in latter centuries in the cross-cultural mission fields, where indigenous forces contested missionary education strategies that hindered the converts' capacity to critically reflect on and experience God within the contexts of their cultures. When the architects of the colonial canopy watched its disheveled collapse in the 1960s, missionaries saw their educational heritage scrambled by new religious forces and experiments on models of theological education. Over the last quarter century African churches have crafted theological education models that could answer the questions raised in the interior of indigenous worldviews and that could empower converts to be truly human, instead of being imitators of Western cultures. There were two dimensions to the problem: first, how to respond to the cultural challenges that daily confront African Christians; and second, how to groom priests who are sensitive to the needs of the indigenous contexts. The challenges proved intractable because of the tensile strength of missionary heritage.

The concern of this chapter is a historical reconstruction of the theological education models practiced by African churches in the postcolonial period. In Africa, theological education models betrayed the heart of the missionary cross-cultural ideology, because it encrusted a conservative multiculturalism that believed in the superiority of Western civilization, locked education into the project of overrule, and created a model of ministerial formation that was less than educational. We will see that today, although vestiges of missionary hardware remain, the experiment with tertiary education by African churches has created a new opportunity for the application of an indigenous model of theological education. In fact, in recent years, young educated Christians have designed a new strategy of "formation-by-engagement."

THE MISSIONARY HERITAGE UNDER THE COLONIAL CANOPY

For the African missionary fields, two types of personnel were recruited and trained: foreign missionary agents and indigenous or "native agents." This reflection focuses on the latter. Theological education flourished in the early Christian era in Africa. The catechetical school in Alexandria produced muscular apologists who consolidated the Jesus movement when it moved out of Palestine. When Europe encountered Africa in the sixteenth century, Portugal established cathedral schools in the Cape Verde Islands, São Tomé, Luanda, and Goa (India) to train priests for Africa. But racist assimilation policy severely restricted ordination to mulatto children and servants of Portuguese traders. The slave trade throttled the missionary enterprise until its resurgence in the nineteenth century. By this time new ideologies colored European-African cultural encounters. Education served as the core instrument in the colonization, civilization, and evangelization projects, and therefore encapsulated the challenges in multicultural theological education.

After the 1885 partition of Africa, European hubris that resulted from technological power, interdenominational rivalry, and the privileging of commercial interests combined to generate a strong racist attitude. Missionary education came to be built on a conservative multiculturalism that disdained indigenous cultures and sought to reproduce the patterns of education practiced in various European centers. Ministerial formation was dovetailed into the school system; schools served as means of evangelization, designed to introduce the new converts to the Bible and other forms of Christian literature and to nurture indigenous Christian leadership. The goal was to "civilize," change the personality of the candidates, and supplant orality with Western literacy, because it was alleged that the vernacular lacked the finesse, the vocabulary, and the potential to serve as a viable mode of teaching and learning in the future. To provide the converts with an access to the Bible, missionaries translated it into many indigenous dialects. However, the vernacular was used for instruction only at the primary levels of education, while European languages were used at the higher rungs.

Just as missionary organizations expanded rapidly into the interior of Africa after the First World War, geopolitical factors hindered their capacity to supply the necessary level of staffing. In some places, the inhospitable climate exacerbated the problem, as, before quinine was discovered, malaria increased the mortality rate of missionary personnel. The need for "native agents" became urgent, and administrators scoured the West Indies for educated Africans.[2] Beyond walled institutions, missionaries trained agents through apprenticeship, as cooks, stewards, interpreters, porters, house boys, and house girls could later become church servants, evangelists, and deacons, and a few might become pastors. All missionary bodies were hesitant to ordain indigenous people as pastors. Some Protestant bodies did ordain them, but many Roman Catholic orders persevered in using foreign agency until the twilight of the colonial period. Racism was rife. The schools' regimen and curricula were designed to groom indigenous leaders as mission agents and teachers in village schools. The curricula not only ignored the cultural environment but set out to undermine indigenous values and cultural traditions. They rejected the indigenous authority structures and created new leadership and ministerial systems along European models. The preference for residential or walled institutions enhanced control, removed the students from their world, and assimilated them into Western culture.

Opinions varied. Some wanted to replicate European education models and produce a native elite that would interpret Western values to their people.[3] Liberal multiculturalists argued in favor of keeping the native agents close to their cultural environment and severely limiting their literacy. Still others, such as the French Holy Ghost Fathers, deployed the method used in juvenile delinquency homes in France, best described by Michel Foucault in *Discipline and Punish*, where the goal was the re-formation of personality and morals. He imaged the enterprise with an apt term: *docile bodies*. A body that is docile may be subjected, used, transformed, and improved. Africans were perceived as plastic, and if chosen young, they would be the recipients of a newly constructed individuality, achieved by the allocation of space, use of time, and other forms of regimen in enclosed school spaces or compounds.

Some missionaries taught physical and industrial education, hygiene, and Bible literacy in enclaves or mission centers. The strategy rejected "book learning" as the chief goal of ministerial formation, because both

colonial officers and missionaries disdained the pretensions of the educated Africans. In 1912, J. R. Mott, the secretary of the International Missionary Council, enthused that "the influence of Western learning has
been in the direction of undermining the faith of the student class in the
non-Christian religions and of breaking up the social and ethical restraints
of the old civilizations."[4] This attitude reflects a rejection of a critical
multiculturalism that would use education to cultivate the knowledge of
self and agency to develop the resources for a truly human life. Instead,
the installation of a common culture remained at the heart of missionary education until the 1940s, when secular intervention differentiated
between teacher training, industrial education, and secondary or grammar schools. Missionary critics insisted that the "fauchet-sponge" model
of education in classroom environment encouraged learning by rote,
stunted creativity, and did little for moral development; that Africans
educated in the old model remained lazy and immoral.

Among Protestants, there were no seminaries, specifically as seminaries in the modern sense, manqué until the late 1940s. The idea arose in
response to the need to train deacons and rural evangelists who could
serve as foot soldiers for competing missionary organizations as they
expanded rapidly in the African interior. Roman Catholics had decided
earlier to counteract government interference by designing seminaries
that served as both grammar schools and undertook priestly formation.
By 1948, the colonial governments buttressed missionary control of primary and secondary levels of education, and responded to African
demand for higher education by establishing universities.

The initial challenge to missionary education came from the first generation of educated Africans. Dubbed "Ethiopians" (because they took
their motto from the promise made to Africa in Ps. 68:31), they objected
to the cultural hubris of missionaries and gave voice to African discon-
tent. Some dared to exit from missionary structures by founding their
own educational institutions without foreign aid. Although they promoted indigenous cultures, as scions of the Western civilization that they
loved to imitate, they failed to design alternative indigenous curricula
and strategies.

TEE AND ITS ENEMIES: THE HEIGHT OF LIBERAL
THEOLOGICAL EDUCATION, 1975–85

A second challenge to missionary education emerged after decolonization, when the proponents of *theological education by extension* (TEE)

contested the predominantly walled institutions: to cure the cultural dislocation of the environment of learning, they proposed placing the students within their own cultural settings so that the educational process could enhance their coping abilities and the quality of their witness. They criticized the increasing cost of education. Indeed, Protestants had tried to save costs by founding ecumenical seminaries, such as Fort Hare in South Africa; Trinity College, Legon (Ghana); Trinity College, Umuahia (Nigeria); St. Paul's, Limuru (Kenya); Faculte de Theologie, Yaounde (Cameroon). All were joint ecumenical ventures. But TEE advocates argued that the ecumenical solution was inadequate, especially when intense rivalry preserved purely denominational institutions, and vitiated ecumenical ventures. Meanwhile, Bible schools emerged among smaller denominations, and institutions for the formation of rural evangelists and deacons sprouted. Many of the colleges/seminaries offered only sub-degree diploma certificates. In the 1960s, the Roman Catholics and some evangelicals founded degree-awarding institutions affiliated with Western institutions such as Concordia University and Urbana University, Rome. Within a decade, the newly independent nations seized mission-founded schools and hospitals, banned these offshore degrees, and insisted on affiliation to local universities.

TEE proposed a multicultural theological education that was sensitive to the learning environment, the cultural imperatives, relevant curriculum, and funding. Its supporters argued that ministerial formation should integrate the academic, moral, and leadership expectations and that creative education should include learning and working, or practicing the *praxis–reflection–praxis* model, and should avoid the dangers of dependency. Dependency bred vulnerability and vitiated the development of selfhood and access to the wealth of indigenous resources and cultural knowledge. The TEE model would combine Western and indigenous models of educating those who would minister among their own peoples, and without it, they argued, the Christian God would remain a stranger among African communities. In the early 1980s the advocacy assumed an evangelical tone as TEE became viewed as a panacea for African ministerial formation. It sought to privilege human experience in the learning process, based on responses to environment and culture, to ensure self-development, liberation, creativity, and spiritual growth. This solution would make theological education more accessible to poorer candidates in the rural areas and would increase the size of a viable leadership cadre.[5]

TEE incorporated some elements of pluralistic multiculturalism that recognized the salience of the many cultural systems in Africa and their value in designing a model of theological education. But it also suffered from many problems related to curriculum, pedagogy, ideology, and funding. Someone had to write the curricula, create access to the materials, and enable dialogue and communal reflection. Costs remained high, and the curricula could not escape a Western orientation, because a host of white missionaries were deployed to work on TEE ministry and write the materials. Logistics based on the level of infrastructure vitiated the possibilities of distributing and retrieving instructional materials, and supervising the students. For instance, the vaunted ideals of refurbishing some radio and taping stations, contacting the students through radio, and distributing materials through audiotapes failed because of lack of funding. Ideologically, a balanced education should expose students to diverse cultural resources and opportunities and enlarge their vision about issues of social justice. Critics alleged, however, that TEE tended to encourage closed, narrow boundaries, and that it resonated with the liberal multicultural model that would keep the participants forever around their rural locations of birth. With increasing urbanization and upward mobility, few students would accept the limited boundaries.

TEE's enemies included the defenders of residential education, who insisted that walled education offered consistent supervision in formation for ministerial leadership, allowing academic studies, devotional life (personal and communal), and practical work to be carried out in a consistent, regular, and in-depth manner that would enable progressive development. Formation in residence particularly, they believed, enables the spiritual development-in-community that is a vital component of congregational life and nurtures fellowship between candidates for the ministry. Formation inside the walls was balanced with ministry in communities during the field work periods.[6]

But TEE's death knell was actually sounded by traditionalism, the internalization of long years of missionary tradition. African theological education sought to shed the vestiges of colonialism and yet perceived TEE to be inferior education whose certificates could not be accredited by "normal" authorities. Like meal tickets, certificates opened the cafeteria doors of modern life. Today accreditation in African ministerial formation is still a problem. Each nation state designs its own rules, and it has been impossible to weave a transnational accreditation system.

From 1965 to 1985, in response to nationalism and the efforts to decolonize the African churches, an outbreak of ecumenism occurred in many African countries. This may have been a survival strategy or passive revolution; nonetheless, by the early 1980s most of the talks about church unity sponsored by the WCC occurred in Africa, with the Church of South India providing a model for Africa. Many efforts failed by the end of the 1980s, as nontheological factors ruined ecumenical endeavors. Years of intense rivalry could not be wiped away by musing on how pleasant it could be for Christians to come together. Moreover, the motivation for ecumenism came externally. To encourage ecumenical theological education, African theological institutions and departments of religion in African universities were grouped into regional associations: southern, eastern, central, western, francophone Africa. The goals were to engage African scholars across denominational lines to design indigenous ministerial formation and escape from the inherited and stultifying models. The focus included reviewing the curricula, staff development, improving library facilities, acquisition of books published outside the regions, Bible translation and writing of Bible commentaries by Africans for African congregations, encouragement of scholarship, and journal publications. In 1980 the regional institutions formed a continental Conference of African Theological Institutions to address broader problems and enable Western bodies to link coherently with the continent, neutralizing the virulent aspects of denominationalism. But by the 1990s these agencies had collapsed, due primarily to the resurgence of denominationalism and leadership failure. A typical African theological educator has many constituencies to serve; many fail to concentrate on onerous tasks such as demanded by international organizations.

In the 1980s, Africans insisted that "mis-formation" was at the root of the failure of African Christian leadership and weakened the churches. They realized that when Western institutions fund the education of Africans, the curricula are not designed to serve African needs, just as diversity in racial population of Western seminaries does not imply diversity in perspectives. Many Africans had to suppress their thoughts and feelings in order to gain the certificate or "golden fleece"; and a patronage system allowed foreign students to graduate despite poor performance, on the understanding that they were going back to their homes. After African bishops pointed to the disadvantages of training priests in Europe, the *Propaganda Fide* section of the Vatican experimented with Catholic Higher Institutes located in Port Harcourt, Nigeria, for west Africa, Nairobi for eastern Africa, and Dakar for francophone Africa. Protestants initiated the *doctorat troisieme* cycle programs for francophone Africans in Younde and Congo Kinshasha.

This is the background to two new developments. First, the 1970s saw the explosion of new evangelical and Pentecostal groups that emphasized evangelization and charismatized the mainline churches. Second, untrained evangelists sprouted with immense implications for ministerial formation. These trends have catalyzed enormous growth of Christianity in Africa and created the need for more pastors than walled schools could produce.[] But growth could be traumatic.

EMERGENT FORMS OF MINISTERIAL FORMATION

The quality of Christianity in Africa depends on how churches train their leadership. The complexity and trauma of church growth are most perceptible in emergent forms of ministerial formation. The Presbyterian Church (U.S.A.) reported in its 2004 Church Development Bulletin that

> Despite the harshness of life in Malawi, rapid church growth has continued. In the CCAP there is a perpetual shortage of ministers and lay leaders. There is just one theological college for the church, Zomba Theological College. It is limited in the number of candidates it can take from each synod and so, from time to time the synods have instituted their own emergency training courses for ministerial candidates.

Massive and unstoppable church growth is yielding a large cache of candidates for the ministry. Can the churches deal with the bulging membership with a ministerial formation strategy based on inherited patterns and walled institutions? Ministerial training used to take a careful selection of candidates for the ministry, followed with a number of years of training. Today, however, the numbers of believers and types of Christian groups have expanded at such an incredible rate that the greatest need is trained personnel. Competition, inherited and conflicting theologies, and jealousy over turf add to the problem. Many people cannot wait for long years of training. Confident of a spiritual experience and a divine call, they start their own ministries without formal training; this is known as *setting up a new altar*. Large numbers of church leaders who work in professional areas such as medicine, architecture, academics, banking, and insurance desert those professions for full-time ministries. Many churches abandon the old strategies of ministerial formation as de-schooling predominates in theological education.

In the scrambled patterns of ministerial formation, many pastors train their own new leaders. This pattern of in-house apprenticeship is often imaged as *gaining a mantle*. The pastor teaches all subjects and does not seek accreditation from an outside body. Some ministries build Bible colleges and seminaries. But the quality has been uneven, and few have accreditation. Governments compel seminaries that have reasonable infrastructure and manpower to affiliate with state-owned universities.

Growth has traumatized theological education in Africa, where church leaders are more interested in certificates, especially from foreign countries, and obtain degrees by taking correspondence courses from American or South Asian institutions. Others simply buy certificates from fake operators. Groups of Americans travel through the Third World ordaining bishops and granting degrees as a way of building a "worldwide network." In bizarre cases, the operators arrive in an African country, hire a hall in an academic institution, pay in foreign currency, and organize a graduation ceremony with gowns, mortarboards, and pomp. Some Nigerian seminaries have taken steps to combat this practice by forming an association, the Nigerian Theological Education Council, and establishing an accreditation body in 1999. It operates under the Accrediting Council for Theological Education in Africa that is run by the Association of Evangelicals in Africa, headquartered in Nairobi. The challenges of theological education in Africa cluster around accreditation and quality control, a curricular ideology that is sensitive to cultural and social justice challenges, and funding for an infrastructure that enables a critical theological formation.

THE RISE OF CHRISTIAN UNIVERSITIES IN AFRICA, 1990–2000

Thus, the context of contemporary Christian education in Africa is characterized by an expanding demand, dwindling government resources, moral discourse, and Afrocentric ideology. In the last two decades, a new phenomenon has emerged: churches spurring the growth of private higher education in Africa. Some of the private universities are secular and "managed by a new group of 'education entrepreneurs' deploying market principles in education."[8] While, as Beth Tavers argues, a majority of the private universities in Kenya are secular, in many other African countries they are largely church operated.

Although African countries took over education from missionaries, recognizing that their goals, ideology, and strategies were not liberating, the hubris of state governments evaporated with population growth and the collapse of economies. Governments could no longer afford to provide adequate tertiary education or to monopolize education. The IMF and World Bank urged African governments to adopt an ideology of liberalization, privatization, and commercialization in their broad economic policies and practices. This affected education policies and funding very dramatically. Education came to be viewed as an investment that should pay its way, as does any other enterprise, and should be privatized and available for those who could afford it. Churches that were pushed away from primary and secondary education during the heydays of decolonization reentered the education field at the tertiary level.

There are other reasons for the rise of Christian universities: Christianity's reengaging the public space after years at the periphery, the collapse of morality in state institutions, a surging demand for education that the existing tertiary institutions cannot adequately meet. This could be partially explained by the youthful bulge in the continent's demographic profile. For instance, in 1999 Central University College opened in Accra with an enrollment of 428 students, which increased to 952 by 2000, and surpassed 2,000 in the 2003–04 academic session.[9] The bachelor's degree in business administration, which includes a computer training component, is the most attractive sector. Some perceive this demand for computer training as being driven by global market economy, but it emerges from the theology of the leader, Mensah Otabil. His concept of "practical Christianity" extols moral and theological values such as self-reliance, human dignity, and excellence. Christians, he asserts, should not romanticize poverty but develop all their God-given resources and strive to succeed; a vital relationship with Christ must result in an abundant and improved quality of life. Though the business sector brings in much of the school's income, there is no attempt to articulate the goals of the institution in an entrepreneurial manner.

In Nigeria, Bishop David Oyedepo describes the vision of Covenant University in similar terms, using the concept of Total Man. This mission statement appears on the Web site and on all the official documents of the school: "This concept centers on developing the man who will develop his world. It is designed to produce students who are intelligently conscious of their environment and who know how to maximize their potentials in life. The programs of the University are first directed at the person before addressing his profession."[10]

Oyedepo insists that the curricula ensure "sound cultural and moral ethic, managerial and sensitive skills and self-development training designed to achieve integrated, holistic life-centered perspective." His vision is the Nehemiah Complex, rebuilding Nigeria's collapsed education structure with a world-class university system. Covenant University, located at Ota, Ogun state of Nigeria, opened its doors in 2003 with 1,360 students: 693 females and 667 males. It has an attractive campus and, by the 2005 National Universities Commission's accreditation report, has adequately met the challenges of an adequate faculty, infrastructure, and funding to match its pace of growth.

The enrollment levels in some institutions such as West African Theological Seminary, Lagos, indicate that many church leaders are hungry for formal theological education. For instance, in the period 2003–05, bishops from Nigeria, Liberia, Sierra Leone, Kenya, and Cameroon oversubscribed a master's degree program designed for ecclesiastical leaders.

Daystar University's mission statement identifies another reason for the rise of Christian universities:

> At Daystar, five African students can be educated for the cost of sending one student overseas. By educating committed leaders in an African context to address the needs and issues of the continent, Daystar is an important solution to Africa's 'brain drain', reversing the loss of its talented young people. Daystar University provides some of the finest Christian education available in East Africa so its graduates are prepared to boldly lead communities, businesses and churches well into the 21st century.[11]

Daystar brags that many of its alumni are serving the nation in parliament, the education sector, relief agencies, indeed the entire society "with leadership rooted in Christian values," echoing the common theme that the problem of the continent is lack of leadership with a strong ethical orientation. It is, therefore, critical for these institutions to distinguish between entrepreneurial goals and Christian goals, especially because higher institutions are cost intensive. Many of the mission statements posted on the websites reflect a theological education for a global pluralistic environment. For instance, Benson Idahosa University, in Benin, has a vision to "raise an army of professionals and academics who would go in Christ's name to the ends of the world with the fire of the Holy Ghost to impart truth by precept and example." Recently, it broadened its curriculum into law, medicine, applied science, and management science.[12]

In Nigeria, the National University Commission has approved about twenty church-related universities and many secular and Muslim ones in the last decade. Among the Christian universities, five are Roman Catholic, three are Anglican; the Methodists, Baptists, Seventh Day Adventists, and Evangelical Church of West Africa own one university each; and the rest are Pentecostal. Ghana has about eleven government-accredited degree-awarding institutions, most of which are church-related. This trend is occurring across the entire continent, as many churches revamp old teachers' colleges and Bible colleges. In many countries, national education watchdogs supervise the expansion to ensure adequate infrastructure, funding, human resources, and academic integrity. The culture of paper qualification, which is an ingrained neocolonial vestige, challenges the ideologies of Christian universities. A degree grants status; a pastor's doctorate degree becomes a marker of the quality of a church.

The pattern of ministerial formation in Africa has been scrambled, reflecting the traumatic effects of growth in African Christianity. Who could control all these institutions and ensure an accredited performance, a liberating curriculum, and adequate infrastructure? In Nigeria and Ghana, the universities are linked to the National University Commissions and, therefore, have strong supervisory bodies. In 2000, the vice chancellors of five private universities in Tanzania met in Dar es Salaam to establish the Tanzania Association of Private Universities to bring some order into the new system. But competition remains rife among the churches and hinders cooperation, because establishing a university constitutes a mark of success in the African environment.

MINISTERIAL "FORMATION-BY-ENGAGEMENT" AND RECOVERY OF MISSIONAL VOCATION

A hopeful dimension in ministerial formation is the intense recovery of the missional vocation of the church among the new Christian groups, a result of the new charismatic spirituality. This has spawned its own model of ministerial formation that is informal, outside the walls, and practical. Instead of sitting in classrooms, many students take a few weeks of preparatory briefing and voyage out into new mission fields where formation occurs *in situ*. Theological education occurs in the midst of the encounter of the gospel and indigenous cultures. The church becomes the presence, witness, representative, and foretaste of the kingdom of God in communities. In the encounter, the missionary becomes a learner who assists communities to experience and receive the gift and resources of the kingdom. This is the essence of *missio Dei*. Rural evangelism is a missionary engagement that requires baptizing the cultures, nations, and peoples; unmasking the powers that dehumanize and deface people; and a holistic and dialogical engagement that identifies and affirms the signals of transcendence in cultures, brings enabling spiritual discernment to people as they cope in challenging environments. This is a major shift in the style of doing mission and ministerial formation. It is not about charity but a different style of presence and empowering agents.

This new strategy has radically reshaped the old missionary model. The transformation is crucial because some Western bodies have given up and others are financially constrained. The trend goes back to the Whitby Conference of International Missionary Council in 1951, when the concept of partnership became important in defining the relationship between the old and emergent centers. Networking, short-term mission, and NGOs now dominate Western missionary strategy. Other strategies include nonproprietary modes of missionary activities and funding of non-Western personnel.

Ministerial formation under the burgeoning African missionary enterprise has eluded scholarly enquiry. There are three dimensions to this missionary work: within a nation, within Africa, and cross-culturally outside Africa. The third dimension, including the African Christian presence in the West, has attracted much attention. Imaged as a "reverse flow," the religion of immigrants attracts attention as a force that reshapes the religious landscapes of Europe and hides the impact of religion's decline in the Northern Hemisphere.[13] Functionalists examine the impact of such ethnic-based expression of Christianity in assisting immigrants to cope with the challenges of their new contexts by providing financial, emotional, and referral services; maintaining and redefining ethnic identity; and creating an enclave that retains connections with the homeland. Despite the growth and importance of emergent immigrant congregations, their capacity to foray beyond racial and ethnic boundaries is questioned.

The concern here is that inadequate attention has been paid to the emergent model of theological education, namely "ministerial formation by engagement"(MFE). As argued earlier, Western models of education erode the sense of the supernatural and eclipse the experiential dimension of the Christian faith. The MFE model counters with a spiritual model of education that advocates dependency on the Spirit.[14] We shall illustrate it with examples from West Africa. Its origin harks back to the youthful, charismatic, university students of the 1970s. These students recovered a spirit of evangelization and regained a passion to evangelize in Muslim enclaves and unreached parts of the nation. Later, many of the resulting ministries consolidated their visions to evangelize other African nations, relocating the sites for multicultural theological education to the missionary fields.

This trend, which has grown through the last three decades, can be illustrated with numerous ministries in Ghana, Kenya, and Nigeria. In

Nigeria, young graduates who were posted by the National Youth Service Corps (NYSC) to serve in northern Nigeria during the mid-1970s started the Calvary Ministries, later known as CAPRO. Both organizations were connected with the Nigerian Fellowship of Evangelical Students (NIFES), and their initial goal was to minister to Muslims a daunting task that collapsed. But they reorganized to include outreach to unevangelized ethnic groups in northern Nigeria.

By the 1980s, CAPRO had broadened their vision, sending missionaries to Gambia and Senegal—Muslim states. In Gambia they cooperated with the British World-wide Evangelization Crusade (WEC) missionaries. WEC turned over the mission field to them. Around the same time, the Christian Missionary Foundation (CMF) was established in Ibadan (southwestern Nigeria). They too started evangelizing parts of rural southwest and central Nigeria, using agricultural projects and health-care delivery as entree into communities. Soon they sent missionaries to Cote d'Ivoire, the Gambia, Republic of Benin, and Liberia, where they assisted the indigenes to form a local branch. For instance, in Benin, Paul Zinsou started as a representative of CFM and later built a local group with fifty-seven missionaries. Similarly, the CFM started the Ministere de l'Evangelisation des Enfants pour l'Afrique Francophone en Cote d'Ivoire and invited the partnership of a local church, Eglise Evangelique de Reveil. Other missionary groups sprouted, such as the Grace Evangelistic Mission, Harvesters Mission, and Children Evangelism and Mission. All these sent missionaries both internally and internationally along the West African coast. The Missionary Crusades Ministry concentrated, in contrast, on reaching some of the sixteen identified unreached peoples in northern Nigeria; their mission to the mountain Koma people won national attention.[15]

In Ghana, the Nigerians catalyzed a similar trend. The Ghana Evangelical Missionary Association, Christian Outreach Foundation (started 1987; focus on church planting), African Christian Mission (1984; education), and Torchbearers (1987; medical work in Mali) are only a few. The ACM co-operated with Action Partners, formerly the Sudan Interior Mission. By the late 1980s a number of Pentecostal ministries started vigorous missionary activities along the coast: The Deeper Life had already distinguished itself as an evangelistic ministry that pushed Pentecostalism from urban to rural areas, grew to almost a million members, and expanded beyond Nigeria. The Church of the Pentecost in Ghana and Redeemed Christian Church of God Mission in Nigeria joined the enterprise. The Redeemed, Deeper Life, and Winners Chapel run television programs in South Africa, Kenya, and many other African countries. Many Liberian and Ivorien missionaries are working among refugees. Deeper Life missionaries from Nigeria went into Burundi refugee camps in Dar es Salaam. (The Christianity of refugee camps is another huge topic in contemporary African Christianity, because of the spate of civil wars in the last two decades.) Malawi missionaries are laboring in northern Ghana just as Congolese Catholic fathers are working in Nigeria. The Holy Ghost Fathers sent Nigerian priests in 1976 to the Gambia to teach in St. Augustine's Secondary School. The real motive was to tour the rural districts and demonstrate that indigenous Africans can serve as priests.

The curriculum in each program is shaped by the challenges. The funding strategy is indigenized to obviate dependency syndrome: charismatic ministries fund themselves; some ask the prospective missionaries to source their funds from a group of supporters/partners; others pay low stipends and honoraria to be supplemented by partners. A group known as Gospel Bankers was formed in Jos to assist such missionaries. But many of the missionary associations encourage professionals to offer short-term free services. For instance, at the end of the Liberian crisis, the Intercessors for Africa (a Nigerian prayer house) sent volunteer professionals to serve for agreed periods of time at their own costs. Doctors, nurses, teachers, and others went to Liberia as led and sustained by the Spirit. Some missionary groups are linked with the Third World Mission Association that was inaugurated in Portland, Oregon, in 1989, others with World Link University, an education project. Some Africans serve as the executives of these associations but these groups are not funding agencies. It should be added that the African missionary enterprise benefited from the precedence of African Indigenous Churches (such as the Church of the Lord Aladura) that started in the 1940s and also from the AD 2000 and Beyond that encouraged many African missionary groups to pick up the gauntlet. As the Ethiopian movement of the 1890s intoned, *Africans must evangelize Africa.* To undertake the arduous evangelization process, many young families undergo an orientation program followed by annual reunions and intensive workshops. They represent how contemporary African Christianity is grappling creatively with the trauma of growth created by the explosion of the numbers of converts.

The encounter with the West ensured that the problem of theological education in Africa would center around the capacity to be multicultural: through interactions among the myriad cultures of Africa; encounters with the gospel and Western cultures; responses to the new states and socioeconomic and political forces; forming theological reflection and practices in the midst of the scourge of poverty, civil wars, abuse of human rights, disease, and legitimacy crises. Since 1975 Africans have experimented with various indigenous multicultural models that liberate them from the vestiges of missionary influence and engage global cultural flows, theories of knowledge, and the urgent need to evangelize.

NOTES

1. Joe L. Kincheloe and Shirley R. Steinberg, *Changing Multiculturalism* (Buckingham, UK: Open University Press, 1997), 2.

2. Daniel Antwi and Paul Jenkins, "The Moravians, the Basel Mission and Akuapem State in the Early Nineteenth Century," in *Christian Missionaries and the State in the Third World,* ed. Holger Bernt Hansen and Michael Twaddle (Oxford: James Currey, 2002), 39–51.

3. J. K. Ade Ajayi, *Christian Missions in Nigeria, 1841–1891: The Making of an Elite* (London: Longmans, 1965).

4. J. R. Mott, *The Decisive Hour of Christian Missions* (New York: Student Volunteer Movement for Foreign Missions, 1912), 114.

5. Ross Kinsler, *The Extension Movement in Theological Education: A Call to the Renewal of the Ministry* (Pasadena, CA: William Carey Library, 1978); Gert J. Steyn, "The Future of Theological Education by Extension in Africa," *Missionalia* 32, no. 1 (April 2004): 3–22.

6. Graham A. Duncan, "Theological Education: Mission Birth–African Renaissance," *Missionalia* 28, no. 1 (April 2000): 23–40.

7. I have discussed these matters more fully in "Elijah's Mantle: Ministerial Formation in Contemporary African Christianity," *International Review of Mission* 94, no. 373 (April 2005): 263–77.

8. Beth Tavers, "Private Higher Education in Africa: Six Country Case Studies," in *African Higher Education: An International Reference Handbook,* ed. Damtev Teferra and Philip G. Altbach (Bloomington: Indiana University Press, 2003), 53–60; Jeffrey S. Hittenberger, "Globalization, 'Marketization,' and the Mission of Pentecostal Higher Education in Africa," *Pneuma* 26, no. 2 (Fall 2004): 182–215.

9. Central University College, *Basic Statistics* (Accra, Ghana, 2003).

10. www.covenantuniversity.com/aboutmain.htm; David Oyedepo, "Influencing the external environment," paper presented at a conference on " Meeting the Challenges of Higher Education in Africa: The Role of Private Universities," Nairobi, Kenya, 2003.

11. www.daystarus.org.

12. www.idahosauniversity.com.

13. Afe Adogame, "African Christian Communities in Diaspora," in *African Christianity: An African Story,* ed. Ogbu U. Kalu (Pretoria: University of Pretoria, 2005): 494–514.

14. See the discussion in Allan Anderson, *An Introduction to Pentecostalism* (Cambridge: Cambridge University Press, 2004): 243–49.

15. See M. Ojo, "The Dynamics of Indigenous Charismatic Missionary Enterprises in West Africa," *Missionalia* 25, no. 4 (December 1997): 537–61.

Bibliography

Adams, Maurianne, Lee Anne Bell, and Pat Griffin, eds. *Teaching for Diversity and Social Justice: A Sourcebook.* New York: Routledge, 1997.

Ahn, Byung Mu. *The Development of the Korean Minjung Theology in the 1980s.* Seoul: Korea Theological Study Institute, 1990.

Ajayi, J. K. Ade. *Christian Missions in Nigeria, 1841–1891: The Making of an Elite.* London: Longmans, 1965.

Akintunde, Omowale. "White Racism, White Supremacy, White Privilege, and the Social Construction of Race: Moving from Modernist to Postmodernist Multiculturalism." *Multicultural Education* 7, no. 2 (1999).

Anderson, Allan. *An Introduction to Pentecostalism.* Cambridge: Cambridge University Press, 2004.

Anderson, Robert G. "The Search for Spiritual/Cultural Competency in Chaplaincy Practice: Five Steps That Mark the Path." *Journal of Health Care Chaplaincy* 13, no. 2 (2004).

Appiah, Kwame Anthony. *The Ethics of Identity.* Princeton, NJ: Princeton University Press, 2005.

Appleby, Joyce, Lynn Hunt, and Margaret Jacob. *Telling the Truth about History.* New York: Norton, 1994.

Aquino, María Pilar. "Theological Method in U.S. Latino/a Theology: Toward an Intercultural Theology for the Third Millenium." In *From the Heart of the People: Latino/a Explorations in Catholic Systematic Theology,* edited by Orlando O. Espin and Miguel H. Diaz. Maryknoll, NY: Orbis Books, 1999.

———, Daisy L. Machado, and Jeanette Rodríguez, eds. *A Reader in Latina Feminist Theology: Religion and Justice.* Austin: University of Texas Press, 2002.

Association of Theological Schools. *Folio on Diversity in Theological Education.* Pittsburgh: ATS, 2003.

Augsburger, David W. *Pastoral Counseling across Cultures.* Louisville, KY: Westminster/John Knox Press, 1986.

Bangert, Mark. "How Does One Go About Multicultural Worship?" In *What Does "Multicultural" Worship Look Like?* edited by Gordon Lathrop. Minneapolis: Augsburg Fortress, 1996.

Banks, James A. "Multicultural Education: Development, Paradigms and Goals." In *Multicultural Education in Western Societies,* edited by James A. Banks and J. Lynch. London: Holt, Rinehart & Winston, 1986.

————, and Cherry A. McGee Banks, eds. *Handbook of Research on Multicultural Education*. San Francisco: Jossey-Bass, 2001.

Barr, James. *Holy Scripture: Canon, Authority, and Criticism*. Oxford: Clarendon, 1983.

Barthes, Roland. *S/Z*. Translated by Richard Miller. New York: Hill & Wang, 1974.

Bastide, Roger. *The African Religions of Brazil: Toward a Sociology of the Interpenetration of Civilizations*. Baltimore: Johns Hopkins University Press, 1978.

Battles, Matthew. *Library: An Unquiet History*. New York: W. W. Norton, 2003.

Bell, Catherine. *Ritual: Perspectives and Dimensions*. Oxford: Oxford University Press, 1997.

Berkhofer, Robert F., Jr. *Beyond the Great Story: History as Text and Discourse*. Cambridge, MA: Belknap Press of Harvard University Press, 1995.

Beversluis, Joel, ed. *Sourcebook of the World's Religions: An Interfaith Guide to Religion and Spirituality*. Novato, CA: New World Library, 2000.

Bhabha, Homi K. *The Location of Culture*. New York: Routledge, 1994.

Blue, Gregory. "Chinese Influences on the Enlightenment in Europe." In *Knowledge across Cultures*, edited by Ruth Hayhoe and Julia Pan. Hong Kong: Comparative Education Research Center, University of Hong Kong, 2001.

Boal, Augusto. *The Rainbow of Desire*. New York: Routledge, 1995.

Bordo, Susan. "Feminism, Postmodernism, and Gender-Scepticism." In *Feminism/Postmodernism*, edited by L. Nicholson. New York: Routledge, 1990.

Botman, Russell. "Should the Reformed Join In?" *Reformed World* 52, no. 1 (March 2002).

Brown, David G., ed. *Ubiquitous Computing*. Bolton, MA: Anker Publishing, 2003.

Browning, Don S. *A Fundamental Practical Theology: Descriptive and Strategic Proposals*. Minneapolis: Fortress Press, 1991.

Brueggemann, Walter. *Cadences of Home: Preaching among Exiles*. Louisville, KY: Westminster John Knox Press, 1997.

————. *Texts under Negotiation: The Bible and Postmodern Imagination*. Minneapolis: Fortress Press, 1993.

Buenker, John D., and Lorman A. Ratner, eds. *Multiculturalism in the United States: A Comparative Guide to Acculturation and Ethnicity*. Westport, CT: Greenwood Press, 1992.

Burke, J., ed. *A New Look at Preaching*. Wilmington: Glazier, 1983.

Burrell, David B., CSC. *Faith and Freedom: An Interfaith Perspective*. Malden, MA: Blackwell Publishing, 2004.

————. *Freedom and Creation in Three Traditions*. Notre Dame, IN: University of Notre Dame Press, 1993.

————. *Knowing the Unknowable God: Ibn-Sina, Maimonides, Aquinas*. Notre Dame, IN: University of Notre Dame Press, 1986.

Carroll, Jackson W. *As One with Authority: Reflective Leadership in Ministry*. Louisville, KY: Westminster/John Knox Press, 1991.

Carter, Robert T. "Reimagining Race in Education: A New Paradigm from Psychology." *Teachers College Record* 102, no. 5 (2000): 864–97.

Castelli, E., and others, eds. *The Postmodern Bible*. New Haven, CT: Yale University Press, 1995.

Chomsky, Noam. "Explaining Language Use." *Philosophical Topics* 20 (1992): 205–31.

Clifford, James. *The Predicament of Culture: Twentieth-Century Ethnography, Literature, and Art*. Cambridge: Harvard University Press, 1988.

Clooney, Francis X., SJ. "Reading the World in Christ: From Comparison to Inclusivism." In *Christian Uniqueness Reconsidered: The Myth of a Pluralistic Theology of Religions*. Faith Meets Faith Series, edited by Gavin D'Costa. Maryknoll, NY: Orbis Books, 1990.

Commission on Theological Concerns of the Christian Conference of Asia. *Minjung Theology: People as the Subjects of History*. Maryknoll, NY: Orbis Books, 1983.

Conway, Ruth. *The Choices at the Heart of Technology: A Christian Perspective*. Harrisburg, PA: Trinity Press International, 1999.

Culler, J. *Structuralist Poetics: Structuralism, Linguistics and the Study of Literature*. Ithaca, NY: Cornell University Press, 1975.

Danielou, J., and H. I. Marrou. *The Christian Centuries, I*. New York: McGraw-Hill, 1964.

Daniels, Lee A., ed. *The State of Black America 2004*. New York: National Urban League, 2004.

De La Torre, Miguel A., ed. *Handbook of U.S. Theologies of Liberation*. St. Louis: Chalice Press, 2004.

Derrida, Jacques. *Margins of Philosophy*. Chicago: University of Chicago Press, 1982.

Dewey, John. *Democracy and Education: An Introduction to the Philosophy of Education*. New York: Free Press, 1944.

DeYoung, Curtiss Paul. *United by Faith: The Multiracial Congregation as an Answer to the Problem of Race*. New York: Oxford University Press, 2003.

Diaz, Carlos F. *Multicultural Education for the 21st Century*. New York: Longman, 2001.

Dube, Musa. "Reading for Decolonization." *Semeia* 75 (1996).

DuBois, W. E. B. *The Souls of Black Folk*. First published 1903. New York: Penguin Press, 1982.

Duncan, Graham A. "Theological Education: Mission Birth–African Renaissance." *Missionalia* 28, no. 1 (April 2000).

Dussel, Enrique. *A History of the Church in Latin America*. Translated by Alan Neely. Grand Rapids: Eerdmans, 1981.

Eco, Umberto. *The Role of the Reader: Explorations in the Semiotics of Texts*. Bloomington: Indiana University Press, 1979.

Eichholz, G. *Einführung in die Gleichnisse*. Neukirchen-Vluyn: Neukirchener Verlag, 1963.

Elizondo, Virgilio. "Benevolent Tolerance or Humble Reverence? A Vision for Multicultural Religious Education." In *Multicultural Religious Education,* edited by Barbara Wilkerson. Birmingham, AL: Religious Education Press, 1997.

Ellacuria, Ignacio, and Jon Sobrino, eds. *Mysterium Liberationis: Fundamental Concepts of Liberation Theology.* Maryknoll, NY: Orbis Books, 1993.

Elliott, Neil. *The Rhetoric of Romans: Argumentative Constraint and Strategy and Paul's Dialogue with Judaism.* Sheffield: Sheffield Academic Press, 1990.

Espín, Orlando. *The Faith of the People: Theological Reflections on Popular Catholicism.* Maryknoll, NY: Orbis Books, 1997.

———. "Toward the Construction of an Intercultural Theology of Tradition." *Journal of Hispanic/Latino Theology* 9 no. 3 (2000): 22–59.

Esposito, John L. *Unholy War: Terror in the Name of Islam.* New York: Oxford University Press, 2002.

Farley, Edward. *Good and Evil: Interpreting a Human Condition.* Minneapolis: Fortress Press, 1990.

———. *Theologia: The Fragmentation and Unity of Theological Education.* Philadelphia: Fortress Press, 1983.

Fenn, Richard. "Diversity and Power: Cracking the Code." In *Making Room at the Table: An Invitation to Multicultural Worship,* edited by Brian K. Blount and Leonora Tubbs Tisdale. Louisville, KY: Westminster John Knox Press, 2001.

Fernández, Eleazar S., and Fernando F. Segovia, eds. *A Dream Unfinished: Theological Reflection on America from the Margins.* Maryknoll, NY: Orbis Books, 2001.

Fish, Stanley. "Boutique Multiculturalism." In *Multiculturalism and American Democracy,* edited by Arthur M. Melzer, Jerry Weinberger, and M. Richard Zinman. Lawrence: University Press of Kansas, 1998.

Fornet-Betancourt, Raúl. *Transformación Intercultural de la Filosofía.* Bilbao, Spain: Desclée de Brouwer, 2001.

Foster, Susan Leigh. "Reading Dancing: Gestures towards a Semiotics of Dance." PhD diss., University of California, Santa Cruz, 1982.

Foucault, Michel. *Power/Knowledge: Selected Interviews and Other Writings, 1972–1977.* New York: Pantheon, 1980.

Franklin, John Hope. *Race and History: Selected Essays 1938–1988.* Baton Rouge: Louisiana State University Press, 1989.

Freire, Paulo. *Pedagogy of the Oppressed.* New York: Continuum, 1984.

———. *The Politics of Education: Culture, Power, and Liberation.* New York: Bergin & Garvey, 1985.

Fulkerson, M. McClintock. *Changing the Subject: Women's Discourses and Feminist Theology.* Minneapolis: Fortress Press, 1994.

Furnish, Victor. *The Love Command in the New Testament.* Nashville: Abingdon, 1972.

Gallagher, Susan. *Postcolonial Literature and the Biblical Call for Justice.* Jackson: University Press of Mississippi, 1994.

Gardner, Howard. *Multiple Intelligences*. New York: Basic Books, 1993.

Gaventa, Beverly Roberts. *The Acts of the Apostles*. Abingdon New Testament Commentaries. Nashville: Abingdon Press, 2003.

Georgi, D. *Theocracy in Paul's Praxis and Theology*. Minneapolis: Fortress Press, 1991.

Gibson, M. A. "Approaches to Multicultural Education in the United States: Some Concepts and Assumptions." *Anthropology and Education Quarterly* 5:94–119.

Goldberg, David Theo. *Multiculturalism: A Critical Reader*. Malden, MA: Blackwell, 1994.

González, Justo L. "Globalization in the Teaching of Church History." *Theological Education* (Spring 1993).

Gooch, P. *Dangerous Food: 1 Corinthians 8–10 in Its Context*. Waterloo, ON: Wilfrid Laurier University Press, 1993.

Griffin, Mark, and Theron Walker. *Living on the Borders: What the Church Can Learn from Ethnic Immigrant Cultures*. Grand Rapids: Brazos Press, 2004.

Groome, Thomas. *Sharing Faith: A Comprehensive Approach to Religious Education and Pastoral Ministry*. San Francisco: HarperSanFrancisco, 1991.

Habermas, Jürgen. *Reason and Rationalization in Society*. Cambridge: Polity Press, 1984.

Hastings, Adrian. *The Church in Africa 1450–1950*. Oxford: Oxford University Press, 1994.

———. *A History of African Christianity 1950–1975*. Cambridge: Cambridge University Press, 1979.

———, ed., *A World History of Christianity*. Grand Rapids: Eerdmans, 1999.

Hawn, C. Michael. *One Bread, One Body: Exploring Cultural Diversity in Worship*. Bethesda, MD: Alban Institute, 2003.

Heim, Mark. *Salvations: Truth and Difference in Religion*. Maryknoll, NY: Orbis Books, 2000.

Helms, Janet E., ed. *Black and White Racial Identity: Theory, Research and Practice*. Westport, CT: Praeger, 1990.

———. "Toward a Methodology for Measuring and Assessing Racial as Distinguished from Ethnic Identity." In *Multicultural Assessment in Counseling and Clinical Psychology*, edited by Gargi Roysircar Sodowsky and James C. Impara. Lincoln, NE: Buros Institute of Mental Measurements, 1996.

Hewitt, Martin, ed. *Culture Institutions*. Leeds: University of Leeds, 2002.

Hiebert, Theodore, and others. *Toppling the Tower: Essays on Babel and Diversity*. Chicago: Paxton Printing, 2004.

Hofstede, Geert. *Culture's Consequences: Comparing Values, Behaviors, Institutions, and Organizations across Nations*. 2nd ed. Thousand Oaks, CA: Sage Publications, 2001.

Hollinger, David. *Post-Ethnic America: Beyond Multiculturalism*. New York: Basic Books, 1995.

Hollis, Martin. "Is Universalism Ethnocentric?" In *Multicultural Questions,* edited by Christian Joppke and Steven Lukes. New York: Oxford University Press, 1999.

Howell, Annie, and Frank Tuitt, eds. *Race and Higher Education: Rethinking Pedagogy in Diverse College Classrooms.* Cambridge: Harvard Education Review, 2003.

Huntington, Samuel P. *Who Are We? The Challenges to America's National Identity.* New York: Simon & Schuster, 2004.

Irizarry, José R. "The Religious Educator as Cultural Spec-Actor: Researching Self in Intercultural Pedagogy." *Religious Education* 98, no. 3 (Summer 2003): 365–81.

Isasi-Diaz, Ada Maria. *En la Lucha: A Hispanic Women's Liberation Theology.* Minneapolis: Fortress Press, 1993.

Iser, W. *The Act of Reading: A Theory of Aesthetic Response.* Baltimore: Johns Hopkins University Press, 1978.

Isichei, Elizabeth. *A History of Christianity in Africa.* Grand Rapids: Eerdmans, 1995.

Jameson, Frederic. "Postmodern and the Consumer Society." In *Anti-Aesthetic,* edited by Hal Foster. Port Washington, NY: Bay Press, 1983.

Jenkins, Philip. *The Next Christendom: The Coming of Global Christianity.* New York: Oxford University Press, 2002.

John, Cheryl Bridges. "The Meaning of a Pentecost for Theological Education." *Ministerial Formation* 87 (October 1999).

Jones, Siân. *The Archaeology of Ethnicity: Constructing Identities in the Past and Present.* London: Routledge, 1997.

Joppke, Christian, and Steven Lukes, eds., *Multicultural Questions.* New York: Oxford University Press, 1999.

Kalu, Ogbu U. "Elijah's Mantle: Ministerial Formation in Contemporary African Christianity." *International Review of Missions* (April 2005): 203–77.

———. *The Embattled Gods: Christianization of Igboland,* 1841–1991. London and Lagos: Minaj Publishers, 1996.

Kang, Won Don. *The Theology of Mul.* Seoul: Han Wool, 1992.

Kant, Immanuel. *Der Streit der Fakultäten.* Translated by Mary J. Gregor. New York: Abaris Press, 1979.

Kaplan, Nancy. "Literacy beyond Books: Reading When All the World's a Web." In *The World Wide Web and Contemporary Cultural Theory,* edited by Andrew Herman and Thomas Swiss. New York: Routledge, 2000.

Karris, Robert. *The Romans Debate.* Peabody, MA: Hendriksen, 1991.

Kelsey, David H. *Between Athens and Berlin: The Theological Education Debate.* Grand Rapids: Eerdmans, 1993.

Kim, Jin Ho. "Minjung as the Subject of History: Reappraisal on 'Minjung' of Minjung Theology." *Theological Thought* 80 (1993).

Kim, Uichol, Harry C. Triandis, Cigdem Kagitcibasi, Sang-Chin Choi, and Gene Yoon, eds. *Individualism and Collectivism: Theory, Method, and Applications.* Cross-Cultural Research and Methodology Series. Thousand Oaks, CA: Sage Publications, 1994.

Kimball, Don. *Emerging Worship: Creating Worship Gatherings for New Generations.* Grand Rapids: Zondervan, 2004.

Kincheloe, Joe L., and Shirley R. Steinberg. *Changing Multiculturalism.* Buckingham, UK: Open University Press, 1997.

King, J., E. Hollins, and W. Hayman, eds. *Preparing Teachers for Cultural Diversity.* New York: Teachers College Press, 1997.

Kinghorn, Johann. "Modernization and Apartheid: The Afrikaner Churches." In *Christianity in South Africa: A Political, Social, and Cultural History*, edited by Richard Elphick and Rodney Davenport. Berkeley: University of California Press, 1997.

Kinsler, F. Ross. *The Extension Movement in Theological Education: A Call to the Renewal of the Ministry.* Pasadena, CA: William Carey Library, 1978.

Knitter, Paul F. *Introducing Theologies of Religions.* Maryknoll, NY: Orbis Books, 2002.

Kraemer, Henrik. *The Christian Message in a Non-Christian World.* Grand Rapids: Kregel Pub., 1938, 1963.

Kukuyama, Mary, and Todd Sevig. "Cultural Diversity in Pastoral Care." *Journal of Health Care Chaplaincy* 13, no. 2 (2004).

Kwok, Pui-Lan. "Reponses to the *Semeia* Volume on Postcolonial Criticism." *Semeia* 75 (1996).

Latourette, Kenneth Scott. *History of the Expansion of Christianity.* New York: Harper & Bros., 1937–1945.

Law, Eric H. F. *The WORD at the Crossings: Living the Good News in a Multicontextual Community.* St. Louis: Chalice Press, 2004.

Lee, Jae Won. "Paul and the Politics of Difference: A Contextual Study of the Jewish-Gentile Difference in Galatians and Romans." PhD diss., Union Theological Seminary, New York, 2001.

Lee, Stacey J. "'Are You Chinese or What?' Ethnic Identity among Asian Americans." In *Racial and Ethnic Identity in School Practices: Aspects of Human Development*, edited by Rosa Hernandez Sheets and Etta R. Hollins. Mahwah, NJ: Lawrence Erlbaum Associates, 1999.

Lock, Don C. *Increasing Multicultural Understanding.* 2nd ed. Thousand Oaks, CA: Sage Publications, 1998.

Lynch, Eleanor W. "Instructional Strategies." In *Multicultural Course Transformation in Higher Education: A Broader Truth,* edited by Ann Intili Morey and Margie K. Kitano. Boston: Allyn & Bacon, 1997.

MacIntyre, A. *Whose Justice? Which Rationality?* Notre Dame, IN: Notre Dame University Press, 1988.

Mamdani, Mahmood. *Good Muslim, Bad Muslim: America, the Cold War, and the Roots of Terror*. New York: Pantheon, 2004.

March, W. Eugene. *The Wide, Wide Circle of Divine Love: A Biblical Case for Religious Diversity*. Louisville, KY: Westminster John Knox Press, 2005.

Marty, Martin E. *The One and the Many: America's Struggle for the Common Good*. Cambridge, MA: Harvard University Press, 1997.

Massey-Burzio, Virginia. "Facing the Competition." *College and Research Libraries News* 63, no. 11 (December 2002).

Mathe, Barbara. "Kaleidoscopic Classifications: Redefining Information in a World Cultural Context." Paper presented at the 64th IFLA General Conference, August 16–21, 1998. http://www.ifla.org/IV/ifla64/109–145e.htm.

Matovina, Timothy, ed. *Beyond Borders: Writings of Virgilio Elizondo and Friends*. Maryknoll, NY: Orbis Books, 2000.

McLaren, P., and P. Leonard, eds. *Paulo Freire: A Critical Encounter*. London: Routledge, 1993.

McManners, John, ed., *The Oxford Illustrated History of Christianity*. Oxford: Oxford University Press, 1993.

Meier, Deborah. *The Power of Their Ideas: Lessons for America from a Small School in Harlem*. Boston: Beacon Press, 2002.

Melzer, Arthur M., Jerry Weinberger, and M. Richard Zinman, eds. *Multiculturalism and American Democracy*. Lawrence: University Press of Kansas, 1998.

Migliore, Daniel. *Faith Seeking Understanding: An Introduction to Christian Theology*. Louisville, KY: Westminster/John Knox Press, 1989.

Mitchell, Leonel L. *The Meaning of Ritual*. Wilton, CT: Morehouse-Barlow, 1977.

Moffett, Samuel Hugh. *A History of Christianity in Asia*. Vol. 1, *Beginnings to 1500*. San Francisco: HarperCollins, 1992.

Moran, Carrol E., and Kenji Hakuta. "Bilingual Education: Broadening Research Perspectives." In *Handbook of Research on Multicultural Education*, edited by James A. Banks and Cherry A. McGee Banks. San Francisco: Jossey-Bass, 2001.

Morris, James H. "Tales of Technology: Consider a Cure for Pernicious Infobesity." *Post-Gazette* (Pittsburgh), March 30, 2003. http://www.post-gazette.com/pg/03089/169397.stm.

Mott, J. R. *The Decisive Hour of Christian Missions*. New York: Student Volunteer Movement for Foreign Missions, 1912.

Muddiman, John. *The Epistle to the Ephesians*. Black's New Testament Commentaries. London: Continuum, 2001.

Nanos, M. *The Mystery of Romans*. Minneapolis: Fortress Press, 1996.

Niebuhr, Reinhold. *The Nature and Destiny of Man: A Christian Interpretation*. New York: Charles Scribner's Sons, 1941, 1964.

Nieto, Sonia. *The Light in Their Eyes: Creating Multicultural Learning Communities*. New York: Teachers College Press, 1999.

———. *What Keeps Teachers Going*. New York: Teachers College Press, 2003.

Novak, Philip. *The World's Wisdom: Sacred Texts of the World's Religions*. New York: HarperCollins, 1994.

O'Donnell, James J. *Avatars of the Word: From Papyrus to Cyberspace*. Cambridge, MA: Harvard University Press, 1998.

Ojo, M. "The Dynamics of Indigenous Charismatic Missionary Enterprises in West Africa." *Missionalia* 25, no. 4 (December 1997).

Oxtoby, Willard G., ed. *World Religions: Eastern Traditions* and *World Religions: Western Traditions*. 2nd ed. Toronto: Oxford University Press, 2002.

Palmer, Parker. *The Courage to Teach: Exploring the Inner Landscape of a Teacher's Life*. San Francisco: Jossey-Bass, 1998.

———. *Let Your Life Speak: Listening for the Voice of Vocation*. San Francisco: Jossey-Bass, 2000.

Park, Andrew Sung. *The Wounded Heart of God: The Asian Concept of Han and the Christian Doctrine of Sin*. Nashville: Abingdon, 1993.

Park, Soon Kyung. "National Reunification and Minjung Theology: Toward a New Development of Minjung Theology." *Theological Thought* 80 (1993).

Parliament of the World's Religions. *Pathways to Peace: The Wisdom of Listening, The Power of Commitment*. Barcelona: Parliament of the World's Religions, 2004.

Patton, John. *Pastoral Care in Context: An Introduction to Pastoral Care*. Louisville, KY: Westminster/John Knox Press, 1993.

Pederson, Paul. *A Handbook for Developing Multicultural Awareness*. Alexandria, VA: American Counseling Association, 1994.

Peters, Ted. *The Cosmic Self: A Penetrating Look at Today's New Age Movements*. New York: HarperCollins, 1991.

Phan, Peter C. *Christianity with an Asian Face: Asian American Theology in the Making*. Maryknoll, NY: Orbis Books, 2003.

Pinn, Anthony B., and Benjamin Valentin, eds. *The Ties That Bind: African American and Hispanic American/Latino/a Theologies in Dialogue*. New York: Continuum, 2001.

Pinnock, Clark H. *A Wideness in God's Mercy: The Finality of Jesus Christ in a World of Religions*. Grand Rapids: Zondervan, 1992.

Pitcher, W. Alvin, and Charles Amjad-Ali, eds. *Liberation and Ethics: Essays in Religious Social Ethics in Honor of Gibson Winter*. Chicago: Center for the Scientific Study of Religion, 1985.

Presbyterian Church (U.S.A.). "A Brief Statement of Faith." In *The Book of Confessions*. Louisville, KY: Presbyterian Church (U.S.A.), 1991.

Pyle, William T. and Mary Alice Seals, eds. *Experiencing Ministry Supervision: A Field-Based Approach*. Nashville: Broadman & Holman, 1995.

Ramsey, Patricia G., and Leslie R. Williams. *Multicultural Education: A Source Book*. 2nd ed. New York: RoutledgeFalmer, 2003.

Reventlow, H. *The Authority of the Bible and the Rise of the Modern World*. Philadelphia: Fortress Press, 1984.

Rhodes, Stephen A. *Where the Nations Meet: The Church in a Multicultural World*. Downers Grove, IL: InterVarsity Press, 1998.

Ricoeur, P. "Biblical Hermeneutics." *Semeia* 4 (1975): 114–28.

———. *The Rule of Metaphor: Multi-Disciplinary Studies of the Creation of Meaning in Language*. Toronto: University of Toronto Press, 1977.

Roy, Olivier. *Globalized Islam: The Search for a New Ummah*. New York: Columbia University Press, 2004.

Sacks, Jonathan. *The Dignity of Difference: How to Avoid the Clash of Civilizations*. London: Continuum, 2002.

Sanders, James. *Canon and Community: A Guide to Canonical Criticism*. Philadelphia: Fortress Press, 1984.

Sanneh, Lamin. *Whose Religion Is Christianity? The Gospel beyond the West*. Grand Rapids: Eerdmans, 2003.

Sawyer, Kenneth. "Multiculturalism Observed." *Journal of Religious and Theological Information* 6, nos. 3–4 (2004)[2005].

Segal, A. *Paul the Convert: The Apostolate and Apostasy of Saul the Pharisee*. New Haven, CT: Yale University Press, 1990.

Segovia, F. "'And They Began to Speak in Other Tongues': Competing Modes of Discourse in Contemporary Biblical Criticism," and "Cultural Studies and Contemporary Biblical Criticism: Ideological Criticism as Mode of Discourse." In *Reading from This Place*, 2 vols., edited by F. Segovia and M. Tolbert. Minneapolis: Fortress Press, 1995.

———, ed. *What Is John? Readers and Readings of the Fourth Gospel*. Atlanta: Scholars Press, 1996.

Segundo, Juan Luis. *The Hidden Motives of Pastoral Action: Latin American Reflections*. Maryknoll, NY: Orbis Books, 1978.

Senn, Frank. *Christian Worship and Its Cultural Setting*. Philadelphia: Fortress Press, 1983.

Skot-Hansen, Dorte. "The Public Library between Integration and Cultural Diversity." *Scandinavian Public Library Quarterly* 35, no. 1 (2002). http://www.splq.info/issues/vol35_1/06.htm.

Sleeter, Christine E., and Carl A. Grant. *Making Choices for Multicultural Education: Five Approaches to Race, Class, and Gender*. 2nd ed. New York: Merrill, 1993.

Smelser, Neil J., William Julius Wilson, and Faith Mitchell, eds. *America Becoming: Racial Trends and Their Consequences*. Washington, DC: National Academy Press, 2001.

Smith, Jonathan Z. *Map Is Not Territory: Studies in the History of Religions*. Chicago: University of Chicago Press, 1993.

Sodowsky, Gargi Roysircar, Edward Wai Ming Lai, and Barbara S. Plake. "Moderating Effects of Sociocultural Variables on Acculturation Attitudes of Hispanics and Asian Americans." *Journal of Counseling and Development* 16 (1991).

Sodowsky, Gargi Roysircar, Kwong-Liem Karl Kwan, and Raji Pannu. "Ethnic Identity of Asians in the United States." In *Handbook of Multicultural Counseling*, edited by Joseph G. Ponterotto, J. Manuel Casas, Lisa A. Suzuki, and Charlene M. Alexander. Thousand Oaks, CA: Sage Publications, 1995.

Spickard, Paul R., and Kevin M. Cragg. *A Global History of Christians: How Everyday Believers Experienced Their World*. Grand Rapids. Baker Academic, 1994.

Spivak, Gayatri Chakravorty. *Other Worlds: Essays in Cultural Politics*. New York. Methuen, 1987.

Starkloff, Carl. *A Theology of the In Between: The Value of the Syncretic Process*. Milwaukee: Marquette University Press, 2002.

Sternberg, M. *The Poetics of Biblical Narrative: Ideological Literature and the Drama of Reading*. Bloomington: Indiana University Press, 1985.

Stewart, David. "Libraries: Western Christian." In *Encyclopedia of Monasticism*, edited by William M. Johnston. Chicago: Fitzroy Dearborn Publishers, 2000.

Steyn, Gert J. "The Future of Theological Education by Extension in Africa." *Missionalia* 32, no. 1 (April 2004).

Sue, Derald Wing, and David Sue. *Counseling the Culturally Diverse: Theory and Practice*. 4th ed. New York: John Wiley, 2003.

Sugirtharajah, R. S. "Imperial Critical Commentaries: Christian Discourse and Commentarial Writings in Colonial India." *Journal for the Study of the New Testament* 73 (1999).

———, ed. *The Postcolonial Bible*. Sheffield: Sheffield Academic Press, 1990.

———. *Postcolonial Criticism and Biblical Interpretation*. New York: Oxford University Press, 2002.

———, ed. *Voices from the Margin: Interpreting the Bible in the Third World*. Maryknoll, NY: Orbis Books, 1995.

Suh, Nam Dong. *In Search of Minjung Theology*. Seoul: Hangil, 1984.

Talvacchia, Kathleen T. *Critical Minds and Discerning Hearts: A Spirituality of Multicultural Teaching*. St. Louis: Chalice Press, 2003.

Tatum, Beverly Daniel. "Talking about Race, Learning about Racism: The Application of Racial Identity Development Theory in the Classroom." In *Race and Higher Education: Rethinking Pedagogy in Diverse College Classrooms*, edited by Annie Howell and Frank Tuitt. Cambridge: Harvard Education Review, 2003.

———. *"Why Are All the Black Kids Sitting Together in the Cafeteria?" and Other Conversations about Race*. New York: Basic Books, 2003.

Tavers, Beth. "Private Higher Education in Africa: Six Country Case Studies." In *African Higher Education: An International Reference Handbook*, edited by Damtev Teferra and Philip G. Altbach. Bloomington: Indiana University Press, 2003.

Tiffin, John, and Lalita Rajasingham. *The Global Virtual University*. New York: Routledge, 2003.

Tomson, P. *Paul and the Jewish Law: Halakha in the Letters of the Apostle to the Gentiles.* Minneapolis: Fortress, 1990.

Torres, Vasti, Mary F. Howard-Hamilton, and Diane L. Cooper. *Identity Development of Diverse Populations: Implications for Teaching and Administration in Higher Education.* ASHE-ERIC Higher Education Report, vol. 29, no. 6. San Francisco: Jossey-Bass, 2003.

TuSmith, Bonnie, and Maureen T. Reddy, eds. *Race in the College Classroom: Pedagogy and Politics.* New Brunswick, NJ: Rutgers University Press, 2002.

Utsey, Shawn O., Carol A. Gernat, and Mark A. Bolden. "Teaching Racial Identity Development and Racism Awareness: Training in Professional Psychology Programs." In *Handbook of Racial and Ethnic Minority Psychology,* edited by Guillermo Bernal, Joseph E. Trimble, A. Kathleen Burlew, and Frederick T. L. Leong. Thousand Oaks, CA: Sage Publishing, 2003.

Valentin, Benjamin. *Mapping Public Theology: Beyond Culture, Identity, and Difference.* New York: Trinity Press International, 2002.

Voorst, Robert E. Van. *Anthology of World Scriptures.* Toronto: Wadsworth, 2000.

Vygotsky, Lev Semenovich. *The Collected Works of L. S. Vygotsky.* Edited by Robert W. Rieber and Aaron S. Carton. New York: Plenum Press, 1987–1999.

———. *The Essential Vygotsky.* Edited by Robert W. Rieber and David K. Robinson. New York: Kluwer Academic/Plenum Publishers, 2004.

Walker, Williston. *The History of the Christian Church.* New York: Scribner, 1985.

Wellman, David T. *Portraits of White Racism.* 2nd ed. Cambridge: Cambridge University Press, 1993.

Wijeyesinghe, Charmaine L., and Bailey W. Jackson III, eds. *New Perspectives on Racial Identity Development: A Theoretical and Practical Anthology.* New York: New York University Press, 2001.

Willard, Louis Charles. "Technology and Educational Practices." *Theological Education* 38, no. 1 (2001): 111–16.

Williams, Rowan. *Seven Words for the 21st Century.* Trowbridge, UK: Cromwell Press, 2002.

Wimberly, Ann E. Streaty. "Hospitable Kinship in Theological Education: Cross-Cultural Perspectives on Teaching and Learning as Gift Exchange." *Teaching Theology and Religion* 7, no. 1 (January 2004).

Yeow, Choo Lak, ed. *Doing Theology with Cultures in Asia.* Singapore: ATESEA, 1988.

Young, Iris. *Justice and the Politics of Difference.* Princeton, NJ: Princeton University Press, 1990.

Contributors

Homer U. Ashby Jr. is W. Clement and Jessie V. Stone Professor of Pastoral Care.

Robert L. Brawley is Albert G. McGaw Professor of New Testament.

Cynthia M. Campbell is President and Cyrus McCormick Professor of Church and Ministry.

Anna Case-Winters is Professor of Theology.

Robert A. Cathey is Associate Professor of Theology.

David D. Daniels III is Professor of Church History.

David V. Esterline is Dean of the Faculty, Vice-President for Academic Affairs, and James G. K. McClure Professor of Theological Education.

Theodore Hiebert is Francis A. McGaw Professor of Old Testament.

José R. Irizarry is Dean of Doctor of Ministry Programs and Associate Professor of Cultural Studies in Religion and Education.

Ogbu U. Kalu is Henry Winters Luce Professor of World Christianity and Mission and Director of the Chicago Center for Global Ministry.

Jae Won Lee is Assistant Professor of New Testament.

Joanne Lindstrom is Director of Experiential Education and Field Studies.

Deborah Flemister Mullen is Dean of Masters Level Programs, Associate Professor of Ministry and Historical Studies, and Director of the Center for African American Ministries and Black Church Studies.

Gary Rand is Seminary Musician.

Luis R. Rivera-Rodriguez is Associate Professor of Theology and Director of the Center for the Study of Latino/a Theology and Ministry.

Kenneth Sawyer is Associate Professor of Church History.

All serve at McCormick Theological Seminary in Chicago.

Index of Names

Index of Subjects